INDEX TO THE WILLS OF MARYLAND

THE AMERICAN
INDEX LIBRARY

MARYLAND

INDEX TO THE WILLS OF:

ALLEGANY COUNTY, 1784-1960

Edited by Joan Hume

Magna Carta Book Company
Baltimore, Md. 21215
U.S.A.
1970

Library of Congress Catalog Number: 78-114225

Standard Book Number: 910946-10-8

FOREWORD

The earliest records of Maryland were the land records. It was extremely important for new title holders of land to have their ownership recorded; and for the Lord Proprietor, it was quite as important because the quit-rents on land were his most important gain for his proprietorship. There was also a need for recording probate records because, however fruitful the land and salubrious the climate, men died, and left estates governed by wills. At first the Secretary of the Province made the probate records and kept them safe. This arrangement continued until about 1671 when an officer was especially appointed to assume these tasks. This officer was known as the Commissary General, who, with the help of the Judges of the Prerogative Court - from one to four - handled all the probate affairs of the Province.

In the 1690's, the country having been settled to the westward, it became more and more difficult for persons, principally executors and administrators, to come all the way to St. Mary's City and shortly thereafter, to Annapolis, to carry on their businesses with the Commissary General and the Prerogative Court. When it became obvious to the Lord Proprietor that this travel imposed an unusual hardship on the colonists, he established county officers known as Deputy Commissaries to be local administrators of probate business. Only unusual estates and confusing wills were thereafter referred to the Prerogative Court.

This system continued satisfactorily until 1776 when the constitution of that year and the laws of 1777 abolished the Court and the Commissary and decentralized probate work altogether by the creation of a Register of Wills for each county and an Orphans' Court. This system has been affirmed by the three constitutions since that time and is still functioning.

All of the records of the Colonial period were preserved in the central probate office - by whatever name it was called. After the Revolution the papers in the Annapolis office were sent to the Register of Wills of each county to be recorded there. As a result, we have two sets of will records preserved for all but two of the counties, Calvert and Dorchester, where later courthouse fires destroyed the local records. The central records, after more peregrination, are now at the Hall of Records.

All but three years (1770-1772) of the colonial wills have been calendared by Jane Baldwin Cotton, Annie Walker Burns and James M. Magruder, Jr. An all-name index was prepared for the Calendar by Magruder, processed and now available in offset.

The county sets have been indexed by the local Registers of Wills offices and microfilmed by the Hall of Records Commission. These indexes are useful because in the transfer to and from the counties after the Revolution, some papers were lost and do not appear in the central records. The wills of the post-colonial period have not been worked on at all, with the exception of those for St. Mary's County, which have been printed in alphabetical order in the St. Mary's Chronicle.

This is the importance of the present printing of the county indexes to the wills of Maryland, which will make them available to interested persons everywhere.

Morris L. Radoff
Archivist of the State of Maryland

EDITOR'S NOTE

Allegany County was formed in 1789 from part of Washington County. Its County Seat is Cumberland, and the searcher should write to the Register of Wills at Allegany County Court House in Cumberland regarding the wills referred to here.

This index of wills is known as a Campbell Index. Under this system, the names are arranged by initial letter of the surname and by initial letter of the given name. Thus, all the decedants whose surnames begin with A and whose given names begin with A will be found on the first page in order of date. Next come those whose surnames begin with A and whose given names begin with B and so on. The reference letter, or first number, is to the liber, or book; the following number is the folio within the liber.

Although this system is not quite as easy to consult as the more usual system of strict alphabetical order by surnames, there are rarely more than two or three pages to be scanned when searching for a name. Moreover, while looking through the names, the searcher sometimes notices names which would have otherwise been overlooked - perhaps a mis-spelled name, which would have been completely lost in an alphabetical system.

The main merit of the system is that it can be compiled directly into a book, rather than on index cards. The time and expense involved in card-indexing would have rendered the present printing impossible.

This index has been copied correctly from a microfilm of a typed index compiled by the office of the Register of Wills for the county. The editor cannot vouch for the correctness of the original index, but where errors have been detected, they have been corrected.

The Magna Carta Book Company is indebted to Dr. Morris L. Radoff, Mr. Gust Skordas and other members of the staff of the Hall of Records in Annapolis, and to the Register of Wills for Allegany County, for their help in the prepartion of this work.

INDEX TO THE WILLS OF ALLEGANY COUNTY, 1784 - 1960

Arnold, Anthony	Aug., 1813	A 118
Arnold, Archibald	June, 1833	A 333
Arnold, Anthony H.	Jan., 1884	E 13
Arnold, Atlee M.	Jan., 1884	E 13
Allee, Annie P.	May, 1887	E 230
Alexander, Ann	July, 1889	F 30
Ash, Amos	Jan., 1901	H 143
Ash, Abraham	April, 1902	H 267
Allen, A.B.	Aug., 1907	I 314
Allerdice, Alexander	Jan., 1908	I 360
Aman, Anna M.	April, 1923	N 34
Appel, Annie	Nov., 1928	O 415
Adams, Alexander	Jan., 1935	Q 570
Arnold, August	July, 1936	R 279
Adams, Annie M.	May, 1940	S 549
Athey, Alice J.	April, 1941	T 124
Amann, Annie P.	Nov., 1949	W 435
Albright, Alice C.	July, 1951	X 205
Alderton, Alice	June, 1952	X 407
Amato, Angelina	May, 1955	Y 588
Althouse, Alfred K.	March, 1957	Z 483

Arnold, Bridget	March, 1908	I 378
Ackerman, Barbara	March, 1917	L 145

Arnold, Charlotte	Feb., 1872	D 7
Arnold, Charles F.	Dec. 1883	E 9
Armbruster, Cath. et al	March, 1885	E 124
Aeschenbreuner, Christina	Aug., 1897	G 246

Ashby, Charles E.	Dec., 1923	N 165
Albright, Charles E.	July, 1929	O 572
Ansel, Chas. Arthur	Aug., 1945	V 18
Alderton, Columbus	Aug., 1946	V 269
Abramson, Celia	April, 1953	Y 27
Ahern, Charles	Nov., 1954	Y 410
Angilletta, Christina	May, 1960	Z 427
Anderson, Deliah	Sept., 1881	D 500
Arnold, David	Dec., 1883	E 9
Annan, Daniel	April, 1921	M 302
Annan, Daniel, Jr.	Nov., 1928	O 426
Arnold, Dessie Irene	May, 1932	P 586
Armstrong, Davisson	June, 1935	R 45
Arnold, Dominick W.	Nov., 1948	W 224
Arnold, Elizabeth A.	May, 1875	D 215
Ash, Eli W.	Oct., 1880	D 454
Anderson, Edward et al		D 502
Arnold, Elbridge L.	Jan. 1884	E 13
Alexander, Edward	July, 1922	M 488
Ash, Edwin F.	March, 1923	N 11
Arnold, Elizabeth Sarah	Nov., 1931	P 477
Avery, Eva M.	Jan., 1945	U 433
Albright, Eliza E.	June, 1945	U 596
Allen, Emily Dongers	Nov., 1950	X 44
Adams, Elizabeth W.	April, 1958	1 231
Alderton, Florida F.	Jan., 1925	N 365
Ankeney, Franklin H.		4 246
Apple, George	Sept., 1869	C 149
Aman, George	July, 1872	D 34
Arnold, George R.	Jan. 1884	E 13
Arnold, George N.	March, 1884	E 35
Anderson, G.Espy	May, 1885	E 114
Armstrong, George	March, 1903	H 328

Andrews, George W.	Feb., 1909	J 7
Anderson, George	Feb., 1931	P 306
Appold, George J.	Dec., 1935	R 148
Aberle, George	Jan., 1939	S 251
Armbruster, Glenn L.	Dec., 1944	U 425
Arbogast, George L.	Feb. 1959	1 565

Albright, Harrison	Feb., 1888	E 307
Ahaus, Henry	Dec. 1891	F 254
Atkinson, Hugh	Jan. 1902	H 243
Ayers, Henry	June, 1907	I 288
Adler, Henry	Nov. 1908	I 474
August, Hattie	Sept., 1909	J 98
Able, Henry	July, 1934	Q 465
Atkinson, Hugh H.	June, 1945	U 588
Askey, Harriet G.	Aug., 1945	V 26
Atkinson, Hugh H.	Nov., 1949	W 427
Appel, Henry	Feb. 1950	W 482
Arnold, Hoye C.	April, 1955	Y 503

Anderson, Ismena	Oct., 1813	A 120
Atkinson, Isabella et al	Feb., 1868	C 123
Addison, Isabel C.	Aptil, 1960	2 366

Allen, James P.	Nov. 1921	M 383
Atkinson, Jacob	Jan. 1922	M 402
Aman, John	Oct., 1922	M 550
Arnold, James	April, 1926	N 585
Atkinson, Jasper M.	May, 1926	O 5
Ash, Jackson McClellan	June, 1928	O 356
Aspinall, John	Oct., 1929	P 27
Appel, John of George	June, 1931	P 385
Abbott, Jacob G.	Sept. 1931	P 444
Anderson, James C.	May, 1932	P 584
Anthony, John	March, 1935	Q 597
Avers, John W.	Dec. 1935	R 138
Allerdice, Jamina	Feb. 1936	R 192
Ash, Jennie	Dec. 1937	S 10

Allen, J.H., Mrs.	April, 1942	T 369
Adams, Jacob Henry	Jan., 1953	X 566
Ayers, Janet C.	July, 1953	Y 87
Ayers, John Henry, Sr.	Feb. 1954	Y 210
Abbott, J.A.	March, 1954	Y 239
Abramson, Julius	Nov. 1954	Y 404
Andrews, John W.	Oct. 1955	Z 94
Allen, Jennie L. McCormick	May, 1956	Z 229
Anderson, John R.	June, 1957	Z 577
Askey, Jane Napier	Oct. 1958	1 442
Armentrout, Jacob K.	Jan. 1959	1 526
Agress, John	June, 1959	2 68

Arnold, Kate	Feb. 1948	W 46

Albright, Laura J.	Oct. 1932	Q 81
Appel, Lucas	April, 1934	Q 416
Arnold, Lillian	May, 1941	T 138
Ash, Lucy B.	Nov. 1941	T 274
Amick, Lillian C.	July, 1946	V 263
Alderton, Lewis V.	May, 1949	W 329

Ayers, Moses	Oct., 1803	A 58
Arnold, Mott H.	Jan. 1884	E 13
Arnold, Margaret		F 77
Same	Feb., 1890	
Ahaus, Mary		F 254
Arnold, Matilda	June, 1897	G 242
Anderson, Matthew	Nov., 1898	G 315
Allen, Mary J.	March, 1919	M 13
Adams, Mary E.	Feb., 1921	M 267
Ash, Martha C.	Dec. 1925	N 500
Albright, Mary A.	Jan., 1929	O 450
Armbruster, Mary	Nov., 1929	P 45
Adams, Margaret Reese	Oct. 1936	R 340
Abbott, Mary Shultice	March, 1937	R 444
Athey, Martha Jane	June, 1944	U 315
Adams, Marion Rubicam	Oct. 1944	U 384

Arnold, Mary L.	Jan. 1945	U 437
Aspinall, Mary	Oct., 1945	V 67
Atkinson, Mary A.	April, 1947	V 438
Arnette, Minnie	Jan., 1948	W 24
Andrews, Mary Jane	July, 1948	W 176
Adams, Mary	Aug. 1950	W 613
Aaron, Mary L.	June, 1959	2 57
Airesman, Mary Grace	Feb., 1960	2 291
Anderson, Nettie	Dec. 1938	S 225
Atwell, Nellie M.	Oct. 1952	X 498
Alburtis, Otho H.	June, 1929	O 563
Armstrong, Robert	April, 1942	T 367
Armbruster, Raymond W.	May, 1947	V 486
Andrews, Robert W.	Dec. 1947	V 599
Alderton, Rebecca Grace	July, 1954	Y 302
Arnold, Simon	Feb., 1872	D 7
Appold, Samuel	Dec. 1899	H 16
Adler, Selig	Nov. 1908	X 470
Amantea, Salvatore	Sept., 1915	K 401
Abernathy, Sarah E.	Feb. 1916	K 485
Arnold, Sarah R.	Aug., 1919	M 72
Anderson, Samuel H.	March, 1937	R 446
Amtower, S.F.	June, 1940	S 589
Appel, Sarah A.	July, 1940	S 604
Arnold, Simon K.	Oct. 1957	1 95
Armstrong, Thomas	March, 1901	H 158
Armstrong, Thomas D.	June, 1911	J 302
Allen, Thomas S.	Feb., 1913	K 1
Allerdice, Thomas	May, 1917	L 183
Athey, Thomas B.	Jan., 1937	R 388
Albright, Thomas P.	June, 1943	U 99

Ashby, William	Sept., 1804	A 80
Armstrong, William	May, 1848	A 650
Arnold, William et al	Sept., 1852	B 53-4
Arnett, William W.	May, 1859	B 158
Armbruster, William	Nov., 1873	D 119
Armbruster, William	March, 1873	D 190
Arnold, William L.	Jan., 1884	E 12
Arnold, William W.	Jan., 1884	E 13
Atkinson, William	Aug., 1911	J 318
Ash, William H.	Aug., 1923	N 115
Andrews, William H.	Oct., 1924	N 331
Adams, W.J.	Jan., 1925	N 364
Allison, William L.	Feb., 1927	O 142
Anderson, Wesley	May, 1927	O 172
Ahern, William H.	June, 1929	O 560
Armbruster, William of H.	Dec. 1929	P. 60
Atkinson, Walter Franklin	June, 1940	S 591
Albright, William F.	Aug., 1944	U 342
Anderson, William	April, 1950	W 532
Abernathy, William	May, 1954	Y 268
Alderton, Walter R.	Jan., 1960	2 261

B

Bruce, Andrew	April, 1815	A 125
same	Sept., 1802	A 143
same	Dec., 1802	A 143
same	Oct., 1803	A 144
same	Dec. 1803	A 144
same	Jan., 1805	A 144
same	Jan., 1806	A 145
same	Jan., 1807	A 145
same	Dec., 1808	A 146
Boyd, Anne Mary	July, 1818	A 168
Blocher, Andrew	Aug., 1837	A 414
Bruce, Andrew	Jan., 1839	A 430
Berry, Amelia	July, 1846	A 600
Beall, Aza	April, 1853	B 59
Blogden, Ann Catherine	Nov., 1857	B 130
Bush, A.M.L.	Dec., 1863	C 34
Bray, Adelia A.	Sept., 1864	C 79
Bennett, Artemas	April, 1866	C 85
Boose, Andrew J.	March, 1867	C 90
Berns, Anna M.	Sept., 1867	C 102
Butler, Alice	July, 1871	C 204
Blackiston, A.H. & R.T. Semmes	Feb., 1875	D 281
Boyd, A.Hunter		D 312
Barrett, Augustus	May, 187-	D 329
Beers, Arabella M.	July, 1878	D 368
Beall, Annie		F 91
Berg, August	Oct., 1893	F 396
Bruce, Ann M.C.	March, 1895	G 104
Bush, Andrew M.L.	May, 1897	G 230
Brailer, Augustine	July, 1898	G 300
Boag, Alexander, Sr.	Feb., 1900	H 42
Barth, Adam	March, 1901	H 160
Beall, Annie	Nov., 1901	H 231
Baker, August	Oct., 1907	I 322
Backhause, Anna	Nov., 1909	J 84
Billmeyer, Andrew H.	Aug., 1912	J 445
Baker, Arthur	Aug., 1916	L 40
Bogart, Anthony	Feb., 1917	L 131

Baker, Alfred	Dec., 1917	L 281
Burkey, Augustine	Jan., 1920	M 112
Berlin, Abram	July, 1920	M 188
Beall, Anna M.	Dec., 1921	M 385
Bannatyne, Annie	Feb., 1922	M 415
Beall, Alpheus	May, 1922	M 463
Boyd, Alexander, Sr.	Dec., 1922	M 567
Burkey, Augustine	March, 1923	N 19
Brown, Amanda A.	Aug., 1925	N 464
Boyd, A. Hunter	Aug., 1925	N 458
Bosley, Amos S.	April, 1926	N 583
Burkhart, Albert E.	Feb., 1927	O 133
Birmingham, Annie B.	Aug., 1928	O 371
Barnes, Albert A.	May, 1931	P 362
Barnes, Annie E.	June, 1934	Q 454
Baker, Annie E.	March, 1936	R 216
Bevans, Annie M.	Jan., 1937	R 376
Barrett, Augustus M.	Feb., 1938	S 58
Brinker, A. John	July, 1940	S 594
Beck, Anna	Jan., 1942	T 308
Banks, Andrew R.D.	April, 1942	T 374
Berry, Albert	Sept., 1942	T 453
Boston, Adam E.	April, 1943	U 52
Bonner, Arbella	May, 1943	U 77
Barncord, Agnes A.	Aug., 1943	U 149
Brennan, Annie	Nov., 1944	U 400
Burkhart, Almena C.	Dec., 1944	U 424
Boyd, Agnes P.	Sept., 1945	V 48
Beall, Annie Elizabeth	July, 1946	V 250
Bechtel, Albert	Jan., 1948	W 15
Brotemarkle, Alla	Feb., 1951	X 105
Bender, Alpha V.	Aug., 1951	X 216
Blonskey, Alice L.	Jan., 1952	X 311
Brady, Annie B.	Aug., 1952	X 468
Brown, Alfred D.	Oct., 1952	X 495
Bordner, Anna Mary	Jan., 1953	X 564
Broadwater, Alfred	July, 1955	Z 33
Berry, Annie Virginia	Dec., 1955	Z 128
Beals, Anna E.	Oct., 1956	Z 362
Bishop, Amanda	Nov., 1956	Z 380
Bonig, Anna Margaret	May, 1958	1 288
Beightol, Alice	May, 1958	1 307
Bruner, Annie	Feb., 1959	1 547
Breighner, Agnes F.	Nov., 1959	2 198

Batie, Albert H.	March, 1960	2 330
Browning, Allen T.	Nov., 1960	3 36

Brown, Benjamin	Feb., 1854	B 76
Baker, Benjamin M. et al	March, 1866	C 89
Blocher, Bell et al	March, 1866	C 89
Blocher, Benjamin M.	Jan., 1866	C 89
Byron, Bridget	May, 1877	D 252
Buskey, Barbara	Jan., 1884	G 13
Barrett, Benjamin	Feb., 1898	G 283
Brooks, Barbarita	Dec., 1902	H 301
Burkett, Benjamin	Dec., 1883	D 569
Bridget, Bernard M.	Aug., 1923	N 105
Benson, Betsie	July, 1927	O 207
Bowers, Bertha M.	Sept., 1929	O 597
Birmingham, Bridget F.	Oct., 1932	Q 94
Boyland, Bernadette L.	Feb., 1937	R 395
Beall, Bertha	May, 1937	R 474
Bradley, Benjamin T.	Oct., 1937	R 585
Browning, Bell	Jan., 1941	T 64
Belfiore, Baldassara	Nov., 1944	U 401
Blonskey, Bertha	Aug., 1950	W 605
Boore, Blanche E.	April, 1952	X 359
Beneman, Barnet	April, 1954	Y 241
Burkey, Bernard E.	Oct. 13, 1954	Y 374
Bridges, Bessie	July, 1957	Z 579
Bennett, Bertha Ann	March, 1958	1 219
Bender, Bruce	June, 1959	2 51

Broadwater, Charles	Sept., 1859	B 162
Boettcher, Charles	July 22, 1873	D 114
Bepler, Charles	Feb., 1877	D 317
Brod, Charles	Jan., 1894	G 6
Bruce, Columbia S.	April, 1895	G 112
Brod, Conrad	June, 1896	G 181
Betzold, Conrad	Jan., 1899	G 331
Barley, Catherine	Feb., 1905	I 76
Brode, Conrad, Sr.	April, 1906	I 198
Burke, Charles Alfred	Nov., 1907	I 335
Bretz, Calton L.	Aug., 1910	J 185

Brode, Catherine	Nov., 1912	J 466
Beeman, Charles H	Dec., 1914	K 257
Barncord, Catherine A.	Jan., 1920	M 110
Blonskey, Charles	March, 1923	N 21
Bopp, Catherine	March, 1926	N 564
Breighner, Charles D.	Sept., 1929	O 594
Bear, Charles H.	Oct., 1929	P 23
Bond, Celia A.	July, 1933	Q 244
Bortz, Christopher C.	Feb., 1934	Q 361
Boon, Charles T.	March, 1934	Q 395
Bowden, Charles	June, 1935	R 51
Bahen, Cornelius	July, 1935	R 55
Buskey, Catherine M.	Jan., 1936	R 162
Broderick, Clare	Oct., 1936	R 325
Boor, Charles G.	Aug., 1937	R 531
Buckingham, Caroline Taylor	Sept., 1937	R 558
Beeman, Charles J.	March, 1938	S 69
Betz, Charles F.	Jan., 1939	S 250
Brode, Charles D.	March, 1940	S 506
Brandler, Charles H.	July, 1941	T 177
Bishields, Congetta	Sept., 1941	T 239
Buskey, Catherine C.	Dec., 1941	T 303
Brashear, Clara	June, 1941	T 415
Bruce, Columbia Sprigg	Oct., 1942	T 500
Browning, Clara E.	Aug., 1944	U 357
Bloss, Carl W.	May, 1945	U 563
Brinkman, Clara W.	Jan., 1946	V 115
Bishop, Charles E.	April, 1947	V 443
Best, Caroline Lucie	May, 1947	V 481
Bowie, Charlotte W.	March 8, 1949	W 284
Baker, Charles L.	Oct. 14,1949	W 417
Bowen, Clara A.	March, 1950	W 508
Bloom, Cecil C.	May, 1950	W 551
Brown, Charles F.	Nov., 1950	X 46
Bender, Christopher C.	Dec., 1950	X 62
Brant, Catherine B.	Sept., 1954	Y 336
Beck, Charles Albert	Jan., 1957	Z 429
Broadstock, Cora E.	Jan., 1958	1 162
Brown, Catherine Davis	Nov., 1959	2 213
Beck, Charles Hermann	July, 1960	2 482
Brown, Charles W.	Sept., 1960	2 550

Blocher, Daniel	May, 1841	A 499
Baker, Dennis et al	March, 1866	C 89
Blocher, Daniel	Jan., 1866	C 89
Bowman, David	May, 1872	D 20
Border, David	June, 1872	D 25
Blocher, Daniel	Jan., 1881	D 465
Brod, Daniel	July, 1886	E 202
Blackiston, David James	June, 1915	K 364
Brode, Daniel C.	Nov., 1920	M 228
Brashears, David W.	March, 1923	N 18
Bittner, David	March, 1923	N 32
Barth, Denton	June, 1933	Q 232
Benson, Davisson Armstrong	May, 1938	S 102
Boyle, Dennis A.	Aug., 1938	S 143
Brady, Darby	April, 1939	S 306
Brotemarkle, David W.	June, 1941	T 167
Bauer, Douglas H.	March, 1943	U 25
Brailer, David	Oct., 1943	U 175
Brinkman, Daniel W.	May, 1945	U 535
Bennett, Dennis	April, 1946	V 194
Bortz, D. Russell	Oct., 1947	V 572
Boal, David	March, 1954	Y 225
Boward, Daisy Pearl	Aug., 1956	Z 327
Bradley, David	Oct., 1958	1 440

Barcus, Ebenezer	July, 1803	A 67
Boyd, Edmund	Sept., 1817	A 159
Bromley, Elizabeth	Dec., 1830	A 305
Bruce, Eleanor	March, 1834	A 347
Brant, Elizabeth	June, 1855	B 95
Bauer, Ernest	June, 1863	C 26
Blocher, Edwin Geo. et al	June, 1866	C 89
Brennan, Edward	Oct., 1870	C 183
Bowman, Elizabeth	May, 1872	D 22
Ball, Edward	Feb., 1897	G 217
Boston, Elizabeth	Sept., 1901	H 215
Blackiston, Elizabeth	April, 1905	I 96
Barth, Ernest	March, 1908	I 375
Bottenfield, Emory E.	Jan., 1910	J 104
Beall, Emma A.	Feb., 1910	J 127
Beachy, Emma L.	May, 1913	K 22
Beaver, Edwin H.	June, 1913	K 39

Beals, Emanuel	Dec., 1914	K 265
Brady, Ellen	June, 1917	L 213
Barton, Elizabeth	April, 1918	L 341
Byrne, Ella P.	Aug., 1918	L 396
Britting, Eva	May, 1919	M 38
Butler, Emma M.	Oct., 1921	M 372
Baker, Eliza L.	Dec., 1922	M 575
Boston, Ella C.	July, 1924	N 284
Broadrup, Emma S.	May, 1926	O 7
Barney, Ella	July, 1926	O 26
Brackett, Elizabeth C.	April, 1929	O 530
Byers, Edna M.	Nov., 1929	P 37
Bradley, Edward R.	June, 1930	P 168
Bone, Emma	June, 1933	Q 240
Barnes, Edward	July, 1933	Q 245
Borgman, Elizabeth F.	Jan., 1934	Q 350
Brown, Elizabeth A.	Nov., 1934	Q 528
Boston, Elliott R.	Dec., 1935	R 144
Blaker, Ethel R.	Oct., 1936	R 324
Barnard, Emma E.	March, 1938	S 68
Balsley, Eli Lee	May, 1938	S 103
Bartol, Elanor H.	Nov., 1938	S 194
Birmingham, Estelle	May, 1939	S 320
Betz, Emma E.	June, 1939	S 335
Bepler, Emma V.	March, 1941	T 110
Browne, Eva P.	Oct., 1942	T 498
Burns, Esther	Dec., 1942	T 545
Bergman, E.L.	Oct., 1943	U 179
Buzzerd, Elizabeth M.	March, 1945	U 490
Burrows, Eleanor Cartmel	March, 1947	V 419
Brannon, Elizabeth	May, 1947	V 476
Bruce, Eleanor Katharine	Aug., 1947	V 530
Blacklin, Eleanora	Feb., 1948	W 28
Barncord, Elizabeth	Feb., 1948	W 34
Beard, Ellen	Feb., 1948	W 39
Buchholtz, Elizabeth C.	March, 1948	W 61
Burket, Elias G.	Oct., 1948	W 200
Browning, Ephraim	Oct., 1949	W 415
Brailer, Ella C.	April, 1950	W 531
Batie, Emma Amelia	May, 1950	W 543
Bullett, Edmonia	March, 1951	X 131
Burnworth, Elizabeth	July, 1951	X 209
Boor, Emma R.	July, 1952	X 446
Beck, Elmer G.	Nov., 1952	X 517

Betz, Emma Morrow	Jan., 1953	X 572
Beckman, Elizabeth M.	March, 1953	Y 4
Baldwin, Elmer A.	April, 1953	Y 26
Bernstein, Emmanuel M.	Oct., 1954	Y 385
Bradley, Emma G.	Dec., 1954	Y 419
Beaver, Ellen E.	Feb., 1956	Z 175
Bruner, Edith Mary	Sept., 1956	Z 335
Burkett, Ellen E.	April, 1957	Z 511
Byrnes, Eleanor C.	July, 1958	1 355
Beck, Elizabeth L.	Dec., 1959	2 231
Buchanan, Elizabeth	Sept., 1960	2 558
Browning, Ernest Herman	Nov., 1960	3 15

Bruce, Francis	Dec., 1833	A 340
Barton, Frances	March, 1862	B 200
Bausch, Frank O.	March, 1885	E 100
Brockman, Francis	March, 1889	E 373
Beall, Franck C.		F 91
Brune, Frederick W.	April, 1899	G 352
Barger, Francis	Dec., 1900	H 134
Banks, Frances	April, 1901	H 171
Bareis, Felix	Sept., 1905	I 140
Brown, Francis F.	Oct., 1907	I 325
Blaul, Frank A.	April, 1915	K 326
Beall, Franklin G.	Oct., 1916	L 68
Beier, Friedericke	April, 1920	M 159
Blaul, Frederick H.	Oct., 1922	M 532
Blaul, Ferdinand	Jan., 1923	M 582
Barnes, Frank J.	March, 1923	N 14
Baxter, Frances	June, 1924	N 272
Beall, Frank C.	June, 1925	N 430
Brackett, Frank E.	Dec., 1926	O 106
Burgee, Frederick	Dec., 1926	O 110
Brewer, Frank L.	Nov., 1927	O 258
Brookman, Frank Joseph	May, 1931	P 370
Bill, Frank	May, 1933	Q 214
Burrows, Fleming W.	Dec., 1933	Q 322
Barnard, Fuller, Jr.	April, 1937	R 457
Barnard, Fuller	May, 1937	R 475
Brookman, Frank Joseph	Feb., 1938	S 45
Brackett, F. Ernest	Jan., 1939	S 242
Bennett, Frances Susan	Oct., 1939	S 398

Billmeyer, Frank	July, 1941	T 186
Buckholtz, F.A.	Oct., 1942	T 508
Bealky, Frank J.	March, 1951	X 123
Burkett, Florence R.	May, 1952	X 389
Burch, Francis M.	Aug., 1955	Z 47
Blackwell, Flora M.	Feb., 1956	Z 167
Blaul, Frank R.	Jan., 1958	1 139

Bruce, George	Dec., 1804	A 150
Brown, George	Dec., 1827	A 270
Brand, George N.	July, 1856	B 116
Brinker, George		C 46
Butler, Jos. R. Guardian	Dec., 1863	C 48
Beall, Gustavus	Jan., 1866	C 63
Beall, G., Jr.	Jan., 1866	C 65
Baker, George et al	March, 1866	C 89
Blocher, George M et al	Jan., 1866	C 89
Beall, Gustavus, Jr.	Aug., 1866	C 186
Beall, George W.	Nov., 1871	C 207
Brinker, George	Feb., 1874	D 147
Beall, George W.		F 91
Boettner, George, Sr.	March, 1893	F 345
Boettner, George	Dec., 1896	G 212
Brown, George Wm.	April, 1899	G 354
Buckell, George	April, 1907	I 268
Banks, George	Jan., 1912	J 371
Bowers, George	Sept., 1915	K 393
Bennett, George	Dec. 1918	L 444
Blume, George E.	Dec., 1922	M 568
Brockey, George H.	April, 1923	N 47
Broadrup, George E.	Dec., 1924	N 347
Beachy, Gideon J.	Aug., 1925	N 461
Bradour, George W.	March, 1928	O 316
Brant, Grafton	Aug., 1915	K 377
Blake, Grover C.	Sept., 1934	Q 499
Butler, G.Stanley	Oct., 1938	S 165
Bloss, George W.	March, 1941	T 112
Beall, George N.	Aug., 1941	T 208
Butler, Gertrude L.	Feb., 1942	T 321
Brailer, George C., Sr.	Dec., 1942	T 564
Broadrup, George L.	June, 1937	R 600
Barth, George G.	May, 1943	U 78

Bowman, George A.	May, 1946	V 233
Barker, George L.	June, 1946	V 249
Burns, Garrett	Aug., 1947	V 531
Barnard, George Wimmel	June, 1949	W 333
Bottenfield, George R.	May, 1951	X 180
Brown, George Walter	Nov., 1954	Y 387
Belfiore, Giuseppina	July, 1958	1 338
Beck, George C.	Oct., 1958	1 426
Beall, Golda Virginia	Nov., 1958	1 448
Buchanan, George L.	Sept., 1960	2 531

Briscoe, Hanson	Jan., 1807	A 145
same	Dec., 1808	A 146
same	Nov., 1809	A 146
same	Dec., 1810	A 147
same	Dec., 1811	A 147
same	Oct., 1817	A 161
Bruce, Helen	June, 1841	A 484
Bevans, Henry	Nov., 1849	B 12
Brown, Horace N.	May, 1858	B 145
Butt, Hazel S.	March, 1860	B 172
Blocher, Hannah et al	1866	C 89
Bishop, Henry et al	Aug., 1869	C 155
Bier, H.M. and wife	Dec., 1873	D 144
Brown, Herman, Sr.	Jan., 1879	D 393
Bucy, Henry	Sept., 1883	D 627
Brotemarkle, Henry	March, 1889	E 374
Brooks, Horace	Nov., 1894	G 82
Betz, Henry	Jan., 1902	H 249
Bucy, Harriet	March, 1906	I 188
Bear, Hartz	Dec., 1907	I 346
Blocher, Henry W.	Dec., 1911	J 363
Brown, Henry B.	Feb., 1914	K 143
Boor, Henry M.	April, 1920	M 160
Bowden, Henrietta	Feb., 1923	N 8
Barncord, Henry Thomas	Dec., 1923	N 166
Brinkman, Harman	Oct., 1926	O 67
Boyd, Herbert S.	July, 1927	O 214
Bell, Harriett Ann	Jan., 1929	O 456
Beall, Horace	Aug., 1931	P 411
Brashears, Howard	May, 1933	Q 206
Bachman, Henry A.	Jan., 1934	Q 351

Bayard, John H. continued	Dec., 1795	A 142
same	May, 1797	A 142
Butler, John George	Jan., 1817	A 155
Barker, John	Nov., 1820	A 190
Bare, Jacob	May, 1823	A 209
Bayard, John H.	Nov., 1828	A 338
Boxwell, Joseph	June, 1838	A 423
Barkdoll, Jacob	Feb., 1848	A 639
Boger, John	Jan., 1850	B 15
Beeghley, Joseph	April, 1852	B 51
Boyer, Jacob	Oct., 1855	B 97
Beall, John	Jan., 1861	B 184
Brobst, John	Jan., 1862	B 195
Bucy, Jesse et al	Oct., 1863	C 33
Beall, Jesse T.	Jan. 1866	C 65
Blocher, John George	Jan. 1866	C 65
same	1866	C 89
Bray, John	Aug., 1866	C 77
Blocher, Jacob et al	1866	C 89
Butler, Jos. R. Guardian	Dec. 1863	C 48
Benenderfer, Jos.	June, 1858	B 146
Brown, Julia Ann	May, 1858	B 145
Buchanan, John M.	Aug., 1854	B 83
Beatty, James	Nov., 1869	C 153
Brook, John R.	June, 1870	C 174
Bryan, John	March, 1865	C 210
Buchanan, John M.	Nov. 1867	C 156
same	March, 1869	C 157
Butler, John	May, 1872	D 19
Barnwell, James	March, 1874	D 151
Brotemarkle, John J.	Aug., 1875	D 240
Bancord, John et al		D 406
Brown, Jacob	July, 1879	D 410
Bell, Jos., (colored)	July 21, 1881	D 491
Boward, John	June, 1882	D 545
Baker, Jacob	Sept., 1882	D 561
Burkett, Benjamin	Dec., 1882	D 569
Barnard, James	Feb., 1884	E 15
Brown, James	May, 1887	E 231
Brandler, J.N.M.	Nov., 1891	F 224
Bachman, John Martin	Jan. 5, 1892	F 251
Blackiston, John T.	Aug. 4, 1893	F 387
Brant, John G.	April, 1894	G 35
Brandler, J.N.M.	Dec. 1, 1899	H 2

Boal, John, Sr.	March, 1899	G 342
Brandler, J.N.M.	Dec., 1899	H 2
Boyce, James	Feb., 1900	H 58
Brailer, Jerome	April, 1901	H 167
Bevans, James H.	Oct., 1904	I 50
Bressler, John M.	June, 1909	J 58
Boor, John T.	June, 1910	J 165
Baker, James	Jan., 1911	J 222
Burkhart, Jacob F.	March, 1911	J 257
Bannatyne, James	July, 1910	J 171
Beck, John D.	Oct., 1911	J 329
Butt, John W.	Aug., 1912	J 447
Bannatyne, John	March, 1914	K 158
Bourne, James M.	July, 1914	K 203
Boyd, John M.	Oct., 1916	L 64
Bopst, Joshua D.	Jan., 1917	L 116
Byrnes, John J.	May, 1917	L 178
Bopp, John A.	Aug., 1917	L 217
Bowden, J.A.B.	Dec., 1917	L 277
Bowser, Joseph	Jan., 1918	L 292
Broadwater, John W.	Jan., 1919	L 461
Briscoe, John	July, 1921	M 348
Blake, John	April, 1922	M 452
Barrett, James, Sr.	March, 1923	N 22
Barnes, Jennie	April, 1923	N 40
Brown, James	April, 1923	N 41
Bopst, Julia E.	Oct., 1923	N 141
Bramble, John T.	Dec., 1923	N 167
Baker, James	Jan., 1924	N 203
Burkett, Josiah	Dec., 1925	N 510
Beeman, James H.	Feb., 1926	N 546
Brown, Joseph	July, 1926	O 39
Barber, John	May, 1928	O 339
Beals, John J.	Jan., 1929	O 457
Bender, Jacob B.	Dec., 1929	P 65
Barncord, John P.	Feb., 1930	P 97
Bradley, James	April, 1930	P 143
Brooks, John J.	June, 1931	P 390
Becker, J. Joseph	Sept., 1931	P 451
Burley, Jennie	Nov., 1931	P 488
Broadwater, Josiah	May, 1932	P 585
Boyd, James Graham	June, 1933	Q 235
Billings, John P.	June, 1934	Q 449
Beard, James William	June, 1934	Q 452

Bowe, John W.	Dec., 1934	Q 556
Barnard, Joshua S.	Sept., 1935	R 93
Bennett, Josephine G.	Sept., 1935	R 111
Bowen, John D.	June, 1936	R 256
Biser, Joseph	Oct., 1936	R 337
Bible, James W.	March, 1937	R 433
Brady, J.P.	Sept., 1937	R 552
Bender, Julia M.	Jan., 1938	S 39
Bepler, J.Harry	Jan., 1939	S 239
Brown, Joseph H.	March, 1939	S 288
Blake, Joseph	April, 1939	S 298
Bedinger, Joseph B.	March, 1940	S 513
Brinker, John A.	July, 1940	S 594
Bell, John W.	August, 1940	S 611
Barry, James J.	Jan., 1943	T 578
Blonskey, John	Sept., 1944	U 368
Burt, James	Nov., 1944	U 406
Bone, John S.	June, 1945	U 570
Brinker, Joseph H.	April, 1946	V 187
Bright, Jesse M.	Oct., 1946	V 302
Brady, James	Dec., 1948	W 249
Bailey, Julia M.	Nov., 1949	W 428
Barnard, John	Dec., 1949	W 442
Bean, John, Sr.	Feb., 1950	W 476
Boyd, J. Thruston	Jan., 1952	X 307
Burkey, Jerome Joseph	Feb., 1952	X 318
Barrett, James P.	May, 1952	X 391
Bucklew, John E.	Sept., 1953	Y 122
Buser, John W.	Jan., 1954	Y 197
Bragg, Joseph C.	Sept., 1954	Y 338
Black, Jessie Gary	April, 1955	Y 544
Brodbeck, Janet Hamilton	Aug., 1955	Z 58
Beck, Joseph Anthony	Jan., 1957	Z 425
Botzum, John R.	Feb., 1959	1 548
Bittner, John Hunter	April, 1960	2 389
Bartlett, Jay O.	July, 1960	2 505
Beeman, Jesse T.	July, 1960	2 469
Bradley, Jenkin	Oct., 1960	2 579
Bond, James Hooper	Oct., 1960	2 583

Balke, Kate	Jan., 1893	F 339
Blonskey, Kate	July, 1938	S 123

Brandstretter, Matthia	Feb., 1791	A 2
Browning, Meshack	Dec., 1859	B 169
Butt, Mary M.	Sept., 1863	C 29
Beall, Mehettable C.	Feb., 1873	D 91
Bier, M.H. and wife	Dec. 1873	D 144
Beers, Martha M.	July, 1878	D 367
Barnes, Melinda (colored)	April, 1883	D 595
Bretz, Mary C.	Dec., 1883	E 9
Baker, Margaret M.	Dec., 1883	E 9
Brooks, Martha	June, 1884	E 66
Bausch, Frank O.	March, 1885	E 100
Barry, Margaret	July 7, 1885	E 130
Beck, Margaretta C.	Oct., 1885	E 138
Brotemarkle, Michael	Nov., 1885	E 146
Bucy, Margaret	Jan., 1886	E 150
Barchus, Mary	June, 1891	F 206
Barger, Mary E.	June, 1891	F 208
Brill, Mary A.		F 218
Broderick, Mary	Sept., 1893	F 392
Beck, Maria Sophia	Feb., 1895	G 96
Bepler, Magdalene	Feb., 1895	G 100
Bevans, Mary Ann	July, 1896	G 182
Bennett, Mary Ann	Dec., 1900	H 139
Black, Margaret M.	Feb., 1901	H 149
Bradburn, Margaret	Oct., 1901	H 224
Beall, Marthy	May, 1902	H 268
Berg, Mary E.	April, 1903	H 331
Bush, Mary L.	June, 1905	I 114
Brinker, Mary	March, 1910	J 134
Barth, Margaret	May, 1910	J 159
Boston, Mary	Feb., 1911	J 244
Brown, Madeone	Nov., 1911	J 350
Bell, Margaret S.	July, 1912	J 435
Brock, Mary	March, 1914	K 145
Beeche, Mary	July, 1914	K 206
Brown, Marion	May, 1915	K 337
Bender, Mary A.	July, 1917	L 212
Bohn, Mary	April, 1918	L 347
Bevans, Mary A.C.	Feb., 1919	L 467
Bealkey, Mary	March, 1919	M 11
Bacon, Mary Jane	Sept., 1921	M 362
Butcher, Margaret O.	Feb., 1922	M 416
Blackiston, Mary J.	May, 1923	N 58
Browning, Meshack	Jan., 1925	N 367

Ball, Maria C.	June, 1927	O 187
Beane, Michael	Sept., 1927	O 248
Bruce, Mary A.	March, 1929	O 501
Bruce, Mary F.	Oct., 1929	P 26
Bowman, Mary A.	Aug., 1930	P 206
Boward, Matilda	May, 1932	Q 6
Brady, Mary A.	Feb., 1933	Q 154
Barrett, Mary Ann	Aug., 1933	Q 262
Brode, Mary D.	Nov., 1934	Q 531
Beggs, Margaret	Nov., 1934	Q 534
Boon, May Smoot	Jan., 1935	Q 559
Becker, Mary	Feb., 1936	R 185
Boyd, Mary A.	June, 1936	R 265
Burns, Mary A.	July, 1936	R 269
Barncord, Martha E.	Feb., 1937	R 418
Brinkman, Marshall A.	Feb., 1938	S 57
Bone, Mary Louise Johnson	Dec., 1938	S 212
Baker, Minnie W.	March, 1939	S 297
Bigler, Maggie	April, 1940	S 531
Bennett, Margaret E.	Nov., 1940	T 32
Brown, Mamie L. Copeland	Jan., 1941	T 74
Beggs, Mary Regina	March, 1941	T 98
Brown, Mary R.	Dec., 1941	T 292
Bayer, Mary E.	Dec., 1942	T 567
Burall, Mary C.	Feb., 1944	U 249
Beeman, Margaret E.	Oct., 1945	V 66
Blaul, Margaret	March, 1946	V 142
Byrne, Mary Ellen	April, 1946	V 181
Bartgis, Michael D.	May, 1947	V 487
Bratt, Mary E.	June, 1948	W 142
Blaul, Martha Flurshutz	March, 1949	W 286
Burns, Michael J.	July, 1949	W 350
Brooks, Margaret T.	May, 1950	W 557
Blaul, Matilda M.	May, 1950	W 559
Bostetter, Margaret L.M.	July, 1950	W 599
Bopst, Mary E.	March, 1951	X 134
Burall, Mary A.	May, 1951	X 170
Barnes, Mabel M.	June, 1953	Y 50
Burkhard, Mina C.	Sept., 1953	Y 113
Bealky, Mary Catherine	Nov., 1953	Y 165
Burgess, Mahlon H.	Jan., 1955	Y 437
Bill, Mary	Sept., 1956	Z 332
Buchholtz, Mary Josephine	Aug., 1957	1 27
Boyd, Margaret G.	Sept., 1957	1 62

Berry, Mary E.	Feb., 1959	1 557
Burns, Margaret A.	May, 1959	2 32
Brailer, Mary F.	Dec., 1959	2 251
Boward, Margaret Ethel	Oct., 1960	3 7
Barber, Melvin	Nov., 1960	3 24

Bryan, Nathaniel	Aug., 1861	B 191
Berkard, Nicholas	March, 1865	C 53
Baird, Nancy M.	March, 1881	D 475
same. Heirs.	March, 1881	D 480
Brandler, Nicholas P. J.		D 502
Beall, Nelson	March, 1886	E 168
Biederman, Norah	June, 1916	L 20
Beck, Nellie S.	Sept., 1932	Q 73
Bowden, Nancy E.	Nov., 1938	S 184
Bittner, Nettie Jeannette	Oct., 1944	U 394
Barnard, Notley	March, 1946	V 160
Broadrup, Nellie D.	Sept., 1949	W 388
Bean, Nora Dale	July, 1954	Y 304
Bawden, Nellie Burgess)	Aug., 1957	1 13
Bowden, Nellie Burgess)	same	1 13
Brinker, Nora Evangeline	March, 1959	1 578
Birch, Naomi E.	April, 1960	2 359
Beeman, Noah	Sept., 1960	2 571
Berkenbaugh, Nellie P.	Oct., 1960	2 595
Bloss, Nettie Virginia	Oct., 1960	3 1

Boor, Oliver Perry	Dec., 1913	K 112
Benson, Ola	Oct., 1932	Q 78
Barncord, Oliver P.	May, 1936	R 243
Berg, Oscar F.	May, 1950	W 536
Boughton, Orble B.	Oct., 1960	2 578

Baumward, Peter	Nov., 1829	A 294
Bucy, Paul, Sr.	March, 1830	A 300
Bray, Philip H.	Aug., 1844	A 540
Bucy, Priscilla J.	March, 1855	B 91
Biddinger, Peter	Oct., 1857	B 127

Bucy, Paul	Nov., 1861	C 2
Bancord, Peter	May, 1879	D 406
Bier, Philip A.	Nov., 1881	F 225
Brown, Peter	March, 1928	O 320
Blank, Perry Franklin	Oct., 1928	O 411
Barnes, P. Clarence	Feb., 1934	Q 354
Benford, Preston L.	Sept., 1938	S 158
Bush, Peter	Nov., 1940	T 29
Brode, Philip	Feb., 1945	U 464
Bradley, Patrick	Nov., 1957	1 121

Beall, Richard	Feb., 1837	A 405
Beall, Rezin	Sept., 1856	B 119
Beall, Rachel	Jan., 1866	C 65
Brant, Rebecca	Jan., 1868	C 109
Bane, Rebecca	Oct., 1873	D 222
Bruce, Robert	Nov., 1875	D 251
same	Nov., 1879	D 417
same	Nov., 1883	E 1
same	Nov., 1887	E 282
same	June, 1890	F 103
Brannon, Robert H.	Nov. 1899	G 397
Burnup, Robert H.	April, 1902	H 266
Bole, Robert A.	Sept., 1924	N 323
Bell, Richard S.	Jan., 1933	Q 142
Beegle, Roland B.	Sept., 1937	R 569
Bucy, R.W.	Oct., 1940	T 20
Bradley, Rebecca	Jan., 1941	T 71
Brode, Rachel	April, 1941	T 127
Burns, Rachel L.	May, 1943	U 85
Brake, Robert Luther	June, 1943	U 98
Byrd, Robert L.	Feb., 1944	U 252
Brady, Rose	Dec., 1944	U 415
Brinker, Rose C.	Aug., 1945	V 23
Barnard, R. Marshall	May, 1946	V 236
Bobo, Robert L.	Feb., 1947	V 399
Bock, Rose B.	June, 1947	V 499
Bradley, Rebecca	Feb., 1948	W 52
Barnard, Robert E.	Nov., 1952	X 522
Barncord, Royal Price	Sept., 1954	Y 354
Broadrup, Ralph D.	Sept., 1957	1 75
Barnes, Robert S.	Oct., 1959	2 179

Borst, Raymond Leroy	May, 1960	2 424
Barth, Robert N.	June, 1960	2 446
Bagley, Ross	Nov., 1960	3 12

Brown, Samuel	May, 1829	A 285
Bucy, Samuel	March, 1840	A 458
Bowden, Samuel	Jan., 1854	B 74
Bowden, Samuel H.O.	June, 1853	B 201
Benenderfer, Sarah	June, 1858	B 146
Brady, Samuel D.	Feb., 1870	C 162
Brady, Susan F.	Feb., 1871	C 186
Biddinger, Solomon H.	Jan., 1872	C 212
Brandt, Susannah	Jan., 1877	D 315
Bluebaugh & wife, Simon et al	May, 1879	D 406
Bluebaugh, Simon (Resident of Somerset Co.)	May, 1879	D 407
Bear, Solomon	July, 1891	F 213
Bucy, Sarah	Oct., 1893	F 395
Blubaugh, Simon (Copy)	March, 1895	G 101
same	Aug., 1895	G 129
Bear, Sarah	Dec., 1897	G 273
Broderick, Stephen	Dec., 1910	J 211
Buchanan, Sarah P.	Dec., 1912	J 475
Beall, Susan	Feb., 1913	J 486
Brinker, Sophia M.	April, 1916	L 1
Buchanan, Sarah	Nov., 1919	M 101
Butler, Sarah E.W.	March, 1924	N 230
Bradley, Samuel	April, 1925	N 419
Brady, Susan E.	March, 1929	O 498
Blubaugh, Sarah	April, 1929	O 534
Bearinger, Suzan	March, 1930	P 122
Beckman, Stephen Eckhart	May, 1930	P 149
Blank, Samuel W.	June, 1930	P 174
Brown, Samuel	July, 1930	P 196
Buley, Sanford	Sept., 1930	P 212
Bittner, Sarah Ellen	June, 1933	Q 227
Blocher, Sophia	Aug., 1933	Q 261
Bowman, Squire	Oct., 1934	Q 501
Brant, Shannon	March, 1935	R 9
Bingham, Susanna	June, 1936	R 267
Byrne, Sarah	July, 1939	S 359
Barncord, Samuel M.	Dec., 1940	T 47

Bowers, Victor C.	March, 1908	I 372
Burkhart, Virginia T.	March 8, 1949	W 281
Black, Van Lear	April, 1955	Y 541
Brant, Videtta I.	Nov., 1955	Z 117

Barnes, William	May, 1821	A 197
Bevans, Walter	April, 1840	A 466
Biddinger, William	Dec., 1862	C 15
Beall, W.R.	Jan., 1866	C 65
Beers, William H.	July, 1878	D 367
Buchanan, William J.	Jan., 1903	H 317
Beall, Walter	June, 1906	I 213
Bohn, William	July, 1908	I 425
Brown, William	June, 1912	J 431
Bachman, William	July, 1919	M 55
Becker, William C.	Dec., 1920	M 237
Bruce, William M.	April, 1923	N 49
Buchholtz, William A.	Oct., 1924	N 327
Bone, William	Nov., 1924	N 337
Broderick, William F.	Nov., 1927	O 264
Barton, William E.	Nov., 1928	O 430
Bradley, William B.	Nov., 1930	P 255
Brown, William W.	Nov., 1931	P 487
Butler, Wright	May, 1932	Q 5
Burns, William L.	April, 1933	Q 189
Bush, William S.	May, 1933	Q 226
Barnard, William W.	May, 1934	Q 430
Burger, William S.	Feb., 1935	Q 594
Brophy, William	Nov., 1937	R 596
Baird, William B.	April, 1939	S 299
Babst, William	June, 1941	T 159
Brown, W.T.	Aug., 1941	
Britzel, William Frederick	Oct., 1944	U 386
Bever, William E.	Jan., 1945	U 439
Boor, William K.	Nov., 1945	V 83
Boward, W. Lester	June, 1946	V 243
Bruce, William Motter	Oct., 1948	W 214
Bowman, Winmer	Jan., 1950	W 459
Beane, W.T.	Feb., 1950	W 480
Bishop, Wilbur K.	April, 1950	W 527
Buchanan, William E.	Dec., 1954	Y 430
Burrell, William C.	Dec., 1955	Z 122

Bothwell, William	Feb., 1957	Z 453
Brandler, Walter W.	Sept., 1950	X 17
Burns, William R.	April, 1957	Z 507
Blake, William H.	April, 1959	2 6
Brown, William	July, 1959	2 116
Breighner, William F.	Sept., 1959	2 149

C

Cresap, Abigail	March, 1843	A 510
Corbus, Ann	Sept., 1859	B 178
Cramer, A.M.C.	Jan., 1873	D 78
Cisel, Anna S.	Feb., 1889	E 365
Coyle, Anthony	Sept., 1907	I 316
Capper, Alfred	May, 1910	J 162
Curran, Ann	Nov., 1910	J 205
Carpenter, Alma J.	March, 1912	J 405
Conway, Annie Mary	June, 1913	K 30
Crump, Amelia	March, 1915	K 300
Cadden, Ann	April, 1917	L 170
Clark, Anna R.	Feb., 1920	M 120
Charles, Albert	Jan., 1924	N 189
Cavanaugh, Annie	April, 1935	R 22
Caton, Annie	March, 1940	S 507
Comp, Adam A.	June, 1941	T 164
Carleton, Annie Laurie	Nov., 1941	T 284
Clark, Alvie A.	Aug., 1943	U 132
Chase, Annie E.	Jan., 1944	U 232
Cook, Anna Mary	May, 1944	U 298
Coulehan, Alice Reid	Sept., 1944	U 359
Carner, Anna R.	Oct., 1944	U 377
Cobler, Anna Down	Sept., 1945	V 35
Clark, Sr., Arnold Gerstell	Nov., 1945	V 80
Caton, Annie C.	May, 1949	W 326
Crosby, Annie G.	Oct., 1949	W 418
Clinedinst, Albert	March, 1952	X 349
Centonfonti, Anna	Aug., 1953	Y 91
Corrigan, Anne S.	Jan., 1954	Y 199
Chorpenning, Alonzo J.	May, 1959	2 19
Clark, Arthur P.	June, 1959	2 70

Coddington, Benjamin	May, 1840	A 463
Collins, Bridget	July, 1899	G 364
Cooney, Bernard F.	Feb., 1906	I 173
Cavanaugh, Bridget	Feb., 1911	J 248
Cole, Barbara E.	Jan., 1919	L 463
Carney, Bridget	Dec., 1924	N 345

Coulehan, Bernard J.	July, 1928	O 369
Clark, Beulah	April, 1930	P 131
Cook, Belle C.	Dec., 1935	R 157
Coyle, Bernard	June, 1937	R 512
Cavanaugh, Bridget E.	June, 1942	T 428
Canty, Bessie	Jan., 1946	V 118
Chestnut, Bruce	March, 1947	V 428
Cupler, Bessie M.	July, 1954	Y 311
Carney, Bertha L.	July, 1956	Z 273
Cunningham, Bessie May	April, 1957	Z 516
Cooke, Benjamin P.	May, 1957	Z 529
Capel, Beatrice Alice	June, 1958	1 316
Carl, B.Harrison	Oct., 1959	2 169

Creighbaum, Conrad	March, 1821	A 193
Chapman, Collimore	April, 1855	B 92
Calmes, Catherine	Nov., 1857	B 131
Conner, Cornelius	Jan., 1872	C 216
Cavanaugh, Charles	March, 1874	D 151
Creitzberg, Casper	Jan., 1886	E 155
Cassen, Caroline S.	March, 1904	I 06
Casperline, Caroline	Aug., 1904	I 37
Clark, Catharine E.	(See Kate E.Clark)	J 86
Cornish, Catharine	Oct., 1911	J 331
Cunningham, Charles L.	Oct., 1913	K 93
Connor, Charles	Feb., 1916	K 483
Conley, Charles E.	June, 1919	M 54
Cullen, Catherine W.	March, 1920	M 136
Cosgrove, Catherine	June, 1925	N 436
Clarke, Cora C.	April, 1926	N 587
Cutter, Charles	Aug., 1928	O 380
Cunrod, Caroline I.	Feb., 1931	P 312
Chestnut, C.B.	Aug., 1934	Q 485
Crawford, Charles P.	Oct., 1934	Q 511
Chappell, Catherine S.	June, 1937	R 504
Cooper, Clara B.	April, 1938	S 76
Childers, Calvin S.	Dec., 1939	S 445
Codire, Christopher J.	Feb., 1940	S 476
Capitale, Charles	May, 1941	T 134
Crowe, Charles C.	Dec., 1941	T 304
Cathcart, Charles	June, 1942	T 420
Conley, Catherine	Oct., 1944	U 396

Cox, Charles W.	Aug., 1947	V 534
Colgate, Charles Henry	Aug., 1947	V 540
Carabine, Charles A.	Jan., 1948	W 25
Clark, Clarence Miller	April, 1948	W 86
Clark, Clarence E.	June, 1951	X 183
Compton, Cora Norris	Feb., 1957	X 456
Cook, Clarence	June, 1956	Z 256
Cooke, Carl Elisha	Jan., 1958	1 160
Carroll, Caroline H.	Feb., 1958	1 201
Clark, Charles Watson	April, 1958	1 254
Callis, Charles B.	July, 1958	1 345
Carnell, Charles F.	Nov., 1958	1 457
Collins, Charles Leo	Sept., 1959	2 159
Critchfield, Clara E.	Dec., 1960	3 65

Cresap, Daniel	July, 1798	A 36
same	Jan., 1792	A 140
same	Dec., 1792	A 140
same	Oct., 1858	B 144
Coddington, David & Elizabeth	April, 1848	C 140
Chaney, David	March, 1880	D 434
Cavanaugh, D.F.	April, 1884	E 40
Conrad, Daniel	Sept., 1899	G 375
Collins, Dennis	May, 1905	I 107
Cessna, Daniel B.	Feb., 1920	M 118
Cronin, Dennis W.	April, 1920	M 153
Cecil, David L.	Aug., 1921	M 353
Coolidge, Daniel	May, 1924	N 265
Cook, David	Sept., 1925	N 469
Cooper, D.M.	Feb., 1931	P 311
Conrad, David	Jan., 1936	R 168
Colborn, Diana Thomas	Dec., 1952	X 547
Cimmino, Dominick	Nov., 1954	Y 407

Custer, Emmanuel	July, 1829	A 288
Chapman, Ellen	June, 1858	B 146
Cross, Elizabeth	Nov., 1862	C 14
Cook, Edward A.	March, 1869	C 133
Chapman, Edward	June, 1865	C 189
Coleman, Eleanor E.	April, 1885	E 107

Calvert, Florence Ann	Oct., 1945	V 55
Colvin, Frank E.	May, 1946	V 203
Carder, Fayette E.	Nov., 1959	2 215

Culp, George	Feb., 1848	A 644
Cresap, Gustavus		B 149
Clary, Gerard	Sept., 1850	B 20
Clopp, George	Feb., 1889	E 367
Chapman, George	March, 1903	H 326
Cecil, George T.	Jan., 1908	I 365
Clauson, George	July, 1908	I 428
Carpenter, George H.	May, 1916	L 9
Chesshire, George W.	June, 1923	N 69
Cook, George O.	May, 1927	O 173
Clise, George	Nov., 1933	Q 306
Clauson, George W.	Sept., 1942	T 481
Clise, George M.	April, 1947	V 452
Cooper, George Watson	March, 1956	X 205
Cox, George D.	May, 1952	X 392
Conley, George W.	July, 1952	X 445
Campbell, George D.	Aug., 1954	Y 330
Chappell, Glen R.	Sept. 1954	Y 368
Carlson, Gunnar Q.	March, 1955	Y 492
Collins, George W.	Nov., 1957	1 103
Clayton, Guy W.	Feb., 1958	1 200
Cunrod, George T.	Aug., 1959	2 136
Cleveland, Grace	Oct., 1959	2 173
Conner, George Lester	May, 1960	2 429

Callan, Harry W.	Sept. 1907	I 315
Cullen, Hannah	Sept., 1910	J 190
Closterman, Henry	Aug., 1913	K 63
Coggeshall, Henry T.	July, 1927	O 216
Colborn, Harry B.	Sept., 1927	O 255
Crabtree, Herbert	Dec., 1929	P 75
Carleton, Hopewell H.	May, 1931	P 359
Cook, Henry F.	June, 1931	P 398
Cooper, H.C.	Jan., 1932	P 515
Campbell, Harry W.	June, 1934	Q 457
Carroll, Howard B.	Sept., 1936	R 316

Clise, Harry, Sr.	Dec., 1938	S 221
Cochrane, Helen Beall	Aug., 1939	S 371
Clark, Haddon L.	Dec., 1942	T 573
Curry, Hattie Jane	April, 1943	U 53
Chaney, Howard E.	April, 1943	U 60
Carpenter, Herbert Guion	July 9, 1943	U 112
Coleman, Hiram S.	July, 1943	U 129
Conway, Henry J.	June, 1948	W 143
Clark, Harry E., Sr.	Aug., 1948	W 186
Cornwell, Harry L.	Dec., 1951	X 274
Cook, Henry L.	July, 1953	Y 76
Chaney, Hudson	Sept., 1953	Y 114
Coughenour, Harriet M. Lannan	Nov., 1953	Y 167
Cook, Henrietta F. Gerdeman	Nov., 1955	Z 108
Cook, Harry O.	July, 1956	Z 301
Colbert, Herman S.	Sept., 1957	1 65

Coddington, Isabella	Aug., 1841	A 497
Cavanaugh, Isaac	April, 1884	E 42
Carabine, Isabell	Dec., 1903	H 382
Cavanaugh, Isaac A.	March, 1906	I 175
Conrad, Iley K.	March, 1939	S 278
Crowe, Isabella Jane	May, 1940	S 552
Clark, I. Fletch	Sept., 1950	W 632
Cunningham, Ida Marguerite	Sept., 1956	Z 334

Con, John	Feb., 1828	A 271
Cresap, James D.	June, 1836	A 392
Crabtree, James	April, 1838	A 556
Clark, Janet	Nov., 1847	A 633
Commission of Judges		B 17
same		B 18
same		B 40
same		B 41
same		B 83
same		B 84
same		B 131
Chapman, Jane et al	June, 1858	B 146
Clark, John	March, 1851	B 30
Cunningham, James	May, 1853	B 65

Combs, John	July, 1859	B 160
Campbell, John B.H.	May, 1860	B 176
same	May, 1861	B 189
Callan, John	July, 1861	B 189
Christy, John	March, 1862	C 1
Campbell, J.B.H.	Nov., 1863	C 34
Coulehan, John	Nov., 1867	C 156
Casteel, Jesse	Jan., 1870	C 161
Coulehan, John	Bov., 1871	C 208
Crable, Joseph	Aug., 1871	C 205
Coulehan, John	Nov., 1875	D 250
Campbell, John B.H.	March, 1876	D 264
same	Feb., 1876	D 265
Creswell, John S. & wife	July, 1878	D 368
Coulehan, John	Nov., 1879	D 416
same	Nov., 1883	E 1
Carleton, James P.	April, 1884	E 50
Combs, John Sampson	Oct., 1885	E 143
Coulehan, John	Nov., 1887	E 281
Craumer, Joseph	July, 1889	F 29
Callahan, James	Aug., 1892	F 305
Campbell, James	June, 1893	F 372
Corrigan, Jane	March, 1894	G 29
Carroll, Julia P.	Jan., 1900	H 36
Clark, John H.	June, 1904	I 27
Connor, John	March, 1905	I 93
Clifford, James	May, 1905	I 109
Cox, Jane	Sept., 1905	I 136
Cavanaugh, James	April, 1908	I 382
Coleman, John	May, 1908	I 404
Cronley, James	June, 1908	I 420
Coleman, Julia Ann	Aug., 1909	J 67
Cavanaugh, John R.	July, 1911	J 306
Cuthbertson, John	Oct., 1913	K 79
Connor, Janet	Aug., 1916	L 45
Connelly, John J.	Oct., 1918	L 415
Close, John D.	Jan., 1919	L 462
Craze, James H.	April, 1919	M 31
Campbell, John	May, 1919	M 45
Cairnes, James H.	Jan., 1920	M 108
Cisel, James	June, 1920	M 172
Carney, John J.	Sept., 1921	M 367
Carroll, John T.	March, 1923	N 31
Carder, Julia A.	May, 1923	N 64

Crosser, James	July, 1948	W 162
Cook, James Wesley	July, 1948	W 166
Conway, James Michael	Jan., 1949	W 255
Cox, John William	Aug., 1949	W 364
Cookerly, John T.	Jan., 1950	W 472
Campbell, John J.	April, 1950	W 534
Close, John R.	Nov., 1950	X 52
Coleman, Joseph A.	Feb., 1952	X 330
Clark, James D.	June, 1954	Y 290
Corfield, James	Sept., 1954	Y 341
Curry, John Rolland	Oct., 1954	Y 375
Cain, John P.	April, 1955	Y 506
Crites, James	Dec., 1955	Z 118
Couter, John Frederick	Dec.,1955	Z 132
Casey, John L.	May, 1956	Z 248
Crump, J.Taylor	Dec., 1956	Z 406
Cowherd, J.Kile	June, 1957	Z 563
Carder, James C.	Oct., 1958	I 420
Campbell, James	Jan., 1959	I 507
Couter, James	June, 1959	2 43
Cataur, Joseph	Nov., 1959	2 199
Coleman, John H.	Dec., 1959	2 229

Clark, Kate E.	Nov., 1909	J 86
Casey, Katherine C.	Aug., 1931	P 414

Crabtree, Lewis	Oct., 1834	A 359
Chapman, Lewis	June, 1858	B 146
Cole, Lydia Ann	June, 1891	F 199
Cresap, Luther M.	March, 1896	G 169
Coleman, Lewis T.	Feb., 1916	K 468
Carter, Levi	May, 1916	L 2
Carpenter, Levi T.	July, 1923	N 92
Connor, Lillian W.	May, 1932	P 589
Clarke, Louisa F.	Feb., 1935	Q 585
Couthard, Louisa H.	June, 1939	S 352
Connor, Lewis B.	July, 1942	T 426
Clites, Lydia M.	Feb., 1945	U 453
Connor, Lillie	July, 1946	V 257
Carroll, Laura V.	Nov., 1946	V 350

Cooney, Margaret C.	Nov., 1939	S 424
Craddock, Michael Joseph	Jan., 1940	S 453
Close, Margaret	Jan., 1941	T 62
Chambers, Mary B.	Aug., 1941	T 197
Carleton, Murray	Nov., 1941	T 280
Contes, Michael B.	April, 1942	T 375
Codire, Margaret	May, 1943	U 72
Conway, Margaret M.	Jan., 1944	U 227
Copeland, Mollie	March, 1944	U 264
Clinedinst, Mollie V.	April, 1944	U 275
Crowe, Mary Ann	March, 1945	U 468
Carr, Mandy Elizabeth	Jan., 1946	V 116
Cosway, Mary Roman	July, 1947	V 517
Carroll, Mary M.	April, 1948	W 76
Cessna, Mollie C.	April, 1948	W 80
Carmack, Mary	Dec., 1949	W 450
Crump, Mary J.	Feb., 1950	W 477
Cosgrove, Morttie S.	Aug., 1950	W 625
Coleman, Margaret A.	July, 1951	X 200
Clingerman, Myrtle L.	May, 1953	Y 36
Corrigan, M. M.	Oct., 1953	Y 132
Cooke, Mary E.	Aug., 1957	1 29
Crites, Mary Elizabeth	Sept., 1958	1 386
Coulehan, Mary Etta Banks	Sept., 1958	1 397
Cox, Mary Berkeley	Oct., 1958	1 416
Couter, Margaret E.	Nov., 1960	3 38

Cochran, Ninian	Sept., 1802	A 143
Chapman, Nathaniel	May, 1858	B 145
Chapman, Nancy	May, 1858	B 145
Casteel, Nathaniel	April, 1866	C 73
Cromwell, Nancy	Feb., 1871	C 186
Clark, Nancy E.	Feb., 1942	T 324
Carder, Newton	July, 1946	V 258
Cadden, Nell	Dec., 1953	Y 172
Carter, Nellie M.	Nov., 1957	1 123
Conley, Nettie Luteman	June, 1959	2 79
Cunningham, Nannie B.	Feb., 1960	2 303

Clark, Robert	May, 1942	T 393
Coyle, Richard Joseph	Nov., 1942	T 533
Cavanaugh, Rose H.	Jan., 1944	U 223
Cole, Robert A.	Aug., 1952	X 461
Callan, Rose B.	March, 1956	Z 196
Coleman, Russell K.	Oct., 1956	Z 373
Clark, Rose B.	Nov., 1956	Z 377

Coddington, Samuel	Jan., 1844	A 527
Cresap, Susannah	June, 1851	B 33
Clark, Stephen J.	Feb., 1913	J 494
Cresap, Stanley	April, 1913	K 20
Castle, Susan M.	June, 1914	K 198
Christie, Sarah R.J.	Jan., 1923	M 588
Coughenour, Samuel A.	Sept., 1931	P 446
Cain, Sarah Elizabeth	Oct., 1932	Q 87
Conners, Sallie A.	June, 1942	T 418
Clise, Susanna Katherine	March, 1944	U 259
Chesshire, Sarah E.	March, 1945	U 476
Chedester, Sallie A.	Nov., 1946	V 340
Casteel, S.H.	Jan., 1953	X 552
Collins, Sanford W.	June, 1953	Y 51
Cook, Sadie Jane	May, 1960	2 416

Cresap, Thomas	Jan., 1790	A 7
Cresap, Thomas	Jan., 1802	A 142
same	Sept. 1802	A 143
same	Dec., 1802	A 143
same	Oct., 1803	A 144
same	Dec. 1803	A 144
same	Jan., 1805	A 144
same	Jan., 1806	A 145
same	Jan. 1807	A 145
same	Dec., 1808	A 146
same	Nov., 1809	A 146
same	Dec., 1810	A 147
same	Dec., 1811	A 147
Cromwell, Thomas	Feb., 1798	A 150
Cresap, Thomas	Dec., 1819	A 187
same	June, 1820	A 190

Cresap, Thomas, continued	Jan., 1821	A 193
same	Jan., 1822	A 200
same	Feb., 1823	A 208
same	Feb., 1824	A 225
same	Nov., 1824	A 229
same	Feb., 1825	A 237
same	March, 1826	A 250
same	Sept., 1826	A 257
same	March, 1827	A 263
same	March, 1828	A 274
same	July, 1828	A 275
same	March, 1829	A 281
same	Feb., 1830	A 300
same	Oct., 1830	A 305
same	Jan., 1831	A 307
same	Feb., 1832	A 324
same	Nov., 1832	A 329
same	Feb., 1833	A 333
same	Feb., 1834	A 345
same	March, 1835	A 370
same	March, 1836	A 384
same	Feb., 1837	A 404
same	June, 1837	A 410
Cheney, Thomas of John	Feb., 1839	A 432
Cresap, Thomas	Jan., 1838	A 417
same	Feb., 1839	A 433
same	Feb., 1840	A 457
same	Feb., 1841	A 479
same	Feb., 1842	A 499
same	Feb., 1843	A 507
same	Feb., 1844	A 534
Chaney, Thomas of N.	Oct. 10, 1843	A 518
Clinton, Thomas	Jan., 1847	A 612
Coulehan, Thomas	Dec., 1867	C 107
Crockett, Thomas D.	Sept., 1870	C 177
Connell, Thomas	Oct., 1891	F 244
Coulehan, T. L.	Feb., 1894	G 22
Connor, Thomas, Sr.	Oct., 1896	G 193
Carr, Thomas (See Court pro-	Nov., 1915	K 438
Carr, Thomas ceedings, Liber 21 F295)	Dec., 1915	K 441
Caudill, Thomas A.	Dec., 1930	P 263
Carabine, Thomas E.	May, 1936	R 237
Clark, Thomas L.	Jan., 1937	R 372

Conroy, Timothy Lawrence	Sept., 1937	R 549
Carr, Thomas	June, 1939	S 355
Cessna, T.B.	July, 1940	S 596
Cooper, Thornton S.	Oct., 1950	X 20
Condon, Thoma E.	June, 1951	X 185
Curtis, Thomas O.	April, 1955	Y 500
Collins, Thomas F.	July, 1959	2 122

Cleppinger, Valentine B.	April, 1867	C 139
Carder, Virginia Blackwell	April, 1909	J 30
Cessna, Viola G.	June, 1930	P 166
Couter, Virgie V.	Jan., 1938	S 29

Coddington, William	June, 1827	A 266
Chambers, William	Nov., 1847	A 632
Calmes, William	Nov., 1849	B 10
Chapman, William H.		B 145
Chisholm, William	April, 1866	C 74
Cowden, William F.	April, 1880	D 440
Crump, William J.	Sept., 1898	G 308
Chapman, William H.	May, 1899	G 351
Coleman, William F.	June, 1903	H 362
Cavanaugh, William	Nov., 1910	I 243
Clark, Walter B.	Nov., 1910	J 207
Coleman, William S.	Jan., 1911	J 216
Collins, Wesley	March, 1921	M 287
Clites, Wesley	Sept., 1922	M 529
Conn, Winfield	March, 1928	O 325
Canty, William	April, 1930	P 145
Cole, William H.	Nov., 1930	P 256
Canty, William H.	Feb., 1931	P 301
Cover, William J.	May, 1931	P 356
Clay, William A.	Jan. 1932	P 504
Clauson, William T.	July, 1932	Q 35
Coulehan, William T.	Jan., 1934	Q 338
Capel, William H.	March, 1936	R 204
Clay, Walter W.	April, 1942	T 379
Crow, William Sherman	Feb., 1943	T 611
Claar, William L.	May, 1944	U 304
Cramer, Ward W.	April, 1945	U 512

D

Davies, Ann	Nov., 1863	C 33
same	April, 1870	C 170
Davis, Amos & wife	Sept., 1874	D 184
Devecmon, Althea M.	March, 1876	D 281
Dowden, Albert H.	Dec., 1887	E 284
Dempsey, Annie	March, 1889	E 369
Devries, Annie M.		F 38
Dowden, Albert H.	Nov., 1893	G 7
Davis, Amos	April, 1896	G 172
Dowden, Albert H.	Oct., 1913	K 78
Dummel, Adelaide C.	Oct., 1913	K 86
Duckworth, Americus	Sept., 1923	N 123
Dunk, Anna E.	July, 1924	N 282
Donnelly, Annie R.	Feb., 1926	N 544
Dorimo, Angelo	April, 1926	N 586
Drenning, Ann Jane	July, 1927	O 205
Darr, Allan H.	March, 1931	P 316
Dilfer, Adam W.	July, 1931	P 402
Davis, August H.	July, 1935	R 73
Dodd, Annie M.	Sept., 1937	R 550
Doub, Anne Cochran	March, 1942	T 336
Davis, Albert M.	Jan., 1944	U 214
Dilley, Annie Agnes	May, 1944	U 301
Doub, Albert A.	Jan., 1947	V 387
Deetz, Annie M.	April, 1947	V 460
Dixon, Arthur P.	Aug., 1947	V 535
Davis, Amos Middleton	Sept., 1947	V 546
Dobbie, Agnes R.	Jan., 1949	W 262
Durst, Allen E.	March, 1949	W 290
Duckworth, Anna V.	Oct., 1949	W 406
Diubaldo, Andrew	Nov., 1949	W 439
Davis, Arch Francis	Aug., 1950	W 607
Davis, Alfred A.	April, 1951	X 157
Davis, Alexander A.	Dec., 1951	X 276
Deneen, Alice	March, 1959	1 571
Dailey, Agnes	May, 1959	2 18
Demarest, Adelaide F.	May, 1960	2 422

Duvall, Benjamin	May, 1820	A 188
Deffinbaugh, Benjamin	Dec., 1850	B 25
Davis, Benjamin	Oct., 1863	C 31
Dawson, Benjamin B.	March, 1872	D 8
Dilley, Barney		E 339
Davis, Benjamin	Feb., 1902	H 257
Duffy, Bridget A.	Nov., 1919	M 93
Devore, Benjamin	Aug., 1938	S 138
Denson, Blanche K.	May, 1943	U 71
Dailey, Bertha K.	Sept., 1954	Y 355
Dick, Bertha B.	Jan., 1957	Z 436
Drenning, Benjamin F.	March, 1957	Z 494
Davis, Bessie May	Sept., 1959	2 155

Duchman, Christina	Feb., 1803	A 51
Deetz, Christian	July, 1808	A 94
Durbin, Comfort	June, 1822	A 206
Dunham, Catherine	Aug., 1866	C 39
Defibaugh, Chenowith	Oct., 1905	I 145
Davis, Caroline A.	Oct., 1913	K 72
Davis, Christopher	April, 1915	K 325
Duckworth, Charles W.	March, 1921	M 280
Dodds, Christopher	March, 1921	M 291
Dilger, Charles E.	July, 1921	M 341
Delbrook, Catherine	June, 1924	N 271
Drewnoski, Christina M.	Aug., 1926	O 46
Derr, Cora Tilghman	March, 1929	O 484
Daniels, Charles Edgar	May, 1933	Q 220
Donnelly, Charles W.	Sept., 1938	S 157
Dellinger, Charles E.	June, 1940	S 583
Defenbaugh, Cecilia M.	Aug., 1941	T 207
Davis, Charles W.	March, 1942	T 338
Dailey, Charles E.	July, 1942	T 432
Dreyer, Catherine	Feb., 1943	T 606
Daehler, Charles	Jan., 1945	U 434
Dillon, Charles S.	July, 1945	V 8
Diehl, Charles Herman	May, 1946	V 216
Drenning, Clara Belle	May, 1947	V 473
Davis, Charles	Aug., 1948	W 178
Deal, Calvin E.	Nov., 1948	W 227
Davis, Cora May	Sept., 1949	W 402
Durvin, Charles W.	June, 1950	W 560

Davidson, Charles Grant	Feb., 1951	X 116
Dillon, Claude	May, 1953	Y 30
Donnelly, Clara W.	July, 1960	2 497

Davis, Daniel et al	July, 1879	D 419
Davies, David J.	June, 1891	F 204
Dixon, David, Sr.	Feb., 1903	H 320
Di Fabio, Dante	June, 1915	K 368
Douglas, Della	May, 1921	M 323
Dixon, Daniel	Nov., 1921	M 380
Deffenbaugh, Daniel Simpson	Jan., 1930	P 76
Dayton, Dollie V.	Jan., 1936	R 172
Dolan, Della I.	Aug., 1957	1 18

Davis, Ebenezer	Jan., 1794	A 10
Durst, Elisha	April, 1867	C 93
Dawson, Eli W.	Aug., 1867	C 101
Dean, Ephraim	Sept., 1845	C 141
Duncan, Ellen	April, 1862	C 148
Davidson, Empson B.	Oct., 1869	C 151
Dawson, Elizabeth	Jan., 1874	D 146
Dodd, Elizabeth	April, 1886	E 228
Dick, Elizabeth	Dec., 1896	G 208
Dufty, Edward	Jan., 1897	G 214
Donahue, Edward	April, 1897	G 222
Douglas, Elizabeth S.	March, 1900	H 72
Dean, Emma L.	June, 1901	H 193
Dawson, Eliza	June, 1904	I 19
Dickinson, Elizabeth	June, 1904	I 22
Davis, Ezra	April, 1906	I 200
Duke, Edgar Thrush	May, 1909	J 47
Dick, Elizabeth	April, 1912	J 417
Drawbaugh, Emma S.	Feb., 1913	J 491
Davis, Eliza	April, 1913	K 12
Dundon, Edmund	July, 1916	L 27
Dufty, Emma	Aug., 1916	L 43
Dolan, Emeline	March, 1918	L 321
Dawson, Eli W.	Feb., 1921	M 272
Dickel, Elizabeth	Feb., 1924	N 217
Drew, Edgar E.	July, 1924	N 288

Dulin, Gabriel M.	Sept., 1906	I 230
Dunk, George H.	May, 1911	J 292
Dowden, George F.	Dec., 1913	K 115
Drees, George H.	June, 1928	O 361
Durst, Gordon	Sept., 1929	O 599
Daisy, George R.	May, 1931	P 355
Dietrich, George Edward	March, 1935	Q 599
Daisy, Georgie	July, 1938	S 121
Dando, Grace H.	June, 1943	U 91
Duvall, George T.	May, 1944	U 300
Dolan, George R.	Nov., 1947	V 576

Dooley, Hester	Feb., 1859	B 181
Dash, Henry	June, 1897	G 240
Dieckman, Henry	July, 1897	G 244
Dreyer, Henry	Oct., 1903	H 378
Dyche, Henry	Aug., 1909	J 65
Dickey, Howard Harlan	July, 1913	K 43
Dawson, Hilleary C.	Jan., 1915	K 267
Delbrook, Henry	April, 1915	K 333
Du Brau, Herman	Nov., 1922	M 563
Dreyer, Henry, Sr.	Oct., 1929	P 24
Donnelly, Harry R.	Sept., 1933	Q 284
Deneen, Helen E.	Aug., 1939	S 368
Davis, Hunter P.	Nov., 1942	T 536
Dye, Herbert A.	Oct., 1951	X 247
Dawson, Harry Alvin	Nov., 1956	Z 394
Davis, Harry M.	Dec., 1957	1 131
Donohoe, Hubert M.	May, 1958	1 260
Deming, Herbert Van Vechten	May, 1958	1 287
Dick, Homer A.	June, 1959	2 74
Duckworth, Harry Thomas	Jan., 1960	2 269

Daniels, Isaac	June, 1859	B 157
Dicken, Isaac	Jan., 1885	E 96
Dickel, Ida	March, 1935	N 393
Dean, Isaac P.	Dec., 1934	Q 546
Deneen, Ira	Dec., 1940	T 52

Dickel, Joseph	Feb., 1924	N 215
Donald, John C.	Feb., 1925	N 380
Dressman, John J.	Jan., 1928	O 289
Deatelhouser, Joseph	May, 1928	O 347
Delaney, John	March, 1929	O 495
Doherty, John W.	April, 1930	P 134
Dick, James R.	Dec., 1931	P 503
Daughtrey, Jane Morris	March, 1932	P 550
Dallard, Jane E.	May, 1932	P 579
Daddysman, John H.	July, 1933	Q 249
Daniels, John J.	April, 1936	R 224
Dobbie, John T.	Oct., 1937	R 579
Davies, Joseph T.	Oct., 1938	S 171
Devecmon, John Semmes	Dec., 1938	S 208
Donahue, James	March, 1939	S 285
Dicken, Jesse M.	Oct., 1939	S 396
Dolan, John Raymond	May, 1941	T 143
Dawson, John A.	Sept., 1941	T 222
Duncan, Jane	Jan., 1942	T 312
Divico, John A.	March, 1942	T 340
Dean, James Mathias	April, 1943	U 64
Duckworth, John Thomas	Dec., 1943	U 213
Dougherty, John J.	Aug., 1945	V 33
Dickle, Julia	Aug., 1947	V 524
Deming, Jane Taylor	Nov., 1948	W 222
Dawson, Jared E.	Feb., 1949	W 268
Dreyer, John G.	Feb., 1949	W 271
Drumm, James L.	April, 1950	W 535
Dorsey, Joseph P.	July, 1950	W 592
Duffy, James P.	Feb., 1951	X 112
Doran, John James	Feb., 1952	X 317
Davis, James S.	March, 1952	X 348
Dean, James W.	May, 1954	Y 266
Dunn, Jennie	March, 1957	Z 469
Dwyer, John H.	April, 1958	1 253

Dawson, Kunigunda	July, 1926	O 33
Diggs, Katherine	May, 1929	O 541
Dorsey, Katherine	Jan., 1942	T 310
Donaldson, Katherine	March, 1953	Y 6
Day, Katharine	Nov., 1954	Y 413

Davidson, Lewis, Sr.	June, 1814	A 123
Davidson, Lewis	Jan., 1859	B 152
Dean, Leonard	Jan., 1889	F 57
Dean, Lewis M.	Nov., 1897	G 267
Duckworth, Lewis Jackson	June, 1907	I 276
Dawson, Louisa	April, 1914	K 166
Durst, Lloyd, Sr.	Nov., 1924	N 341
Dunn, William V.	Oct., 1926	O 62
Dishong, Lillie E.	April, 1931	P 349
Dicken, Lucy E.	July, 1931	P 404
Downey, Leo T.	May, 1945	U 534
Dubel, Leslie S.	April, 1948	W 89
Dela Grange, Louis A.	April, 1950	W 526
Determan, Lena	Feb., 1952	X 334
Dela Grange, Louise Elizabeth	June, 1953	Y 49
Dove, Lory D.	Nov., 1953	Y 170
Deffinbaugh, Leroy W.	June, 1956	Z 261

Davis, Mary	June, 1812	A 111
Donaldson, Margaret	March, 1847	A 614
Davidson, Margaret	May, 1852	B 164
Duncan, Margaret	June, 1869	C 142
Dye, Mary	March, 1876	D 263
Dean, Mary	July, 1877	D 334
Dockeny, Marks	Jan., 1880	D 422
Doerner, Mary C.E.	June, 1892	F 300
Dolan, Michael	July, 1894	G 51
same		G 54
Dougherty, Michael H.	Sept., 1898	G 311
Dietrich, Mary Sophia	Feb., 1904	H 396
Dailey, Mary	March, 1907	I 265
Danner, Mary N.	Sept., 1907	I 320
Defibaugh, Mary	July, 1909	J 59
Dowden, Mary	Aug., 1910	J 187
Dixon, Mary	Sept., 1911	J 322
Dailey, Michael	Aug., 1914	K 215
Davis, Millard F.	May, 1917	L 175
Dicken, Martin L.	May, 1918	L 365
Dailey, Mary L.	July, 1920	M 177
Deekins, Mary S.	Feb., 1923	N 3
Danby, Mark	July, 1923	N 102
Dorn, Mary	Oct., 1926	O 63

Dehler, Mary	Dec., 1927	O 279
Dickey, Minnie H.	Dec., 1929	P 67
Deetz, Mary	Feb., 1932	P 526
Dorsey, Margaret	April, 1932	P 570
Diehl, Michael E.	July, 1932	Q 44
Dawson, Minerva E.	Nov., 1933	Q 301
Dowden, Margaret J.	May, 1936	R 238
Deininger, Mary Virginia	April, 1938	S 78
Davis, Mary J.	Feb., 1939	S 260
Daugherty, Marie J.	Feb., 1939	S 262
Dilley, Mary Clem	June, 1941	S 578
Damm, Mary L	Sept., 1941	T 232
Darr, Mary Ellen	Aug., 1943	U 135
Delbrook, Martha E.	Oct., 1945	V 62
Duckworth, Mary Ann	Sept., 1946	V 281
Dillon, May	Aug., 1949	W 363
Deal, Margaret L.	March, 1950	W 504
Dolan, Mary E.	March, 1951	X 144
Donahoe, Martha M.	April, 1955	Y 507
Dyche, Mary Agnes	July, 1955	Z 29
Debelock, Marie (Dibilobe)	Dec., 1955	Z 121

Davis, Nathaniel	July, 1868	C 145
Donevan, Nancy	Nov., 1877	D 346
Dunn, Nathaniel	Oct., 1939	S 405
Di Marco, Nick	April, 1946	V 182
DeLuca, Nellie	July, 1955	Z 28
Dubbs, Nettie	Sept., 1960	2 552

Damm, Otto	Nov., 1894	G 72
Dawson, Orpah T.	Jan., 1911	J 227
Dawson, Orpah	Feb., 1911	J 249
Deffinbaugh, Oliver C.	Aug., 1913	K 59
Damm, Otto	Aug., 1941	T 199
Dean, Oswald Carl	July, 1952	X 431

Drane, Priscilla	May, 1836	A 388
Deffenbaugh, Peter	Nov., 1868	C 128
Durst, Philadelphia	Dec., 1927	O 276

Dick, Samuel A.	Feb., 1918	L 313
Dawson, Sarah	Oct., 1920	M 216
Davis, Sarah E.	Nov., 1925	N 484
Duggan, Silas W.	Dec., 1925	N 505
Denson, Samuel, Sr.	Dec., 1928	O 433
Dennis, Samuel L.	July, 1930	P 187
Danby, Sarah A.	July, 1932	Q 36
Davis, Susan	July, 1934	Q 466
Deal, Sophie Ford	Sept., 1934	Q 487
Davis, Samuel F.	April, 1937	R 467
Diehl, Solomon S.	June, 1939	S 338
Devore, Samuel	Feb., 1943	T 609
Duncan, Sara McCleave	March, 1945	U 471
Dibert, Susanna	Sept., 1948	W 194
Durst, Sally W.	June, 1953	Y 65
Dolan, Susannah	Aug., 1959	2 128
Devecmon, Thomas J.	Aug., 1827	A 267
Devecmon, Thomas	Dec., 1862	B 200
same	June, 1863	B 201
Davis, Thomas	May, 1862	C 4
Devecmon, Thomas	Dec., 1864	C 46
Dawson, Thomas W.	Jan., 1880	D 430
Doyle, Thomas	May, 1880	D 447
Davis, Thomas B.	Jan., 1912	J 377
Dillon, Thomas G.	March, 1924	N 231
Duncanson, Thomas	April, 1951	X 150
Dailey, Theodore Thomas	Feb., 1953	X 590
Dixon, Thomas A.	July, 1953	Y 86
Donahue, Teresa	July, 1954	Y 313
Devlin, Terance J.	Jan., 1956	Z 156
Dawson, Upton Benjamin F.	March, 1950	W 511
Dennison, Virgie Montrose	Dec., 1951	X 278
Dawson, William	July, 1802	A 50
Davis, William	June, 1843	A 517
Durst, William	Feb., 1858	B 134

E

Emerick, Andrew	Aug., 1938	A 621
Ebert, Adam	Nov., 1907	I 333
Eichhorn, August, Sr.	March, 1915	K 304
Eschenbacher, Anna M.	Sept., 1915	K 395
Elosser, A.L.S.O.	March, 1921	M 279
Ebbert, Anna	March, 1925	N 391
Evans, Arch. M.	April, 1926	N 592
Everline, Anna	Feb., 1930	P 91
Eyler, Annie E.	April, 1934	Q 405
England, Alexander	Aug., 1936	R 294
Edwards, Annie	Oct., 1939	S 416
Edmunds, Annie	July, 1950	W 601
Evans, Agnes	July, 1953	Y 70
Eskin, Albert C.	July, 1958	I 330

Eschenbrenner, Balthazar	Feb., 1886	E 163
Eckshaw, Barbara Ellen	Nov., 1932	Q 102

Everstine, Clara L.		F 262
Everline, Charles	July, 1893	F 380
Eschenbrenner, Christine	Aug., 1897	G 246
Eschenbrenner, Christine	Sept., 1897	G 255
Ebbert, Conrad	June, 1908	I 422
Engle, Christian L.	Dec., 1925	N 512
Eyler, Charles R.	Dec., 1929	P 72
Emerick, Clara Jane	April, 1936	R 226
Eckshaw, Charles H.	July, 1936	R 276
Everstine, Clara J.	March, 1937	R 448
Earle, Charles H.	May, 1938	S 97
Eisler, Charles	April, 1941	T 120
Eppler, Catherine A.	Oct., 1941	T 256
Emerick, Clara Alberta	Feb., 1948	W 47
Evans, Cora H.	July, 1948	W 151
Eisenberg, Carrie	May, 1951	W 176

Entler, Hannah	April, 1821	A 195
Elbin, Henry B.	Aug., 1889	F 33
Evans, H. Clay	Aug., 1926	O 47
Evans, Harriet	May, 1928	O 348
Evans, Horace G.	July, 1939	S 357
Engle, Hattie	April, 1940	S 529
Everline, Henry A.	July, 1950	W 576
Evans, Hannah T.	Feb., 1952	X 328

Elrick, Isabelle L.	Nov., 1935	R 124
Everline, Ida B.	March, 1955	Y 495

Ervine, James	April, 1813	A 116
Easter, Jacob	Nov., 1860	B 182
Edwards, John T.	June, 1871	C 197
Eckhart, John		D 502
Englar, James W. J.	Sept., 1883	D 624
Edwards, John E.	April, 1920	M 163
Engle, James	July, 1923	N 96
Evans, Joseph William	May, 1926	O 11
Elder, Jasper W.	Oct., 1929	P 29
Everett, John	Sept., 1932	Q 72
Evans, John O.	May, 1938	S 95
Eagan, John	Nov., 1942	T 535
Engle, Jane M.	June, 1943	U 103
Eckshaw, James Thomas	Feb., 1915	K 275
Edmunds, John Charles	Aug., 1945	V 14
Ebert, J. Gale	Sept., 1948	W 187
Ellis, John D.	March, 1950	W 499
Emerick, James J.	March, 1952	X 342
Estes, Jessie Vada	Feb., 1955	Y 465
Eyman, James Franklin	May, 1959	2 25

Ewald, Karl E.	May, 1959	2 27

Eisentrout, Lepold	July, 1910	J 173
Elosser, Lewis F.	April, 1912	J 415
Engle, Lewis, Dr.	July, 1946	V 264

Eckles, Samuel	Oct., 1874	D 178
Earsom, Samuel H.	March, 1883	D 589
Edwards, Samuel J.	May, 1908	I 402
Eisenberg, Samuel	Dec., 1918	L 446
Eyler, Sarah A.	Dec., 1922	M 576
Evans, Sidney H.	Oct., 1934	Q 505
Engle, S. Athalia	June, 1940	S 581
Engle, Sophia	June, 1951	X 190
Eichner, Sarah E.	Oct., 1951	X 251
Elbin, Silas	July, 1956	Z 279
Evans, Sheridan	May, 1960	2 430

Evans, Thomas E.		D 510
Evans, Thomas B.	Feb., 1925	N 377
Emmart, Thomas P.	March, 1925	N 397
Elder, Thomas W., Jr.	Jan., 1936	R 173
Emery, Thelma Ridgeley	Jan., 1958	1 145

Engle, William	Nov., 1891	F 242
Emerick, Wilson	March, 1921	M 293
Eppler, William F.	June, 1930	P 177
Emerick, William H.	Nov., 1935	R 135
Ewald, William	Dec., 1948	W 236
Emerick, William J.	Jan., 1952	X 301
Englehart, William M.	May, 1952	X 393
Ewing, William	July, 1955	Z 26
Everett, William	July, 1957	Z 588
Emerick, William H.	March, 1960	2 334

F

Faw, Abraham	July 8, 1828	C 79
Frost, Albert G.	Nov., 1883	D 635
Faherty, Anna	July, 1908	I 433
Fesenmeier, Adelheit	June, 1911	J 304
Filer, Alfred W.	March, 1914	K 147
Fisher, Anthony	Jan., 1917	L 113
Foreman, Angelina	Sept., 1919	M 76
Farrell, Annie E.	July, 1920	M 189
Frey, Adolph C.	Dec., 1926	O 98
Fuller, Adah L.	June, 1931	P 395
Frantz, Alva M.	Dec., 1932	Q 120
Flurshutz, Annie Catherine	Jan., 1933	Q 149
Franklin, A. Leo	Nov., 1934	Q 538
Fisher, Anna D.	June, 1935	R 52
Fradiska, Anna	May, 1937	R 499
Freal, Annie	Oct., 1942	T 517
Fisher, Annie	Sept., 1943	U 164
Fogtman, August H.	Oct., 1946	V 299
Fogle, Arthur B.	Oct., 1947	V 564
Fuller, Althea R.	May, 1953	Y 29
Frenzel, Albert Leander	May, 1953	Y 40
Fowler, Arthur G.	May, 1954	Y 271
Feeley, Annie	May, 1955	Z 1
Flake, Argyle T.	April, 1958	1 244

Free, Bessie M.	Jan., 1910	J 113
Foxall, Benjamin	Oct., 1923	N 144
Fogarty, Bartley	May, 1938	S 94
Flake, Benjamin Holiday	Sept., 1946	V 280
Flood, Blanche McFarland	June, 1955	Z 10
Filer, Benjamin	Feb., 1959	1 566

Frye, Conrad	Oct., 1812	A 113
Frantz, Catherine	June, 1851	B 31
Fisk, Charles B.	Jan., 1866	C 113

Fisher, Christian		F 193
Fisher, Christian	May, 1891	F 193
Feichtner, Catherine	Oct., 1905	I 158
Fay, Charles L.	June, 1922	M 481
Frey, Conrad	Jan., 1928	O 297
Floto, Charles A.	Oct., 1930	P 230
Fadley, Charles E.	April, 1934	Q 426
Finzel, Carrie M.	Sept., 1937	R 556
Franze, Catherine	Nov., 1940	T 33
Fadely, Charles E.	Dec., 1942	T 555
Fraley, Clarence F.	Nov., 1947	V 575
French, Chrissie A.	Nov., 1952	X 519
Fletcher, Courtney A.	April, 1955	Y 515
Fuller, Charley W.	June, 1957	Z 570
Fuller, Clifton E.	Sept., 1958	1 393

Fayerweather, Daniel B.	May, 1893	F 355
Forney, Daniel C.	April, 1914	K 170
Fletcher, Daniel	Sept., 1916	L 49
Fisher, Daniel E.	March, 1918	L 318
Fletcher, Daniel A.	Jan., 1939	S 249
Footer, Daisy V.	Dec., 1954	Y 425

Fisher, Eleanor	Sept., 1841	A 496
Friend, Elijah	Dec., 1869	C 158
Foundling, Elizabeth	July, 1890	F 106
Fisher, Elizabeth F.	Nov., 1911	J 348
Flaccus, Edward C.	Sept., 1914	K 227
Furlow, Elisha H.	Feb., 1915	K 287
Fleckenstein, Elizabeth	Aug., 1920	M 197
Frenzel, Elizabeth	April, 1921	M 307
Field, Emily	Aug., 1927	O 233
Foley, Ellen M.	April, 1933	Q 201
Flynn, Ellen	March, 1938	S 63
Finch, Ernest E.	Dec., 1938	S 200
Farber, Emma P.	Aug., 1942	T 444
Fowler, Edith Edwards	July, 1943	U 120
Fritch, Elue Oscar	Jan., 1950	W 465
Fredrickson, Elizabeth B.	Dec., 1953	Y 183
Free, Emily V.	July, 1954	Y 318
Fisher, Ella Lavin	Oct., 1960	2 597

Foor, Francis	Sept., 1854	B 82
Fogtman, Frank	Feb., 1880	D 428
Frantz, Flavilla P.	Oct., 1892	F 321
Finkeldey, Frederick A.	April, 1915	K 335
Flurshutz, Frederick W.	May, 1924	N 268
Frey, Frank A.	Feb., 1941	T 88
Fittro, Fred G.	Feb., 1943	T 608
Fleckenstein, Frances	Aug., 1944	U 346
Forbeck, Frank J.	March, 1945	U 491
Fisher, Florence V.	June, 1946	V 240
Fisher, Florence Gertrude M.	Nov., 1955	Z 101
Fisher, Frank L.	Dec., 1957	Z 420
Flurshutz, Fred W.	March, 1958	1 220
Fazenbaker, George	May, 1810	A 102
French, George	Nov., 1831	A 322
Fisher, George E.	May, 1910	J 161
Frost, Gottlieb	Dec., 1920	M 241
Fuller, Guy N.	Jan., 1927	O 114
Fraley, Gilbert B.	Aug., 1930	P 197
Felker, George	April, 1932	P 559
Fazenbaker, George W.	Nov., 1934	Q 540
Froehlich, George Edward	Oct., 1944	U 382
Frenzel, George C.	April, 1953	Y 14
Fisher, Grace M.	Jan., 1954	Y 195
Froelich, George S.	Aug., 1956	Z 309
Fletcher, Gretchen Legoria	Sept., 1957	1 80
Fletcher, Grace M.	Nov., 1959	2 212
Farrell, Honora E.	Oct., 1869	C 150
Fogtman, Henry	Sept., 1872	D 43
Freel, Hugh A.	Sept., 1884	E 80
Flury, Henry	Feb., 1887	E 224
Fey, Henry	June, 1887	E 239
Firle, Henry	Nov., 1896	G 194
Fisher, Helen M.	Feb., 1923	N 5
Fries, Henrietta H.	Nov., 1926	O 77
Frank, Henry	June, 1928	O 358
Fischer, Henry	July, 1929	O 581
Finzel, Henry L.	Sept., 1940	T 3

Footer, Harry	Oct., 1945	V 57
Flurshutz, Harmon U.F.	Jan., 1946	V 96
Frost, Isaiah	Nov., 1848	A 672
Falkner, Ida E.	Jan., 1927	O 120
Frye, Isabella	Jan., 1929	O 438
Feidt, Isabel	Oct., 1958	I 431
Felker, Isabelle	Dec., 1958	1 479
Finan, Irene A.	Dec., 1958	1 490
French, James	Feb., 1815	A 129
Frost, Josiah	Sept., 1819	A 180
Fouty, Jacob	Feb., 1828	A 278
Fike, John, Sr.	Sept., 1829	A 290
Fearer, John, Sr.	Jan., 1830	A 298
Frantz, John	Nov., 1846	A 603
Fitzpatrick, James	March, 1848	A 646
Friend, John	April, 1849	A 694
Fisher, John	Nov., 1850	B 24
Frantz, Jonathan	Feb., 1854	B 77
Friend, Jacob B.	Sept., 1861	B 191
Fike, John	Sept., 1862	C 11
Fitzpatrick, James	March, 1865	C 54
Fenton, Josiah J.	July, 1867	C 100
Friend, John S.	March, 1868	C 111
France, John	June, 1848	C 142
Folck, John	Feb., 1873	D 85
Fairbanks, John	Nov., 1876	D 308
Folck, John Heirs	Jan., 1881	D 469
Fisher, Joseph	April, 1885	E 109
Ford, John	June, 1886	E 194
Fisher, John D.	Jan., 1887	E 216
Fitzpatrick, John	March, 1889	E 371
Fichtner, Johanna	Dec., 1891	F 249
Firle, John Henry	May, 1893	F 366
Folck, Jacob	Aug., 1897	G 248
Fries, Jacob	Nov., 1906	I 242
Fleegle, John	Dec., 1907	I 337
Fischer, Jacob	Dec., 1907	I 341
Findlay, James	Jan., 1909	I 493

Fichtner, Jonathan	Feb., 1909	J 10
Forster, John P.	June, 1916	L 21
Farber, Joseph	Oct., 1918	L 420
Ford, Josiah	Jan., 1924	N 179
Farber, J. Matthew	Jan., 1926	N 521
Freithof, John J.	Dec., 1929	P 68
Flick, Jacob M.	Nov., 1930	P 249
Franklin, John	Feb., 1931	P 299
Fisher, J. Conrad	April, 1933	Q 197
Farrell, John P.	Aug., 1933	Q 273
Fulton, John A.	Feb., 1934	Q 375
Ford, James K.	Oct., 1934	Q 507
Fisher, John V.	July, 1935	R 65
Farrady, John	Dec., 1935	R 147
Fisher, James L.	Jan., 1936	R 178
Farrell, John D.	Jan., 1937	R 379
Fisher, Jesse R.	Feb., 1938	S 53
Faherty, James J.	June, 1938	S 601
Free, Jared B.	Oct., 1940	T 19
Flynn, Johanna	March, 1941	T 99
Fisher, Julia Ann	Oct., 1941	T 254
Feldman, Joseph A.	Dec., 1942	T 548
Finan, Joseph B.	Aug., 1943	U 137
Fogle, Jefferson Bascom	March, 1944	U 261
Forbeck, James A.	Oct., 1944	U 388
Footen, Julie	May, 1946	V 221
Footer, Joseph W.	May, 1947	V 483
Franklin, Joseph P.	June, 1947	V 497
Frankfort, John W.	July, 1948	W 159
Fisher, John L.	Jan., 1949	W 260
Fazenbaker, James Edward	July, 1952	X 414
Finan, John F.	May, 1953	Y 42
Fair, Jane	Nov., 1955	Z 106
Fowler, Julia M.	Aug., 1957	1 47
Fleegle, John William	Oct., 1957	1 89
Fradiska, Joseph M.	Feb., 1958	1 186
Foote, John R.	March, 1960	2 314
Fletcher, Julia B.	March, 1960	2 350

Flannigan, Katherine	Sept. 4, 1928	O 394
Fetzer, Katherine	Oct., 1953	Y 139
Fletterman, Karl E.	Oct., 1957	1 98

Frostburg Lutheran E. Church	Aug., 1869	C 155
Fyan, Louis N.	April, 1876	D 275
Fechtig, Levi R.	July, 1889	F 27
Ford, Lewis G.	Jan., 1923	M 592
Fisher, Louis	April, 1925	N 402
Falkner, Levi S.	Nov., 1926	O 93
Filsinger, Louise	Nov., 1934	Q 523
Fuller, Laura B.	Jan., 1943	T 594
Force, Luther D.	Feb., 1943	T 602
Fogle, Laura V.	Sept., 1949	W 396
Firlie, Louis A.	April, 1955	Y 524

Fisher, Michael	Sept., 1796	A 25
Fisher, Michael	Oct., 1848	A 666
Flannagan, Michael	Oct., 1888	E 345
Fallon, Michael		E 378
Farrell, Margaret	June, 1890	F 96
Foley, Matilda C.		F 203
Fechtig, Mary E.	March, 1897	G 220
Feeley, Michael	Oct., 1899	G 382
Firle, Margaret	June, 1902	H 274
Freithof, Mary A.	Jan., 1913	J 484
Fisher, Margaret	June, 1914	K 187
Faherty, Mary C.	June, 1917	L 205
Fahey, Michael P.	April, 1919	M 22
Fogerty, Mary Ann	April, 1926	N 597
Flora, Mary Martha	Aug., 1927	O 231
Fox, Margaret Emily	May, 1931	P 369
Fleegle, Mary C.	Sept., 1931	P 454
Fradiska, Michael	Dec., 1932	Q 127
Furlow, Mary Elizabeth	Feb., 1933	Q 159
Fesenmeier, Michael L.	Aug., 1934	Q 471
Frey, Margaret C.	April, 1936	R 222
French, Martha Catherine	June, 1938	S 114
Foreman, Mary Bridget	Nov., 1938	S 193
Frantz, Mary Ellen Egolf	Feb., 1940	S 500
Forbeck, Minnie	Oct., 1941	T 246
Fradiska, Mary T.	May, 1945	U 551
Filer, Marian	May, 1946	V 219
Frost, Meshack S.	Nov., 1946	V 346
Frey, Mollie A.	July, 1947	V 521
Feeney, Margaret E.	June, 1950	W 565

Friend, Mary J.	July, 1951	X 211
Fram, Morris D.	July, 1953	Y 81
Fischer, Mary E.	Oct., 1953	Y 150
Fike, Mildred F.	Jan., 1959	1 533

Furlong, Nicholas	May, 1893	F 362
Fitzpatrick, Nora	May, 1936	R 244
Flick, Nellie	Sept., 1950	X 2
Felton, Nina May	April, 1957	Z 517
Fleming, Nora C.	Nov., 1957	1 113
Footer, Nellie Wilson	March, 1958	1 229

Fosha, Obadiah	March, 1827	A 262
Flynn, Owen	Aug., 1907	I 312
Frost, Ora M.M.	Sept., 1923	N 130

Fireboh, Philip	May, 1809	A 97
Ferrell, Patrick O.	June, 1825	A 237
Freithof, Peter	May, 1885	E 112
Fator, Peter	Jan., 1901	H 141
Fletcher, Philip H.	Feb., 1914	K 135
Fletcher, Philip	Feb., 1921	M 264
Friel, Patrick	May, 1922	M 459
Farrell, Patrick H.	Aug., 1924	N 306
Fisher, Permelia R.	May, 1926	O 3
Faherty, Philomena	May, 1934	Q 434
Frenzel, Pauline A.	April, 1942	T 378
Firlie, Peter V.	Feb., 1946	V 126
Frenzel, Pauline Johanna	Nov., 1946	V 352
Fetzer, Philip A.	Dec., 1946	V 369
Feeney, Patrick L.	Jan., 1952	X 290

Fairall, Richard M.	Aug., 1919	M 69
Floto, Ruth	May, 1940	S 567
Farrell, Rush Hubert	Feb., 1943	T 604
Fisher, R. Walter	April, 1943	U 45

Filsinger, Raymond H.	Dec., 1953	Y 186
Frantz, Robert L.	March, 1960	2 353

Fouty, Stephen	Feb., 1834	A 344
Fiery, Samuel M.	Jan., 1866	C 65
Fichtner, Sylvester	March, 1886	E 171
Furlow, Samuel D.	Jan., 1892	F 258
Flanagan, Solomon	April, 1928	O 332
Fisher, Sanford S.	March, 1931	P 328
Fleegle, Sarah C.	April, 1932	P 575
Finley, Susanna	Oct., 1932	Q 83
Fuller, Samuel H.	April, 1933	Q 190
Fine, Samuel	March, 1940	S 503
Felten, Susanna	April, 1943	U 33
Free, Sadie E.	May, 1945	U 556
Fazenbaker, Stella F.	Oct., 1950	X 36
Fowler, Sila F.	Nov., 1954	Y 405

Frants, Thomas B.	Jan., 1868	C 108
Fisher, Thomas	Feb., 1918	L 301
Foutz, Tobias	March, 1922	M 441
Footer, Thomas	Aug., 1923	N 120
Finan, Thomas B.	June, 1939	S 354
Frankhouse, Truman H.	Jan., 1944	U 234

Froelich, Valentine	Oct., 1898	G 314
Fleegle, Valentine	Oct., 1913	K 81
Fadley, Victoria V.	July, 1952	X 441
Fleegle, Vonder Smith	March, 1954	Y 226
Fogtman, Viola May	April, 1959	1 587

Firley, Wendeline	June, 1869	C 138
Fike, William	June, 1870	C 175
Foley, William D.		F 203
Findley, William	March, 1894	G 26
Frantz, William B.D.N.	June, 1901	H 194

G

Gonder, Andrew	May, 1863	C 8
Gonder, Andrew	July, 1863	C 27
Gonder, Andrew	April, 1871	C 194
Gummert, Annie V.	March, 1873	D 98
Gonder, Andrew	Dec., 1878	D 378
Green, Adam, Heirs of	Aug., 1886	E 208
Gardner, Annie G.	Dec., 1886	E 214
Gruber, Annie C.	Nov., 1887	E 276
Gruber, Annie C.		E 283
Guhtman, Appollonia	Feb., 1894	G 18
Guhtman, Appollonia	Feb., 1894	G 18
Guhtman, Appollonia	Feb., 1894	G 18
Gum, Ann Elizabeth	Dec., 1897	G 276
Gardner, Alexander	April, 1898	G 289
Gerloch, Anna Mary	May, 1903	H 336
Gillies, Alexander	March, 1907	I 267
Gephart, Annie	Feb., 1908	I 368
Griminger, Anna C.	May, 1908	I 407
Gramlich, Anna E.	Feb., 1911	J 262
Gross, Amos C.	July, 1915	K 375
Gannon, Annie M.	June, 1916	L 16
Green, Alcinda	Jan., 1918	L 286
Gross, Andrew	Nov., 1918	L 433
Geisler, Alice	Sept., 1924	N 313
Gross, Abraham Prager	Jan., 1927	O 122
Grim, Ada M.	March, 1927	O 156
Getson, Annie	July, 1927	O 208
Griffith, Annie	Oct., 1927	O 256
Greene, Annie	June, 1928	O 362
Grabenstein, Anna M.	June, 1929	O 564
Glisan, Albert E.	Feb., 1930	P 95
Getty, Alvin F.	Aug., 1930	P 199
Gerdeman, Almira	March, 1934	Q 390
Grant, Albert C.	May, 1934	Q 439
Glotfelty, Albert A.	Sept., 1934	Q 495
Green, Amanda	Sept., 1935	R 106
Grimm, Aria Ann	March, 1936	R 219
Grabenstine, Annie C.	March, 1938	S 64
Gardiner, Alexander	Sept., 1939	S 376

Gorsuch, Arabella L.	June, 1945	V 1
Growley, Anna	Sept., 1945	V 51
Gatehouse, Annie B.	June, 1947	V 501
Gillies, Annie	Feb., 1948	W 31
Grayson, Arlettie M.	Feb., 1953	X 579
Grove, Aden C.	Feb., 1955	Y 463
Goetz, Alice L.	March, 1957	Z 473
Gunnett, Annie K.	April, 1957	Z 501
Gank, Anna Alden	Dec., 1957	1 126
Glantzer, Anna Elizabeth	Jan., 1958	1 164
Goodwin, Alice F.	Sept., 1959	2 148
Garrett, Anne DeWitt	June, 1960	2 464

Ganley, Bridget	Nov., 1900	H 128
Gerdeman, Bernard J.	April, 1927	L 168
Gannon, Bridget A.	June, 1926	O 25
Griffith, Bardin	Oct., 1928	O 409
Gillum, Brace	June, 1938	S 108
Gibbs, Bradford L.	May, 1941	T 136
Guistwhite, Bruce H.	Aug., 1942	T 449
Gatrell, Bessie Donna	Feb., 1947	V 410
Gooding, Bernadette Rafferty	Oct., 1954	Y 382
Gano, Belle	Feb., 1955	Y 468

Griffith, Charles	March, 1869	C 168
Guire, Catherine	Oct., 1870	C 182
Graham, Curtin M.	Sept., 1883	D 624
Grady, Catherine	March, 1884	E 29
Graham, Curtin M.	Sept., 1885	E 136
Gonder, Catherine A.	Oct., 1887	E 267
Groening, Charles	Dec., 1896	G 198
Gardner, Charlotte A.	March, 1906	I 187
Glime, Christianna	Aug., 1916	L 37
Gantt, Conrad	March, 1918	L 331
Griffey, Charles H.	May, 1918	L 364
Griffey, Catherine	April, 1918	L 353
Gurley, Charles R.	Aug., 1922	M 511
Geatz, Catherine	Sept., 1923	N 135
Gritzner, C.W. (Mrs.)	July, 1927	O 200
Gross, Catherine	Nov., 1929	P 55

Gilpin, Clara E.	Jan., 1911	P 271
Gover, Charles D.	Oct., 1935	R 117
Groves, Catherine	June, 1936	R 268
Grant, Catherine Smith	April, 1939	S 305
Getty, Charles Wilmot	Dec., 1942	T 560
Garland, Clara	Nov., 1943	U 190
Graham, Catherine	July, 1944	U 335
Gloss, Cephas H.	Dec., 1944	U 408
Graham, Charles Cleveland	Dec., 1945	V 89
Gunter, Charles	June, 1946	V 246
Green, Charles A.	Nov., 1946	V 355
Gross, Charles L.	May, 1951	X 163
Garlick, Christopher C., Sr.	Jan., 1952	X 305
Geare, Cyril B.	April, 1954	Y 254
Gabler, Charlotte Josephine	May, 1955	Y 572
Gehr, Clarence E.	July, 1956	Z 295
Gottschall, Clarence H.	Aug., 1956	Z 305
Ginevan, Carrie V.	April, 1957	Z 509
Greitzner, Claude	Jan., 1958	1 156
Gray, Catherine C.	March, 1958	1 217
Gillies, Christina	Nov., 1960	3 40
Green, Duff	June, 1876	D 269
Green, Duff	June, 1876	D 269
Gallagher, Dominick	June, 1905	I 117
Graham, Doodridge F.	Feb., 1916	K 474
Gates, David	July, 1940	S 606
Garlick, Darlie	April, 1943	U 59
Green, D.E. Mrs.	Sept., 1944	U 361
Glorius, Dalia	March, 1948	W 63
Glick, DeSales	April, 1955	Y 501
Gainer, Delvin C.	Jan., 1959	1 520
Grimes, Edward	March, 1808	A 88
Gwynn, Evan	Dec., 1795	A 141
Gwynn, Evan	May, 1797	A 141
Gwynn, Evan	Dec., 1801	A 141
Gwynn, Evan	Jan., 1802	A 142
Gwynn, Evan	Dec., 1794	A 142
Gwynn, Evan	Nov., 1818	A 171
Glasgow, Elizabeth	March, 1866	C 89
Griesman, Eva	Feb., 1889	E 362

Gault, Elizabeth C.	Aug., 1889	F 34
Garman, Emma L.	Jan., 1914	K 123
Grady, Ella	Dec., 1915	K 448
Garlitz, Enoch A.	Oct., 1922	M 536
Gilpin, Edward Scott	May, 1926	O 9
Gunning, Edward E.	June, 1931	P 381
Gilpin, Edward M.	Dec., 1931	P 498
Garland, Ellen	Sept., 1932	Q 71
Gross, Eliza A.	May, 1933	Q 225
Gleichman, Emma C.	Jan., 1938	S 43
Greitzner, Effalista Tate	Feb., 1938	S 155
Griffith, Ella B.	Feb., 1939	S 265
Goetz, Edwin G.	June, 1939	S 341
Gard, Edwin S.	Jan., 1940	S 462
Gardner, Ellen	Jan., 1943	T 590
Gaither, Ella	Jan., 1945	U 441
Gates, Edward, Sr.	July, 1945	V 12
Gerstell, Eleanor F.P.	Oct., 1952	X 492
Gaston, Edna M.	Nov., 1952	X 512
Grabenstein, Edward F.	Feb., 1953	X 587
Glover, Emily	Aug., 1954	Y 328
Gooding, Edward L.	March, 1955	Y 481
Gatehouse, Edna David	March, 1958	1 226
Grimes, Elizabeth B.	May, 1958	1 300
Gramlich, Emma M.	Oct., 1959	2 181
Grove, Ethal G.	Aug., 1960	2 518
Gauntz, Earl	Dec., 1960	3 69

Gellner, Francis X.	July, 1875	D 219
Grimes, Frances	Nov., 1882	D 566
Gramlich, Francis M.	May, 1892	F 286
Glick, Frank J.	March, 1899	G 344
Grever, F.Henry	Jan., 1902	H 234
Grove, George W.	Sept., 1904	I 43
Gramlich, Francis M.	Jan., 1915	K 272
Giles, Floyd W.	Oct., 1918	L 413
Grote, Francis J.	Feb., 1919	L 487
Gottlieb, Fannie	Feb., 1919	L 492
Goellner, Frank	Jan., 1924	N 201
Grimes, Frank R.	Jan., 1932	P 513
Glick, Francis J.	June, 1932	Q 22
Green, Franklin P.	Feb., 1934	Q 355

Gurley, Fannie S.	Sept., 1935	R 94
Gross, Florence Almeda	July, 1936	R 282
Graney, Frank P.	April, 1937	R 452
Glotfelty, Frances Alverda	May, 1939	S 326
Gales, Frances Rebecca	May, 1955	Y 576
Grabenstein, Frederick J.	July, 1956	Z 276
Growden, Frederick William	Nov., 1959	2 210
Gellner, Frank J.	June, 1960	2 441

Geary, George P.	May, 1876	D 282
Gray, George W.	April, 1900	H 82
Gardner, George	Oct., 1902	H 297
Grove, George W.	Sept., 1904	I 43
Griffey, George A.	May, 1910	J 163
Gephart, George F.	Aug., 1917	L 223
Golden, George O.	April, 1924	N 241
Glos, G. Frank	May, 1925	N 421
Gessner, George	Sept., 1925	N 470
Grove, George	June, 1926	O 12
Gonder, Grace Louisa	June, 1929	O 553
Gowans, George	Nov., 1936	R 352
Geatz, George P.	Nov., 1937	S 2
Gonder, Genevieve M.	Oct., 1938	S 161
Gross, George C.	July, 1947	V 522
Gunnette, George M.	March, 1953	Y 7
Gore, George C.	Feb. 1960	2 297

Griffith, Hiram	Jan., 1870	C 168
Goldsmith, Hannah	Aug., 1874	D 172
Gaton, Hugh	April, 1901	H 163
Gattens, Hugh		H 163
Grever, Henry	Jan., 1902	H 234
Gerdeman, Henry	Feb., 1904	H 400
Goebel, Henry August	Aug., 1908	I 446
Gerken, Henry	Nov., 1909	J 85
Grindel, Hubert	June, 1915	K 348
Gasenhaus, Harman H.	Aug., 1917	L 218
Gates, Henry	June, 1931	P 392
Groves, Harry A.	June, 1935	R 46
Green, Horace Joseph	April, 1944	U 281

Gaither, Herbert	Sept., 1947	V 543
Garlitz, Harvey H.	Jan., 1950	W 460
Gordon, Harry McClellan	March, 1953	Y 1
Greenlees, Helen H.	Feb., 1960	Z 286

Getson, Isabela	Aug., 1924	N 301
Geiger, Irvin	July, 1957	1 12
Greitzner, Ida M.	May, 1958	1 284
Gibbons, Irene S.	May, 1959	2 22

Gross, John	June, 1804	A 68
Garey, John	May, 1836	A 390
Gephart, John	June, 1837	A 410
same	Jan., 1838	A 417
same	Feb., 1845	A 545
same	Feb., 1846	A 591
same	Feb., 1847	A 616
Glass, John	April, 1845	A 551
Gorman, John	April, 1861	B 187
Getty, J.H.C.	Aptil, 1870	C 172
Goodman, John G.	May, 1870	C 172
Grable, Joseph	Aug., 1871	C 205
Gonder, Joseph	June, 1872	D 22
Getz, John	Oct., 1885	E 139
Gates, Jane	Jan., 1888	E 293
Groser, James	May, 1889	E 384
Goodwin, Janet	April, 1890	F 85
Giles, James L.	Jan., 1881	F 170
Gaitley, John T.	March, 1893	F 349
Gardner, James	Dec., 1898	G 321
Grimes, John	March, 1902	H 258
Graim, John	Aug., 1902	H 284
Gloyd, John	June, 1903	H 352
Grim, John C. F.	April, 1904	I 2
Garrett, Joseph	July, 1905	I 118
Getty, John H.C.	Jan. 1907	I 256
Gardner, John	July, 1908	I 426
Grabenstein, Justus	April, 1909	J 31
Gattens, James	Nov., 1913	K 94
Garman, Jacob R.	Feb., 1914	K 142

Griffin, John T.	June, 1915	K 355
Grant, James	Oct., 1915	K 413
Gaffney, James P.	Feb., 1917	L 138
Grose, John	July, 1918	L 393
Grove, Jesse	Sept., 1919	M 82
Grose, James	Jan., 1920	M 109
Gonder, Joseph A.	Feb., 1920	M 115
Glenn, John	Feb., 1920	M 125
Griffith, Joel L.	Aug., 1921	M 349
Grimm, John Irvin	July, 1923	N 99
Gall, Joseph	Jan., 1924	N 181
Gross, Jacob	Dec., 1926	O 102
Gank, John	March, 1928	O 319
Gallaway, James W.	Oct., 1928	O 409
Grim, John T.T.	Feb., 1929	O 474
Gellner, John	Feb., 1929	O 476
Grabenstein, Julius	Oct., 1930	P 231
Garlets, Jesse	Jan., 1931	P 285
Gardner, John	Oct., 1931	P 458
Grapes, James E.	Feb., 1933	Q 157
Green, John W.	Jan., 1934	Q 337
Grabenstein, Joseph	Feb., 1936	R 189
Grant, John Francis	April, 1937	R 464
Graham, James	Aug., 1937	R 535
Good, John Joseph	Oct., 1937	R 576
Garlick, Joseph	Dec., 1938	S 210
Gordon, John	Feb., 1939	S 273
Green, Joseph Jacob	Oct., 1942	T 513
Getty, Joseph P.	Jan., 1944	U 225
Gunning, John B.	Sept., 1944	U 370
Gottlieb, Jacob	Nov., 1946	V 343
Gunning, J.Harry	May, 1948	W 97
Graham, James T.	Nov., 1948	W 231
Geary, John L.	March, 1949	W 291
Grose, James H.	July, 1949	W 343
Grabenstein, John William	Sept., 1949	W 398
Gross, James	June, 1950	W 571
Glover, John Wallace	July, 1950	W 600
Green, John A.	April, 1952	X 361
Gaughan, John	May, 1952	X 388
Goodman, Jacob	July, 1953	Y 68
Gallen, John A.	May, 1954	Y 263
Green, John Joseph	Jan., 1955	Y 441
Gurley, J. Frank	Sept., 1955	Z 68

Grant, Margaret Smith	July, 1933	Q 255
Grimes, Martha Ann	April, 1936	R 221
Gerson, Myer	April, 1938	S 90
Griffin, Margaret A.	Sept., 1939	S 389
Garritano, Margaret Anna	Oct., 1939	S 399
Gloss, Mary B.	June, 1940	S 584
Glodfelty, Margaret	Jan., 1941	T 73
Getty, Michael A.	Aug., 1941	T 215
Gross, Mary	Sept., 1941	T 218
Galloway, Malinda	March, 1942	T 351
Gordon, Margaret	Nov., 1943	U 184
Gellner, Mary C.	May, 1945	U 557
Gross, Mary A.	Aug., 1945	V 29
Greenfield, Mary C.	Nov., 1945	V 73
Geis, Mary C.	Oct., 1946	V 297
Gunter, Mary	Feb., 1950	W 479
Green, Mahala Jane	Sept., 1951	X 242
Gillette, Mary C.	Dec., 1952	X 529
Grahame, Margaret C.	Jan., 1953	X 558
Goldsworthy, Margaret E.	Nov., 1954	Y 400
Guggenheimer, Madeline B.	March, 1957	Z 475
Gordon, Mary Ellen	June, 1957	Z 560
Grubb, Mary T.	July, 1957	Z 596
Goodrich, Mary A.	April, 1958	1 239
Gordon, Moses A.	May, 1958	1 292
Glick, Mary M.	June, 1958	1 320
Garrett, Myrtle May	Aug., 1958	1 378
Getty, Margaret Loretta	Aug., 1959	2 137

Grove, Nancy	May, 1874	D 157
same	May, 1877	D 361
Garrett, Nancy		D 502
Guggenheimer, Nathaniel S.	April, 1946	V 192
Graney, Nell J.	July, 1952	X 413

Gephart, Oliver C.	Nov., 1891	F 223
Gephart, Oliver C.	Aug., 1917	L 233
Gerlach, Olin	April, 1925	N 403
Gurley, Oscar	Feb., 1957	Z 455

Gebhart, Peter	Feb., 1826	A 247
Garey, Peter	Aug., 1870	C 176
Glenn, Patrick	March, 1891	F 178
Grant, Patrick	April, 1902	H 263
Griffin, Patrick	Feb., 1905	I 79
Gill, Peter	Feb., 1914	K 132
Gallagher, Patrick H.	Nov., 1918	L 435
Goldsworthy, Paul	April, 1926	N 595
Getzendanner, Phineas D., Sr.	Feb., 1929	O 462
Goldsworthy, Paul F., Sr.	May, 1946	V 225
Gelwick, Paul	May, 1951	X 166

Gunter, Richard	May, 1908	I 403
Gordon, Robert H.	May, 1910	J 158
Gantt, Rachel M.	Nov., 1919	M 99
Garlitz, Richard	Aug., 1932	Q 55
Gunter, Richard W.	April, 1934	Q 412
Grace, Rosetta Catherine	May, 1940	S 560
Grace, Robert C.	Feb., 1944	U 239
Graham, Robert, Sr.	Jan., 1953	X 560
Gerdeman, Rose	Oct., 1958	1 423

Grove, Solomon	May, 1874	D 140
same	May, 1877	D 361
Goldsmith, Solomon	Sept., 1874	D 171
Graham, Susannah W.	May, 1878	D 359
Green, Susan M.	Feb., 1910	J 117
George, Solomon	Sept., 1914	K 222
Grimminger, Samuel	Feb., 1915	K 279
Goodrich, Solomon	Sept., 1920	M 203
Gephart, Susan M.	Jan., 1921	M 250
Green, Samuel	April, 1922	M 455
Gross, Solomon	Dec., 1934	Q 543
Grobstein, Simon H.	March, 1938	S 65
Gannon, Sarah P.	Oct., 1938	S 175
Grabenstein, Sebastian A.	Dec., 1944	U 419
Griminger, Samuel E.	May, 1948	W 107
Gottlieb, Sarah	March, 1951	X 148
Grim, Stanley Edwin	Sept., 1953	Y 131
Gunnette, Sarah Weems	Feb., 1954	Y 219

Gary, Samuel W.	Jan., 1956	Z 147
Gillespie, Sara B.	April, 1960	2 392
Green, Simeon W.	July, 1960	2 490
Greenwell, Thomas	March, 1831	A 307
Gunter, Thomas	Sept., 1891	F 228
Gray, Thomas S.	Sept., 1906	I 222
Gears, Thomas	Aug., 1907	I 308
Griffith, Timothy	March, 1916	K 490
Gray, Thomas A.	June, 1917	L 196
Grindell, Thomas R.	Feb., 1923	N 5
George, Theophilus	March, 1926	N 559
Gormley, Thomas	Jan., 1928	O 293
Glass, Thomas	March, 1931	P 338
Gatehouse, Thomas	April, 1932	P 567
Griffith, Thomas	Nov., 1932	Q 101
Grubb, Verlinda A.	Jan., 1952	X 291
Grindage, William	Oct., 1850	C 78
Groves, William	May, 1886	E 190
Griffith, William E.	June, 1886	E 207
Gunter, William	Sept., 1891	F 228
same	Sept., 1891	F 228
Green, William H.	April, 1906	I 197
Gunning, William	April, 1913	K 15
Giles, William V.	May, 1918	L 362
Green, William	Feb., 1924	N 211
Griffiths, William	March, 1929	O 494
Grabenstein, William H.	Feb., 1930	P 102
Grimes, William	March, 1930	P 113
Gillum, William G.	Dec., 1930	P 270
Green, William	Sept., 1932	Q 76
Glodfelty, William A.	May, 1933	Q 203
Gunter, William R.	June, 1933	Q 233
Green, William C.	Jan, 1935	Q 569
Garrett, William Mahone	April, 1936	R 232
Giles, Wilbur T.	March, 1944	U 273
Geppert, William L.	July, 1946	V 255
Getson, William F., Sr.	March, 1947	V 424

Gurd, William H.	Aug., 1950	W 609
Grimm, William Walter	April, 1953	Y 24
Gormley, William Thomas	April, 1954	Y 253
Gornall, William F.	Nov., 1956	Z 382
Goebel, William	Feb., 1958	1 209
Gunther, William Arnold	Feb., 1959	1 546

H

Hoye, Ann	Sept., 1825	A 242
Harden, Abraham	Dec., 1838	A 428
Hinkle, Alpheus B.	Jan., 1861	B 188
Hall, Anna G.	April, 1880	D 435
Halle, Albert, Sr.	April, 1887	D 482
Hess, Andrew	April, 1882	D 536
Hetzel, Anna M.	Jan., 1884	E 3
Halpin, Andrew	Feb., 1884	E 20
Hammon, Andrew	Feb., 1887	E 221
Hoffman, Azalia		F 195
same		F 246
Holle, Albert	Jan., 1892	F 253
Harris, Aubrey W.	March, 1893	F 344
Hartman, Ann Martha	June, 1897	G 239
Humbertson, Ann M.	April, 1901	H 164
Humbertson, Ann M.M.	Dec., 1902	H 298
Holzen, Anton, Sr.	Jan., 1904	H 385
Hagan, Alice	Jan., 1906	I 165
Hensler, Agatha	Nov., 1906	I 245
Hitchens, Adam E.	Dec., 1906	I 252
Hixson, Anderson	Nov., 1908	I 466
Haverstick, Alexander C.	May, 1909	J 52
Hauser, August	Jan., 1911	J 224
Haselberger, Agatha	April, 1912	J 411
Hammon, Anna M.	Oct., 1912	J 463
Hook, Anna M.	Oct., 1914	K 238
Hilton, Andrew J.	Nov., 1917	L 266
Hefelbower, Anna E.H.	Dec., 1922	M 569
Hitchins, Aminta E.	Jan., 1924	N 197
Hendley, Annie	March, 1925	N 398
Heller, Andrew	May, 1925	N 425
Hermann, Annie M.	Dec., 1925	N 499
Hehn, August	Jan., 1927	O 118
Handle, Anna C.	Jan., 1929	O 441
Holzen, Anna M.	Jan., 1929	O 455
Henkel, Arnold Carl	Dec., 1929	P 73
Hohing, Anna Eliza	Nov., 1930	P 252
Hawkins, Alvin G.	Jan., 1938	S 37
Heinrich, August W.	June, 1938	S 116

Heck, Charles	Oct., 1818	A 170
Heck, Charles	Jan., 1819	A 177
Heck, Charles	June, 1841	A 483
Hart, Casper	Aug., 1885	D 235
Hurley, Catherine	Oct., 1887	E 269
Holzshu, Charles L. vs. Richard Jacob Eilas		F 150
Hansell, John O.	(Error - See J folio 267)	F 209
Holzshu, Charles L.	Sept., 1891	F 231
Holzheimer, Christopher	Nov., 1892	F 329
Handel, Conrad	Aug., 1899	G 365
Hammersmith, Catherine	Nov., 1901	H 230
Hedges, Charles N.C.	Feb., 1905	I 80
Hedges, Charles N.C.	Feb., 1905	I 83
Hamill, Charles H.	June, 1907	I 275
Hetzel, Christian F.	Jan., 1908	I 351
Hohing, Conrad	Nov., 1910	J 199
Hartig, Christena	Dec., 1912	J 479
Hinkle, Clarence M.	June, 1915	K 358
Himmler, Catharine	June, 1915	K 369
Hess, Charles	July, 1915	K 384
Harding, Clara E.	Feb., 1916	K 467
Hobrock, Catharine	July, 1916	L 31
Himmer, Catharine	Sept., 1921	M 370
Hume, Catherine V.	March, 1924	N 226
Hayden, Charles T.	Oct., 1926	O 71
Hawkins, Charles	March, 1927	O 154
Hensel, Catherine V.	May, 1929	O 540
Hitchins, Clayton S.	March, 1930	P 128
Hoblitzell, Charles M.	June, 1930	P 178
Hartung, Christina	May, 1932	Q 1
Herpich, Conrad	Aug., 1932	Q 53
Hice, Charles Adam	Dec., 1933	Q 324
Hohing, Conrad	April, 1934	Q 410
Hauger, Charles C.	Dec., 1934	Q 557
Haller, Charles W.	March, 1935	R 8
Herpick, Catherine S.	Aug., 1937	R 545
Hice, Cora E.	Nov., 1937	S 6
Herpich, Christopher G.	Aug., 1938	S 136
Hartsock, Clara Jeannette	Sept., 1938	S 149
Hinze, Charles W.	Sept., 1938	S 151
Hetzel, Carl C.	April, 1939	S 311
Hartig, Catherine	April, 1940	S 539
Harden, Carrie M.	Aug., 1941	T 204

Huntsman, Clem B.	Sept., 1942	T 456
Harrison, Carrie	March, 1944	U 258
House, Charles W.	July, 1946	V 259
Hamilton, Charles H.	Dec., 1946	V 363
Holben, Calvin A.	April, 1947	V 437
Hebner, Charles O.	July, 1947	V 508
Heier, Charles C.	Feb., 1951	X 115
Hyde, Catherine	Nov., 1952	X 523
Hazelwood, Clare A.	Oct., 1953	Y 156
Hext, Carrie B.	Jan., 1954	Y 203
Hobell, Casper C.	Nov., 1954	Y 408
Hartman, Charles C.	Jan., 1955	Y 450
Hout, Charles John, Sr.	May, 1955	Y 581
Huston, Charlotte Louise	Jan., 1956	Z 133
Hitchins, Chester A.	July, 1956	Z 278
House, Charles D.	Aug., 1956	Z 325
Hayden, Caroline Hortense	Jan., 1957	Z 437
Hart, Cecilia Anna	Sept., 1958	1 382
Hiner, Charles E.	Jan, 1959	1 519
Hartig, Charles M.	Dec., 1959	2 228
Haller, Curtis Lee	Dec., 1959	2 249

Hoffman, David, Sr.	Sept., 1848	A 660
Hedges, Decatur	Jan., 1866	C 65
Hinkle, David	Feb., 1873	D 83
Howell, David M.	Jan., 1880	D 427
Hartnett, Daniel	March, 1881	D 474
Huebner, Daniel	Aug., 1883	D 619
same	Aug., 1883	D 621
Hartzell, David P.	April, 1886	E 189
Habig, Damian	Jan., 1911	J 218
Haworth, Dorcas	March, 1926	N 570
Houck, Daniel	June, 1926	O 16
Hardesty, David W.	June, 1937	R 515
Huffman, Daniel F.	Feb., 1941	T 84
Hammond, Daisy A.	Dec., 1950	X 70

House, Enoch	June, 1840	A 708
Hoffman, Elizabeth	Oct., 1858	B 142
Hoye, Edward	Oct., 1849	B 15

Hambright, Emanuel	Jan., 1866	C 89
Hamilton, Elizabeth	May, 1870	C 173
Howell, Elizabeth	Jan., 1872	C 214
same	Jan., 1872	C 214
Hall, E.W.	Nov., 1879	D 415
Healey, Ellen E.	May, 1887	E 235
Hoffman, Eugene E.		F 195
same		F 246
Harbaugh, Ellen	Sept., 1906	I 231
Hosken, Elizabeth Anne	Nov., 1914	K 250
Howard, Edward S.	May, 1916	L 7
Hext, Ellen	March, 1919	M 10
Henckel, Emma C.	May, 1920	M 165
Hotchkiss, Elizabeth McL.	May, 1921	M 318
Hartig, Elizabeth	July, 1921	M 340
Hanly, Eudora W.	Nov., 1922	M 552
Hendley, Elizabeth	Oct., 1923	N 138
Hoffman, Effie M.	March, 1924	N 228
Hunter, Elizabeth	Aug., 1924	N 310
Holzen, Elizabeth F.	Nov., 1924	N 339
Hinkle, Ellen	July, 1925	N 456
Harrison, Elizabeth	Oct., 1925	N 475
Hast, Emanuel E.	Feb., 1926	N 541
Hammond, Eugene	Jan., 1927	O 115
Hawse, Enos T.	April, 1929	O 529
Hartsock, Emory R.	March, 1932	P 542
Hart, Elizabeth	April, 1932	P 557
Hanna, Ella Lee	Aug., 1932	Q 51
Haines, Edward H.	Jan., 1933	Q 137
Heller, Elizabeth	June, 1933	Q 229
Hawkins, Esther	June, 1934	Q 447
House, Etta B.	Dec., 1934	Q 553
Holzen, Edward A.	Feb., 1935	Q 591
Hartung, Edward H.	April, 1939	S 307
Heavner, Ella	May, 1940	S 557
Hambright, Emma Sophia	Sept., 1941	T 226
Hileman, Emma R.	Oct., 1942	T 504
Hamilton, Emma	Feb., 1944	U 248
Hershberger, Eva M.	June, 1944	U 308
Heber, Edward M.	July, 1944	U 338
House, Emilie J.	Nov., 1944	U 407
Hartman, Ernest	June, 1945	U 584
Heier, Elizabeth	July 13, 1945	V 4
Harvey, Edwin John	Jan., 1946	V 109

Hebb, George, continued	Feb., 1833	A 333
same	Feb., 1834	A 345
same	March, 1835	A 370
same	March, 1836	A 384
same	Feb., 1837	A 404
same	June, 1837	A 410
same	Jan., 1838	A 417
Hinkle, George P.	July, 1837	A 411
Hoffman, George	March, 1846	A 592
Harn, George R.	June, 1857	B 139
Hutson, George W.	Aug., 1874	D 208
Hoover, George W.	July, 1883	D 623
Himmler, George	Feb., 1884	E 23
Henderson, George, Jr.	March, 1884	E 30
Hinkle, George P.	March, 1888	E 309
Herpich, George H.	March, 1891	F 182
Hammersmith, George	Dec., 1893	G 4
Hosken, George	April, 1897	G 223
Hamilton, George	Dec., 1900	H 136
Hensler, George	June, 1902	H 271
Hoover, George W.	April, 1912	J 413
Humberston, Greenbury	Oct., 1916	L 61
Hamilton, George R.	June, 1917	L 208
Haines, Georgia P.	April, 1924	N 245
Hart, George X.	July, 1924	N 286
Hartig, George, Sr.	Sept., 1924	N 315
Hansel, Garrett H.	April, 1925	N 413
Helmstetter, George	Jan., 1929	O 440
Hice, George T.	June, 1933	Q 239
Hammond, Gabriel E.	Aug., 1934	Q 469
Holzen, George	Jan., 1935	Q 575
Henderson, George M.	Oct., 1936	R 330
Hosken, George K.	April, 1938	S 86
Henry, George W.	June, 1939	S 340
Hopwood, Goldie A.	Nov., 1941	T 272
Hinkle, George Arnette Lee	April, 1945	U 525
Helfrich, George Francis	Aug., 1945	V 19
Hast, G. Louis	Jan., 1948	W 18
Habig, George M.	Oct., 1953	Y 157
Hocking, George Dud	Nov., 1953	Y 159
Hiser, Grace	Dec., 1956	Z 403
Hammann, George Edward	May, 1957	Z 531
Hartman, George V.	Jan., 1958	1 150
Hamilton, Gertrude Scott	Aug., 1959	2 127

Hosken, Ida	Nov., 1945	V 72
Holtzman, Ida W.	March, 1949	W 293
Huff, Isaac T.	July, 1953	Y 88
Hirsch, Isaac	Feb., 1958	1 191
Holland, Irving T.	Feb., 1958	1 211
Horton, Irene	Feb., 1960	2 275

Hoffman, Jacob	March, 1824	A 225
Hook, John S.	Nov., 1826	A 258
Hook, James	April, 1834	A 355
Hendrickson, James	Jan., 1835	A 366
Hamilton, John	June, 1835	A 375
Hays, John	Feb., 1839	A 433
same	Feb., 1840	A 457
same	Feb., 1841	A 479
same	Feb., 1842	A 499
same	Jan., 1843	A 507
same	Feb., 1844	A 535
same	March, 1848	A 646
Hare, Jacob	April, 1844	A 535
Hook, James	June, 1845	A 566
Hook, John L.	June, 1845	A 569
Hook, James	June, 1845	A 569
Hoye, John	June, 1849	A 697
Hughes, Joseph	May, 1845	A 655
Hoye, John	July, 1850	B 18
Hays, John	Feb., 1850	B 17
Hays, John	May, 1850	B 17
Hoye, John of Wm.	Feb., 1852	B 43
Holmes, Joanna	Aug., 1856	B 117
Hilleary, J.G. (Wm.)	March, 1860	B 138
Herpich, John M.	March, 1860	B 173
Henry, James H. et ux.	June, 1863	B 201
Hambright, Julia	Jan., 1866	C 89
Hoffman, John A.	May, 1862	C 5
Heier, John	July, 1865	C 60
Hays, John	Feb., 1872	D 3
Hinkle, Jesse	Sept., 1872	D 50
Hartzell, Jennie L.	March, 1865	D 154
Hoop, John	May, 1877	D 326
Helber, John	Jan., 1879	D 381
Hicks, Joseph	May, 1880	D 446

Hast, John G.	Nov., 1880	D 458
Hartman, Joseph	Aug., 1881	D 495
Hodel, John, Sr.	Feb., 1884	E 17
Hobrook, John Adam	Oct., 1884	E 82
Hinkle, Jaritta	Nov., 1887	E 280
Hinkle, J.T.		E 284
Humbird, John, Jr.		F 38
Humbird, J.B.		F 38
Hoffman, John	March, 1890	F 80
Hoffman J.C.		F 150
Hansell, John O.		F 209
Huff, Jasper	March, 1892	F 277
Hinkle, John	Aug., 1892	F 308
Humbird, Jacob Will	June, 1893	F 374
same. Codicil	June, 1893	F 376
Hart, John	April, 1897	G 226
Hill, James Thomas	Dec., 1898	G 320
Herpich, John Frederick	Jan., 1900	H 39
Hinkle, John F.	July, 1901	H 199
Heinrich, John H.	March, 1902	H 261
Hosken, John	Jan., 1903	H 318
Harris, John	April, 1904	I 8
Hughes, James	March, 1906	I 191
Hansel, Jacob	May, 1906	I 203
Hedding, John S.	July, 1907	I 294
Hartig, John	Dec., 1909	J 102
Hartley, James T.	Sept., 1912	J 450
Hoban, John F.	March, 1914	K 150
Hackett, Jessie Macbeth	Jan., 1915	K 273
Harris, Joseph S.W.	May, 1917	L 173
Hogan, John	June, 1917	L 202
Handle, Jacob	Dec., 1918	L 437
Hartman, Joseph H.	Aug., 1919	M 65
Hardman, John P.	June, 1920	M 173
Hanson, James	June, 1920	M 176
Heck, John W.	July, 1920	M 185
Herrick, John A.	Sept., 1922	M 525
Hughes, Joseph, Sr.	Oct., 1922	M 542
Helmstetter, Joseph	March, 1923	N 29
Houck, Jane Ann	Nov., 1923	N 164
Hitchins, Joseph H.	Dec., 1924	N 359
Holzen, John	April, 1925	N 405
Hughes, Jacob W.	June, 1925	N 432
Hamilton, John K.	June, 1925	N 440

Hoenicka, John A.	June, 1925	N 442
Hart, John W.	Dec., 1925	N 495
Hermann, John G.	Jan., 1926	N 524
Hogan, James	Feb., 1926	N 534
Haus, Jennie	Oct., 1926	O 70
Harper, James A.	Oct., 1926	O 76
Hoffman, John	March, 1927	O 145
Holtzman, James L.	June, 1927	O 190
Hymes, John	Oct., 1927	O 257
Hammon, J. Conrad	Dec., 1927	O 287
Houck, J. Holmes	April, 1928	O 328
Herboldsheimer, John B.	April, 1928	O 329
Holahan, Josephine	Aug., 1928	O 375
Hirsh, Joseph	Jan., 1929	O 447
Herring, John C.	Oct., 1929	P 30
Hopcraft, Jane	March, 1930	P 123
Hoopengardner, James	Nov., 1930	P 248
Hannan, John J.	May, 1932	P 590
Heinrich, J. Philip	July, 1932	Q 37
Hale, John R.	Feb., 1936	R 193
Helmstetter, Josephine	Aug., 1936	R 300
Humbird, J. Wilson	May, 1937	R 492
Herwig, John H.	May, 1937	R 497
Hauser, Joseph C.	Oct., 1937	R 587
Hershiser, James F.	Dec., 1937	S 21
Hendra, John H.	April, 1939	S 304
Hammersmith, Joseph C.	Feb., 1942	T 331
Hardy, John W.	Oct., 1942	T 509
Hull, Jane	June, 1943	U 96
Hinkle, Jarilla Janet	Oct., 1944	U 391
Howe, John	June, 1945	U 585
Howe, John J.	May, 1946	V 214
Hughes, James Henry	Aug., 1946	V 267
Hausrath, John J.	Oct., 1946	V 316
Hogan, John W.	Oct., 1948	W 210
Hensell, John M.	May, 1949	W 327
Hamilton, James	Aug., 1952	X 460
Harrison, Joseph Meredith	Dec., 1956	Z 405
Hitchins, James J.	Feb., 1957	Z 439
Hessinger, Julius Henry	March, 1957	Z 480
Hirsh, Jesse	July, 1958	1 340
Hewett, Jacob Calvin	Dec., 1958	1 500
Holzen, John Francis	Feb., 1959	1 543
Hawk, J. Milton	Feb., 1959	1 562

Hoenicka, Jessie V.	April, 1960	2 397
Harris, Joseph	Oct., 1960	3 6
Hook, Keziah	June, 1845	A 569
Haupt, Kate	Feb., 1916	K 481
Helmstetter, Karl	May, 1929	O 548
Haller, Kate M.	Feb., 1930	P 98
Hodgson, Katherine Elizabeth	July, 1953	Y 79
Hare, Katherine J.	March, 1957	Z 470
Hast, Katherine	Dec., 1959	2 247
Hilleary, Levi		B 99
Hurn, Levi (Harn)		B 139
Hinkle, Leonard	Oct., 1878	D 373
Hummelshine, Levi K.	March, 1899	D 395
Hitchcock, Lydia H.		F 38
Hoffman, Leonard	June, 1890	F 104
Hansell, Laura		F 209
Hinkle, Louisa	April, 1894	G 33
Hinkle, Leonard	Feb., 1898	G 279
Hartley, Lavinia	Nov., 1900	H 132
Hamilton, Lewis M.	Feb., 1905	I 77
Harbaugh, Lewis Frank	May, 1910	J 155
Huber, Louis	March, 1911	J 282
Hughes, Lewis Napoleon	Feb., 1912	J 394
Himmler, Lepotina	Feb., 1918	L 299
Helmer, L. Leslie	Jan., 1925	N 374
Hughes, Letitia Ann	Aug., 1927	O 226
Hilleary, Levi S.	June, 1929	O 556
Hepburn, Louisa Lowndes R.	Aug., 1933	Q 266
Hansrote, Laura B.	May, 1935	R 34
Hillery, Louise B.	March, 1939	S 294
Hansrote, Lawrence J.	April, 1944	U 285
Hohing, Lenore	Oct., 1944	U 393
Holmes, Lilla May	June, 1947	V 490
Henderson, Louisa P.	June, 1948	W 115
Hart, Louise C.	June, 1951	X 188
Hadley, Lottie	Aug., 1951	X 219
Hitchcock, Lydia H.	Aug., 1953	Y 99
Hardesty, Lillie	June, 1955	Z 20
Henckel, Lawrence	July, 1959	2 85

Hays, Michael		A 273
Hilleary, Margaret		A 275
Hoff, Morgan		A 324
Harden, Margaret		A 430
Haldeman, Mira B.		B 67
Hazelhurst, Maria E.		B 192
Hammill, Mary		C 11
Hedges, Margaret H.		C 65
Hardinger, Mary	April, 1873	D 103
Hoye, Mary E.		D 245
Hoye, Mary E.	Oct., 1875	D 245
Helber, Magdalene E.	Jan., 1879	D 383
Healey, Maurice A.	July, 1879	D 408
Hicks, Mary Jane	May, 1880	D 445
Henninger, Mary A.	April, 1887	E 228
Hinkle, Mary E.		E 284
Hamilton, Maxwell, J.		E 327
Hodel, Mary Ann	Jan., 1890	F 59
Hoffman, Matilda		F 195
same		F 246
Hansell, Margaret		F 209
Hinkle, Minerva J.	May, 1892	F 296
Harvey, Mary	Aug., 1894	G 58
Hinkle, Morgan	Feb., 1895	G 98
Hebb, Mary Duncan	Dec., 1895	G 152
Hoban, Michael J.	March, 1899	G 343
Hartnett, Mary	May, 1899	G 356
Hinkle, Mary	June, 1901	H 197
Harvey, Margaret	April, 1905	I 102
Holzen, Mary G.	Nov., 1905	I 161
Hinkle, Mary A.	Aug., 1907	I 309
Hodel, Mary Ellen	April, 1908	I 392
Hopwood, Mary Ann	June, 1908	I 409
Hutson, Mary D.	Aug., 1908	I 450
Hesser, Minta M.	Jan., 1909	I 484
Hill, Mary E.	Jan., 1910	J 110
Hewitt, Mary Frances	April, 1912	J 410
Herpich, Margaret	Nov., 1912	J 464
Hartig, Martin	Feb., 1914	K 137
Hamilton, Mary K.	June, 1914	K 184
Hein, Matilda	July, 1914	K 209
Higgins, Michael J.	Dec., 1914	K 261
Herpich, Margaret	Jan., 1916	K 462
Humbertson, Mary C.	June, 1916	L 18

Hast, Mary Effie May	Oct., 1949	W 409
Haslbeck, Mathew J.	March, 1951	X 138
House, Mary Jane	Oct., 1951	X 257
Harris, Mary	Jan., 1952	X 297
Hermann, Maggie	Oct., 1952	X 500
Holzshu, Mary E.	April, 1953	Y 20
Hivick, Merl Newton	Aug., 1953	Y 94
Hughes, Matilda	Oct., 1953	Y 158
Hughes, Minna	April, 1954	Y 249
Hayden, Margaret Virginia	April, 1954	Y 255
Huster, Mary Helen	Jan., 1955	Y 452
Hartzell, Margaret Elizabeth	July, 1956	Z 272
Hodges, Mary E.K.	July, 1957	Z 593
Holliday, Melvin E.	Jan., 1958	1 155
Harbaugh, Marion Lee	Jan., 1958	1 167
Henckel, Margaret Edna	April, 1959	2 2
Hitchins, Mabel L.	Oct., 1959	2 175
Harbaugh, Margaret Hudson	Oct., 1959	2 180
Hamill, Mary A.	Dec., 1959	2 244
Haslacker, Marie Parks	April, 1960	2 391
Hoban, Margaret P.	July, 1960	2 484
Harvey, Marshall N.	Oct., 1960	2 584
Harriman, Mary G.	Oct., 1960	2 587

Hartsock, Nathan		B 102
Hodel, Nicholas		B 193
Hartzell, Nannie	April, 1886	E 188
Husband, Nancy	Sept., 1916	L 54
Hitchins, Nancy P.	June, 1926	O 15
Hendley, Noah	Dec., 1935	R 155
Hewitt, Nora	Sept., 1950	X 1
Hughes, Nell	Sept., 1951	X 231
Hauger, Nina Louise	Aug., 1957	1 15
Hitchins, Nannie B.	April, 1959	1 589

Heffner, Oliver	June, 1848	C 142
Hitchens, Owen	March, 1893	F 347
Hohing, Otto, Sr.	March, 1915	K 315
Hymes, Oliver	Oct., 1922	M 537
Hohing, Otto, Sr.	Sept., 1941	T 219

Hogan, Richard	Sept., 1927	O 249
Himmler, Robert G.	Jan., 1930	P 79
Hoy, Ralph Totton	April, 1933	Q 193
Harvey, Rachel C.	June, 1934	Q 450
Helbig, Rosalie	March, 1941	T 114
Hawkins, Richard James, Sr.	May, 1941	T 129
Hess, Rose L.	March, 1943	U 9
Hedrick, Rosa Belle	Sept., 1944	U 367
Hilleary, Richard P.	June, 1948	W 147
Hill, R. Mason	Nov., 1948	W 233
Henrickson, Russell C.	Sept., 1953	Y 123
Hardman, Raymond Guy	Dec., 1956	Z 399
Hitchins, Rosina	Nov., 1957	1 115

Hazlet, Samuel		A 536
Hite, Sarah E.		D 486
Humbird, Sallie V.		F 38
Humbird, Sarah A.	Jan., 1891	F 160
same		F 160
Hammersmith, Sebastian		G 47
same	June, 1894	G 47
Humbertson, Salem	April, 1898	G 288
Hardman, Sarah Rebecca	Aug., 1898	G 303
Hocking, Sarah J.	Oct., 1899	G 378
Humbertson, Susan L.	July, 1901	H 206
Hume, Simeon R.	Nov., 1904	I 59
Hinkle, Susan V.	March, 1905	I 90
Hamburger, Seligman	March, 1907	I 266
Hardy, Sallie E. E.	Jan., 1909	I 494
Horn, Susan	March, 1915	K 307
Hansel, Solomon	Dec., 1916	L 87
Hinkle, Summerfield	Jan., 1917	L 107
Haus, Samuel C.	March, 1918	L 323
Hill, Sarah C.	Aug., 1918	L 394
Hershberger, Susan M.	May, 1923	N 55
Hopcraft, Sarah J.	Oct., 1923	N 151
Holmes, Susan	Feb., 1925	N 385
Heck, Sarah Elizabeth	April, 1925	N 406
Hartman, Samuel J.	Jan., 1932	P 509
Hamilton, Samuel	May, 1932	Q 8
Harvey, Susan	Jan., 1935	Q 578
Hanekamp, Sarah Ann	July, 1935	R 62

Hoffman, Valentine		A 486
Haversack, Valentine	April, 1872	D 17
Heber, Vernie K.	March, 1944	U 255
Habeeb, Victoria	Jan., 1951	X 98
Hartsock, Virgil L.	May, 1956	Z 241

Howell, William		A 109
Hoblitzell, William		A 251
Hoye, William W.		A 385
Harness, William		B 87
Hilleary, William J.G.		B 138
Hooper, William Henry		C 10
Holle, William	April, 1885	D 207
Hildebrand, Wilimina	Sept., 1876	D 295
Hammersmith, Wolfgang	April, 1879	D 404
Haddock, William		F 66
same	Jan., 1890	F 66
Hansell, William A.		F 209
Hartung, Wolfgang	June, 1893	F 369
Hamilton, William A.	March, 1894	G 24
Himmler, William	Oct., 1904	I 47
Henckel, William P.	May, 1908	I 400
Holle, Wilhelmina	Feb., 1910	J 121
Hiner, William Henry	Feb., 1911	J 256
Hitchins, William A.	June, 1919	M 49
Hilton, Warren E.	Oct., 1928	O 406
Harrison, William J.	Jan., 1929	O 458
Hoffman, Will O.	March, 1929	O 496
Himmler, Wilhelmina	Feb., 1930	P 104
Harper, William	July, 1930	P 183
Hammersmith, Wolfgang	March, 1933	Q 181
Henderson, William G.	June, 1935	R 40
Hill, Walter T.	Aug., 1935	R 91
Hammers, William Francis	Oct., 1935	R 119
Hardy, Wilbert D., Sr.	Nov., 1936	R 346
House, William A.	July, 1937	R 526
Hodges, Wyllys R.	July, 1938	S 134
Hixon, William T.	Feb., 1940	S 474
Harr, Warren	March, 1940	S 518
Hammond, William J.	April, 1943	U 42
Hopwood, William W.	Sept., 1943	U 166

Henry, William C.	Nov., 1944	U 402
Holland, William Rankin	Nov., 1945	V 70
Haines, William L.	March, 1941	V 157
Hunter, William C.	Sept., 1946	V 291
Hauger, Ward N.	July, 1947	V 516
Hast, William H.	Nov., 1947	V 585
Holsinger, William I.	April, 1950	W 537
Huster, William A.	Aug., 1950	W 615
Hocking, William C.	April, 1954	Y 258
Hartman, William E.	Dec., 1958	1 467
Hay, William N.	June, 1960	2 439

I

Iiams, Amos		B 39
Indolfi, Antanetta	July, 1948	W 152
Irons, Asa	June, 1950	W 566
Imes, Benjamin	May, 1949	W 320
Isaacs, Charles B.	March, 1909	J 16
Irons, Candace	Dec., 1926	O 112
Inskeep, Charles M.	March, 1932	P 553
Imes, Daniel L.	Nov., 1943	U 187
Isenhart, Elizabeth	Feb., 1874	D 221
Imbrogna, Filomena	Sept., 1928	O 403
Iiams, Hiram		B 92
Irvine, Harry	Aug., 1942	T 438
Ireland, Isabel	Jan., 1944	U 215
Irons, John		B 22
Imel, Jacob		F 189
Inskeep, John Scott	Jan., 1895	G 89
Ingles, James, Sr.	March, 1911	J 260
Inskeep, James William	Dec., 1914	K 251
Imel, Mary Jane		F 189
Isaacs, Mary Elizabeth	March, 1908	I 373

Inskeep, Otho	Jan., 1940	S 470
Irvine, Sophia M.	Sept., 1942	T 486
Inskeep, Sarah	March, 1947	V 413
Iames, Theodore S.	March, 1946	V 152
Iiams, William		A 313
Inskeep, William V.		B 154
Izzett, William	Nov., 1895	G 144

J

Johnson, Abraham		A 47
Jackson, Ann		A 284
Jones, Arthur	Aug., 1912	J 443
Jenkins, Ann	May, 1913	K 24
Jones, Alice Ann	Feb., 1927	O 138
Jamison, Alice R.	May, 1943	U 75
Joyce, Anna	April, 1949	W 294
Johnson, Alex H.	Aug., 1951	X 225
Jones, Annie Ford	March, 1952	X 344
Jones, Albert E.	July, 1956	Z 296
Johnson Ada B.	July, 1958	1 329
Jacopi, Alfred	May, 1960	2 426

Jadwin, Bartholomew		A 184
Jones, Benjamin K.	Jan., 1912	J 375
Jenkins, Benjamin	June, 1935	R 38
Jones, Bertha V.	Dec., 1938	S 215

Jamison, Cecilia E.	March, 1880	D 432
Jones, Carlton S.	Feb., 1913	J 496
Jones, Cecelia F.	Nov., 1920	M 231
James, Catherine	July, 1927	O 209
Johns, Catherine	Oct., 1932	Q 95
Jackson, Clara	March, 1938	S 72
James, Claiborne M.	Aug., 1940	S 610
Johnson, Clara I.	Jan., 1943	T 589
Jones, Cora L.	Nov., 1946	V 341
Judy, Cora M.	May, 1950	W 549
Jolley, Charles P.	June, 1950	W 568
Jewell, Charles Alexander	Oct., 1953	Y 142
Johnson, Clyde R.	Feb., 1957	Z 444
Jeffries, Charles S.	June, 1959	2 44
Johnson, Crates S.	June, 1960	2 460

Jeffries, George Garfield, Jr.	March, 1954	Y 224
Jenkins, Gertha V.	April, 1955	Y 516

Jacob, Hannah	Rejected	A 136
Jamison, Henry A.		C 92
Johnson, Henry J.	March, 1886	E 175
Jones, Harry, Sr.	May, 1911	J 296
Jammer, Henry	Jan., 1912	J 369
Jones, Harriett	Nov., 1928	O 429
Johnson, Henry	Nov., 1929	P 36
Jenkins, Henry A.	March, 1937	R 428
Judy, Harris Edward	Jan., 1938	S 34
Johnson, Henry J.	July, 1941	T 179
Jacob, Helen McMullen	June, 1958	1 318

Jacobs, Ida M.	April, 1932	P 577
Johnson, Ida C.	Dec., 1947	V 592

Jacob, John J.		A 442
Johnson, Joshua		B 84
Johnson, John C.	Feb., 1872	D 1
Johnson, John F.	Aug., 1876	D 292
Johnson, Joseph	Jan., 1879	D 387
Johnson, James S.	Jan., 1879	D 387
Johns, Juliana	April, 1884	E 44
Johnson, John L.	Jan., 1887	E 218
Jandorf, Joseph		F 197
Jenkins, Joseph	June, 1891	F 210
Jones, James	June, 1899	G 360
Johnson, Jane	Oct., 1899	G 386
Johnson, Joshua	March, 1904	H 403
Jacobs, James H.	Sept., 1910	J 189
Jones, James S.	Jan., 1912	J 365
Jose, James	Dec., 1915	K 444
Jones, Jane H.	March, 1917	L 141
Johnson, James S.	March, 1918	L 329
Jeffries, Jabez	Oct., 1919	M 90
Johnston, James S.	Dec., 1927	O 284

Jeffries, Jabez	Oct., 1919	M 90
Johnston, James S.	Dec., 1927	O 284
Jeffery, John	Jan., 1931	P 287
Jenkins, Joseph Thomas	Sept., 1931	P 447
Jones, James	Jan., 1937	R 385
Johnson, James T., Sr.	April, 1938	S 87
Johnson, James Roddy	Aug., 1940	S 608
Johnson, Josephine	Jan., 1941	T 61
Jack, John, Sr.	Aug., 1949	W 366
Jammer, Jacob Suter	July, 1952	X 422
Jones, John T.	April, 1955	Y 511
Jackson, James A.	June, 1955	Z 5
Jukes, Josephine P.	March, 1958	1 222
Johnson, Jerome J.	Feb., 1960	2 293

Jesinofsky, Ludwig	Jan, 1872	C 214
Johnson, L. Emma	March, 1904	G 22
Jamesson, Lionel P.	Feb., 1911	J 246
Jukes, Lucy, Helen	Jan., 1919	L 458
Joblinskey, Leva (Blonskey)	Jan., 1924	N 196
Johnson, Lelia A.	July, 1954	Y 317

Johnson, Mary Ann	Oct., 1872	D 52
Jones, Matilda	March, 1901	H 161
Johns, Mary Martha	Jan, 1908	I 362
Johns, Mary	March, 1916	K 488
Johnston, Mary Ann	April, 1920	M 152
Jacobs, Margaret J.	May, 1921	M 326
Jamison, Mary J.	Feb., 1922	M 405
Jeffries, Mary Susan	Feb., 1924	N 214
Johnson, Mary S.	Sept., 1924	N 316
Jacobs, Martha	Nov., 1927	O 269
Johnson, Margaret	June, 1932	Q 15
Jones, Malcolm S.	Aug., 1935	R 80
Jones, Mary J.	Dec., 1942	T 541
Judy, Mary A.	Jan., 1945	U 446
Jeffries, Mary Jane	July, 1948	W 164
Jones, Matthew A.	May, 1954	Y 262
Jamesson, Mary A.	March, 1956	Z 197
Jones, Mary Shaffer	April, 1958	1 257

Johnson, Nicholas	Jan., 1880	D 423
Johnson, Oscar Leroy	March, 1927	O 146
Jenkins, Obed	April, 1931	P 347
Jameson, Priscilla C.		A 386
Jenkins, Philip	Jan., 1911	J 217
Jukes, Priscilla	Nov., 1935	R 126
Jeffries, Robert		A 82
Jacobs, Richard		A 226
Jenifer, Ruth	April, 1848	C 140
Johnson, Reverdy	Dec., 1872	D 303
Johnson, Richard D.	Oct., 1900	H 126
Johnson Rachel	Oct., 1914	K 220
Johnson, Richard D.	May, 1918	L 354
Johnson, Rosalie J.	Dec., 1924	N 343
Jeffries, Richard H.	March, 1931	P 329
Jackson, Robert	May, 1948	W 95
Jenkins, Robert T.	Sept., 1952	X 488
Jamison, Samuel		A 312
Jackson, Samuel		A 337
Jacobs, Susannah	June, 1839	A 447
Jackson, Samuel	April, 1846	A 607
Jamison, S.J.	April, 1853	B 57
Jenkins, Sarah	June, 1887	E 242
Johnson, Samuel	June, 1904	I 20
Johns, Sarah M.	May, 1923	N 60
Jankins, Savila	Nov., 1927	O 267
Jackson, Sarah	Aug., 1941	T 216
Johnson, S.Sylvia	June, 1955	Z 22
Jeffries, Samuel Bolitho	June, 1959	2 62
Jamison, Tobias B.	April, 1853	B 57
Johns, Thomas	June, 1882	D 541
Johnson, Thomas	Nov., 1883	D 636

K

King, Alexander		A 415
same	Nov., 1859	B 172
same	Nov., 1855	B 98
same	Dec., 1873	D 138
King, Alexander, Jr.	Dec., 1873	D 140
Kolb, Andrew		F 151
Kolb, Anna M.		F 151
Kean, Annie	Jan., 1891	F 166
Kalberg, August	Aug., 1890	F 181
Kiernan, Ann	Oct., 1894	G 70
Karig, Adam	April, 1900	H 78
Kean, Anthony	Aug., 1901	H 211
Koelberg, Ann	April, 1905	I 103
Kastner, Anton	May, 1910	J 156
Kienhofer, Anthony	Dec., 1914	K 253
Krause, August	Dec., 1914	K 260
Kabosky, Anna	Feb., 1915	K 291
Keller, Anna M.	Jan., 1918	L 294
Kiser, A.V.	Jan., 1922	M 393
Kraft, Andrew	Jan., 1924	N 194
Kammauf, Adam	Jan., 1929	O 462
Kroll, Annie Elizabeth	Aug., 1931	P 439
Kalbaugh, Alexander B.	June, 1932	Q 20
Kinloch, Anne	July, 1932	Q 43
Krauss, Anna K.	Nov., 1934	Q 530
Kerber, Anna C.	Oct., 1935	R 121
Kolb, Anna M.	Feb., 1938	S 51
Kuhlman, Adeline F.	Dec., 1942	T 544
Kight, Anna Catherine	Nov., 1945	V 75
Kintner, Adrian C.	Oct., 1946	V 336
Kolb, Annie M.	Dec., 1946	V 370
Kelly, Agnes	Sept., 1949	W 400
Kinney, Annie S.	April, 1950	W 521
Kotschenreuther, Anna	Jan., 1954	Y 202
Kraft, Appollonia	May, 1955	Y 577
King, Annie S.	July, 1956	Z 268
Kaplon, Abram	Jan., 1959	1 515

Kelley, David		B 126
Kerr, David, Sr.	June, 1915	K 350
Koch, Diana T.	May, 1917	L 172
Keplinger, Daniel W.	May, 1925	N 424
Keating, Delia G.	Jan., 1927	O 113
Kuykendall, David F.	Oct., 1933	Q 297
Kauffman, David	Oct., 1956	Z 367

Kight, Enoch	Feb., 1869	C 131
Knapp, Elizabeth	April, 1883	D 598
Kolb, Elizabeth		F 151
Kane, Ellen M.	Sept., 1891	F 226
Kean, Eliza	Aug., 1893	F 391
Keller, Edward T.	Feb., 1911	J 252
Kelly, Eliza	Oct., 1919	M 87
Kammauff, Elizabeth	Sept., 1920	M 202
Kallmyer, Eliza	Jan., 1924	N 185
Kaefer, Eva B.	Dec., 1932	Q 118
Kelley, Ella Mason	March, 1933	Q 164
Kolb, Emma E.	Dec., 1936	R 359
King, Elmira	Oct., 1938	S 173
Kyle, Edward McC.	Jan., 1940	T 60
Kelly, Ella B.	Feb., 1941	T 90
Kuhn, Emma C.	Jan., 1944	U 229
Kenny, Emma C.	March, 1947	V 430
Kroll, Ellen	July, 1947	V 514
Kight, Eliza A.	Jan., 1949	W 263
Kabosky, Elizabeth E.	May, 1953	Y 39
Kelly, Elsye Twigg	June, 1953	Y 55
Knieriem, Elizabeth M.	Sept., 1954	Y 357
Keifer, Erma H.	Oct., 1954	Y 379
Keller, Emma M.	Jan., 1956	Z 144
Kooken, Ethel Cornelia	Jan., 1957	Z 416
Koontz, Emma Elizabeth	Oct., 1958	1 414

Kasecamp, Frederick	April, 1873	D 107
Kuhn, Frank C.	Jan., 1910	J 107
Kaiser, Frederick T.	June, 1914	K 200
Kelley, Fannie S.	May, 1920	M 166
Kean, Frank T.	Feb., 1932	P 524

Knippenberg, Frederick	April, 1933	Q 188
King, Francis William	Feb., 1934	Q 357
Knight, Floyd	Feb., 1937	R 402
Kastner, Frank M.	May, 1947	V 464
Kelley, Florida L.	Oct., 1947	V 563
Kunes, Floyd Ernest	June, 1948	W 137

Kook, George, Sr.		A 49
King, George		A 659
Kolb, George		F 151
Kuhn, George W.	May, 1911	J 297
Kean, George A.	Oct., 1917	L 255
Klitsch, Gottlieb	April, 1923	N 37
Kight, Gilbert B.	Dec., 1923	N 170
Krouse, George	Aug., 1924	N 295
Keedy, George	Feb., 1926	N 542
Kean, George E.	April, 1929	O 524
Kotschenreuther, George	March, 1934	Q 384
Korns, George H.	April, 1934	Q 414
Klencke, George E.	Nov., 1935	R 128
Kumm, George A.	Aug., 1936	R 307
Kolb, George	Dec., 1936	R 357
Kober, George M.	May, 1937	R 482
Kintner, Gertrude B.	Dec., 1938	S 203
Kreitzburg, George L.	Feb., 1948	W 56
Knieriem, George	Oct., 1950	X 25
Kirkwood, George W.	May, 1957	Z 538
Keller, George W.	Aug., 1958	1 372

King, Hester M.		A 456
Koontz, Henry, Sr.		C 99
Korns, Henry	March, 1878	D 349
Knatz, Henry	April, 1890	F 87
Kane, Harriet A.	Dec., 1909	J 100
Keller, Harry P.	May, 1910	J 154
Kuhn, Henry	Feb., 1911	J 240
Knippenberg, Henry F.	Dec., 1911	J 356
Kight, Howard R.	March, 1920	M 147
Krumbine, Henry S.	March, 1924	N 221
Krauss, Henry	July, 1925	N 455

Kamens, Harry A.	Nov., 1927	O 260
Kaiser, Henry C.	March, 1931	P 315
Kelso, Hugh	July, 1933	Q 250
Kuehn, Herman	Nov., 1933	Q 311
Kight, Harry Silas	Dec., 1934	Q 542
Knieriem, Henry J.	May, 1940	S 551
Kuhn, Henry B.	April, 1942	T 386
Kohl, Henry J.	Feb., 1944	U 247
Kuhn, Henry E.	April, 1948	W 79
Kuhn, Henry	Feb., 1960	2 282

Kight, Isabel	May, 1883	D 602
Keady, Isaac	Sept., 1926	O 49
Kempner, Isidor	Feb., 1931	P 305
Karns, Irene M.	Dec., 1955	Z 129

Kimes, John		A 100
Koontz, Jacob, Sr.		A 524
King, Joseph		B 54
Kessler, John		B 94
Koontz, Jacob		B 126
Kelley, James		C 38
Kenard, John	Oct., 1873	D 121
Kelenbeck, John H.	June, 1877	D 329
Kolb, John Adam	July, 1877	D 332
Kight, James	May, 1883	D 600
Klein, John	Dec., 1886	E 212
Kolb, John	Jan., 1888	E 285
Korns, Jesse	Feb., 1888	E 301
Kolb, John A.		F 151
Keller, John J.	Nov., 1881	F 239
Kolb, John N.	Feb., 1892	F 263
Knode, Joseph	Feb., 1892	F 266
Kelso, John	Dec., 1892	F 333
Kuhnle, J.C.	Jan., 1893	F 339
Kuhnle, Joseph	Jan., 1893	F 339
Koegal, John	Feb., 1893	F 343
Kane, James	Jan., 1894	G 11
Keating, John		G 54
Kienhofer, John M.	Feb., 1896	G 157

Kuffner, John) Keefner, John)	Aug., 1896	G 185
Kuhn, John	May, 1901	H 187
Kirk, James	Dec., 1906	I 251
Kroll, John	March, 1910	J 139
Kesser, Jacob	July, 1910	J 175
Kelley, John	April, 1911	J 287
Kiper, Jacob	May, 1912	J 424
Kabosky, John	July, 1914	K 207
Kuhnle, J. Christopher	Sept., 1914	K 225
Kenney, James	Feb., 1915	K 276
Kirk, John	July, 1915	K 378
Kesler, John	Feb., 1918	L 305
Kearchner, John H.	April, 1918	L 349
Kight, Joenna	Feb., 1920	M 116
Keady, James	Dec., 1920	M 244
Kight, Jessie C.	Nov., 1925	N 480
Kinloch, John	Dec., 1925	N 497
Korns, John Wilson	Sept., 1926	O 52
Keating, John	Nov., 1926	O 94
King, James R.	Feb., 1927	O 131
Kerr, Jane M.	Dec., 1928	O 434
Kifer, Jesse	June, 1929	O 559
Keech, James Edward, Sr.	Sept., 1929	P 11
Kirk, James E.	Nov., 1930	P 247
Kane, Joseph P.	Nov., 1930	P 257
Kemphfer, John A.	March, 1931	P 323
Kirkwood, John Forrest	May, 1931	P 361
Kelly, Julia A.	March, 1932	P 538
Keller, John S.	May, 1932	P 583
Kabosky, Julia A.	Oct., 1932	Q 85
Kesner, Jacob	March, 1934	Q 398
Kyne, Johana	April, 1939	S 306
Kreitzburg, John W.	May, 1940	S 572
Kelso, John H.	Dec., 1940	T 57
King, James Nelson Garfield	Jan., 1943	T 597
Kile, Jacob H.	March, 1943	U 10
Kiiffner, John W.	April, 1943	U 47
Kenny, John T.	Feb., 1944	U 251
Kreiling, John P.	Oct., 1944	U 380
Kyle, Jeanette M.	Aug., 1948	W 177
Keech, James Edwin	Aug., 1950	W 617
Kuhn, Jessie Estelle	Nov., 1951	X 264
Kelly, James F.	April, 1952	X 368

Kight, James Elmer	May, 1952	X 397
Kline, John W.	July, 1953	Y 72
Keller, John D.	Oct., 1954	Y 371
Kaplon, Jacob Lewis	Dec., 1954	Y 423
Klawan, Joseph	Jan., 1955	Y 448
Kenney, James P.	Feb., 1956	Z 179
Keller, John	June, 1957	Z 571
King, John T.	Sept., 1957	1 63
Kenney, James E.	Feb., 1958	1 185

Karpf, Kathleen Keating	July, 1935	R 67
Koch, Katharine C.	Nov., 1945	V 78
Kalbaugh, Katherine N.	April, 1947	V 446
Kerscher, Katherine	Oct., 1947	V 558

King, Lavinia M.	April, 1880	D 442
same		D 444
Kuhnle, L.F.	Jan., 1893	F 339
Kreiling, Louis	July, 1905	I 119
Kalbfus, Lavinia E.	March, 1909	J 24
Keyes, Louis	Aug., 1912	J 441
Kifer, Leonidas	Jan., 1925	N 362
Kimes, Lawrence L.	Jan., 1929	O 443
Kolmer, Leonard	Sept., 1932	Q 63
Knott, Lucy B.	March, 1933	Q 184
Kifer, Lemma H.	June, 1939	S 336
Knight, Lucy Hughes	March, 1944	U 267
Kisamore, Leo Riffle	April, 1945	U 511
Kline, Louis	May, 1945	U 555
Kraft, Lucy E.	April, 1943	V 195
Krantz, Lucille	Aug., 1948	W 184
Kabosky, Louis Aloysius	March, 1950	W 496
King, Lillian M.	Jan., 1956	Z 148
Knippenberg, Leona Maud	July, 1958	1 351
Kelso, Lemuel S.	Dec., 1958	1 481

Kershner, Michael		A 254
Kelley, Minerva M.	Dec., 1888	E 352

Kesser, Martha A.	Sept., 1892	F 311
King, Matilda	Oct., 1892	F 322
Kalbaugh, Michael	March, 1896	G 166
Karig, Margaret	Sept., 1900	H 122
Knight, Mary C.	Oct., 1902	H 294
Kegg, Mary A.	Dec., 1905	I 162
Kroll, Minnie	March, 1906	I 186
Koontz, Margaret	May, 1907	I 272
Kelley, Mary Clare	Jan., 1911	J 213
Kitzmiller, Mary A.	March, 1911	J 266
Kuykendall, Martha	May, 1917	L 177
Kelly, Malinda J.	Dec., 1925	N 503
Koelker, Mary J.	July, 1927	O 191
Keyser, Mary Ellen	Nov., 1930	P 254
Kerr, Marion R.	Sept., 1931	P 452
Keefer, Mary	March, 1932	P 543
Kroll, Mary	May, 1933	Q 207
Kearney, Matthew J.	Aug., 1934	Q 468
Keys, Minnie Helen	Jan., 1936	R 181
Kean, Mary	April, 1937	R 454
Koegel, Mary Elizabeth	Jan., 1939	S 231
Kelley, Mary Clara	Oct., 1939	S 417
Koffar, Mike	March, 1940	S 511
Keating, Margaret Mary	May, 1940	S 558
Keefer, Margaret	Nov., 1940	T 33
Kolb, Mary Ann	Sept., 1941	T 240
Kerber, Mary	Dec., 1941	T 293
Keller, Martha Resaca	June, 1942	T 414
King, Minnie E.	Sept., 1942	T 457
Kumm, Mary	Feb., 1943	T 605
Knippenberg, Maria	Jan., 1946	V 111
Kelso, Minnie	Feb., 1948	W 41
Kearsing, Margaret Alice	Dec., 1952	X 536
Kraft, Mary M.	March, 1955	Y 479
Kirkwood, Mary	May, 1957	Z 536
Kinnear, Margaret M.	Nov., 1958	1 455
Keller, Mary H.	July, 1960	2 476

Koontz, Nicholas		A 137
Knowles, Naomi J.	Aug., 1921	M 359
Koontz, Nancy	April, 1932	P 565
Karacatsanes, Nicholas	Aug., 1938	S 139

Kraff, Nettie	Jan., 1948	W 12
Kiddy, Nina M.	July, 1954	Y 310
Kelly, Nellie B.	Dec., 1960	3 49

Kinham, Peter		C 95
Kirk, Patrick	June, 1894	G 49
Kelley, Patrick	Jan., 1903	H 316
Knieriem, Peter	Dec., 1924	N 350
King, Patrick	May, 1930	P 158
Kohl, Philip G.	June, 1933	Q 231
Kinney, Patrick J.	Feb., 1934	Q 382
Kean, Patrick E.	March, 1955	Y 487
Klavuhn, Peter M.	Jan., 1960	2 273

Kennedy, Robert		A 531
Keller, Reuhanna	Jan., 1898	G 278
Kiddy, Robert	Sept., 1908	I 453
Kay, Robert	Oct., 1915	K 419
Keller, Ruth E.	Feb., 1925	N 383
Kline, Rachel	Nov., 1932	Q 104
Keller, Robert M.	Nov., 1934	Q 541
Karns, Reuben	Oct., 1936	R 326
Kiefer, Rose	Jan., 1937	R 375
Koontz, Rachel	March, 1937	R 442
Kean, Raymond L.	March, 1939	S 289
Kaplon, Rebecca	March, 1943	U 30
Kerr, Robert M.	Sept., 1943	U 155
King, Robert	Aug., 1945	V 28
Kellough, Robert Elmer	Jan., 1946	V 373
Kiddy, Russell	Sept., 1947	V 545

Koontz, Sarah	Feb., 1884	E 14
Keech, Susan	July, 1895	G 126
Keller, Susan	March, 1903	H 329
Kirby, Sarah J.	Feb., 1919	L 472
Klosterman, Sarah A.E.	Feb., 1920	M 123
Keyser, Sarah F.	July, 1922	M 499
Kraft, Sarah A.	Aug., 1922	M 508

Kline, Samuel E.	July, 1928	O 367
Kelso, Scott	Jan., 1936	R 176
Kauffman, Samuel F.	Dec., 1936	R 356
Knotts, Stephen Ellsworth	Oct., 1939	S 418
King, Stephen	Nov., 1941	T 277
Kennell, Samuel	Jan., 1943	T 591
Koegel, Sophia	March, 1943	U 28
Kelso, Sarah M.	Jan., 1947	V 378
Kaplon, Samuel W.	Aug., 1953	Y 96
Kirby, Sarah Day	July, 1954	Y 307
Knippenberg, Stephen A.	July, 1955	Z 35
Kerns, Sadie	March, 1960	2 349
Kreitzburg, Sarah A.	Nov., 1960	3 14

Kiddy, Thomas	Oct., 1908	I 462
Kean, Thomas S.	July, 1915	K 383
Klosterman, Thomas A.	Feb., 1927	O 139
Kuhlman, Theresa	Aug., 1932	Q 57
Korns, Thomas J.	Feb., 1939	S 271
Kean, Thomas B.	Feb., 1941	T 81
Kelley, Thomas J.	March, 1941	T 107
Kuehn, Theresa	June, 1941	T 169
Kennell, Theodore	Sept., 1941	T 241
Koon, Thomas W.	Dec., 1946	V 366
Kooken, Thomas Z.	Jan., 1949	W 253

Knight, Valeria	Feb., 1937	R 403
Knippenberg, Verna	Nov., 1949	W 441
Koch, Verda O.	Nov., 1951	X 259

Kennedy, William	April, 1869	C 135
Koenig, William	April, 1872	D 16
Keefer, Winietine	1881	D 492
Kight, William	Sept., 1885	E 141
Koegal, Wilhelmina M.	July, 1893	H 367
Kent, William	Oct., 1904	I 55
Keech, Walter Daniel	Nov., 1911	J 343
Knieriem, William	June, 1912	J 429

Kight, William of E.	Nov., 1914	K 242
Kornhoff, William H.	Oct., 1918	L 423
Kiefer, Wendelin	April, 1921	M 304
Koppen, William P.	June, 1928	O 357
Keeling, William	March, 1930	P 125
Kalbaugh, William L.	June, 1931	P 386
Korns, William C.	Nov., 1936	R 342
Keller, Walter F.	June, 1941	T 174
Kirby, William C.	Feb., 1945	U 450
Koch, William H.	June, 1945	U 577
Kight, William	Feb., 1952	X 338
Kirtley, William A.	Oct., 1953	Y 147
Kolberg, William	Feb., 1956	Z 169
Kraft, Zacharias	Aug., 1922	M 524

L

Luke, Bernhard	Jan., 1876	D 254
Long, Barbara E.	Oct., 1916	L 69
Laley, Bathsheba	April, 1930	P 132
Laffey, Bridget	March, 1937	R 436
Levin, Benjamin	Aug., 1960	2 516

Leasure, Catherine E.		C 114
Leasure, Cassa	Nov., 1868	C 127
Lutheran Evan. Church	Aug., 1869	C 155
Little, Charles	July, 1872	D 28
Lottig, Conrad	Nov., 1884	E 81
Lottig, Conrad	Dec., 1884	E 88
Lippold, Catherine	Nov., 1889	F 44
Laing, Catherine E.		F 255
Lindner, Christina	Feb., 1903	H 323
Lynch, Cornelius	Jan., 1904	H 391
Leech, Charles	Aug., 1906	I 217
Leatham, Charles H.	April, 1909	J 38
Little, Charles H.	June, 1909	J 56
Lapp, Conrad, Sr.	April, 1913	K 18
Laing, Catharine A.	Sept., 1913	K 66
Leasure, Caroline	Oct., 1913	K 91
Linn, Caroline	Sept., 1913	L 236
Langer, Christina M.	Nov., 1919	M 95
Lowndes, Charles T.	Jan., 1923	M 584
Little, Catherine	Aug., 1923	N 114
Lennan, Clara	Nov., 1926	O 81
Livingstone, Charles	July, 1927	O 211
Loar, C. Wesley	July, 1929	O 574
Leibel, Charles	Nov., 1932	Q 116
Lester, Charles E.	May, 1933	Q 210
Lavin, Catherine	March, 1937	R 443
Lapp, Conrad	April, 1937	R 462
Lam, Charles H.	April, 1938	S 91
Lapp, Conrad A.	Dec., 1940	T 49
Longerbeam, Charles	April, 1941	T 122
Laughney, Catherine	Nov., 1941	T 273
Lowery, Charles Nicholas	Oct., 1944	U 390
Lantz, Charles Henry	Dec., 1944	U 416
Lynch, Charles F.	Jan., 1946	V 105
Langer, Charles A.	Oct., 1946	V 314
Lindeman, Cynthia	Nov., 1947	V 579

Lashley, Conda G.	Nov., 1947	V 586
Laffey, Cecelia E.	Nov., 1949	W 430
Lee, Clayton C.	March, 1951	X 140
Laughlin, Catherine McG.	Sept., 1951	X 235
Lippold, Caroline B.	Jan., 1955	Y 438
Leary, Clarence G.	Nov., 1956	Z 390
Lippold, Charles W.	Aug., 1957	1 59
Loy, Claggett Levi	Dec., 1959	2 222

Lynn, David		A 372
Lynn, David, Jr.		B 169
Luther, D. W.	Feb., 1876	D 260
Lear, Dietrich	April, 1880	D 440
Link, Dominick	Nov., 1898	G 316
Long, Daniel R.	Nov., 1901	H 227
Linaburg, Danforth	Oct., 1908	I 459
Lear, Dietrich H.	April, 1909	J 39
Lambert, David	Feb., 1912	J 395
Levy, David L.	Jan., 1914	K 126
Linn, David M.	June, 1917	L 200
Long, Dayton J.	Dec., 1917	L 274
Lechliter, Daniel T.	March, 1924	N 224
Lewis, David H.	Jan., 1926	N 525
Linn, David Edward	Feb., 1943	U 2
Lewis, Daniel W.	March, 1952	X 353
Lewis, David J.	Aug., 1952	X 465

Lloyd, Edward	Aug., 1861	
Lingo, Eunice		A 383
Loar, Elijah	Oct., 1873	D 222
Lavin, Elizabeth	May, 1879	D 407
Loeber, Elizabeth	Oct., 1890	F 133
Loar, Enoch	March, 1892	F 274
Lottig, Eliza Jane	March, 1902	H 260
Lambie, Elizabeth	Jan., 1917	L 101
Lehman, Espy A.	Dec., 1920	M 242
Lowndes, Elizabeth T.	Jan., 1922	M 396
Layman, Elizabeth	June, 1924	N 279
Loeber, Emma Josephine	April, 1927	O 165
Linn, Elizabeth M.	May, 1927	O 176

Lewis, Edward	Sept., 1927	O 251
Lippold, Edward J.	Jan., 1929	O 444
Lutz, Emma F.	July, 1933	Q 248
Lewis, Edmund	Nov., 1933	Q 303
Laney, Ellen Belle	Feb., 1939	S 256
Logsdon, Elizabeth	May, 1941	T 144
Lester, Elizabeth	June, 1944	U 309
Luhrman, Emma G.	Jan., 1946	V 100
Longridge, Elizabeth	March, 1947	V 417
Ludwig, Emma B.	Feb., 1948	W 37
Liles, Ethel B. Gunning	July, 1948	W 163
Lichtenstein, Elsa L.	Aug., 1953	Y 103
Little, Eugenia S.	April, 1955	Y 521
Lepley, Earl T.	March, 1957	Z 479
Layman, Eugene	Sept., 1958	1 400
Leiws, Elizabeth S.	Jan., 1959	1 512
Lester, Elizabeth B.	July, 1960	2 509

Laing, Francis X.		F 255
Luttrell, Frederick B.	July, 1895	G 122
Laing, Francis	July, 1896	G 184
Leasure, Frazy	April, 1899	G 350
Litfin, Frank M.	Dec., 1899	H 14
Laing, Francis, Sr.	Jan., 1902	H 240
Laing, Frederick	May, 1904	I 16
Lambert, Fannie	Dec., 1907	I 338
Linderman, Fredericka	Aug., 1916	L 41
Leidinger, Frank W.	Dec., 1925	N 509
Lashley, Frances C.	June, 1931	P 396
Leonard, Florence A.	Aug., 1931	P 441
Lilya, Frank H.	Feb., 1934	Q 363
Lininger, Floyd Russell	April, 1938	S 89
Lueck, Frank J.	May, 1949	W 321
Lloyd, Fanny B.	Feb., 1951	X 114
Laird, Fannie Ellen	Jan., 1952	X 300
Lewis, Frances E.	May, 1953	Y 43
Lookenott, Frederick Frank	July, 1953	Y 69
Lehman, Flora K.	May, 1954	Y 260
Lookenott, Frances M.	Aug., 1956	Z 316
Lichtenstein, Francina Freese	Feb., 1958	1 179
Langen, Florence E.	May, 1958	1 306
Lindner, Frank L.	July, 1958	1 350

Luhrman, Frederick A.	Nov., 1959	2 203
Leasure, Frank R.	Feb., 1960	2 307
Lloyd, Fannie	Aug., 1960	2 521

Lynn, George		B 128
Lottig, George	June, 1876	D 285
Leibrandt, George	Sept., 1876	D 297
Loar, George	March, 1885	E 104
Lyons, George W.	Aug., 1891	F 216
Lashley, George	Jan., 1892	F 256
Lammert, George A.	Sept., 1897	G 253
Long, George T.	April, 1900	H 85
Lemmert, George	April, 1910	J 146
Leibrant, George	Hov., 1913	K 107
Little, George W.E.	March, 1915	K 316
Linn, George	Nov., 1915	L 307
Langham, George C.	May, 1918	L 361
Laing, George M.	June, 1918	L 388
Langham, George	July, 1918	L 392
Ludwig, George W.	Sept., 1920	M 209
Landwehr, George D.	April, 1924	N 236
Lewis, George W.	April, 1924	N 246
Longerbeam, George H.	Feb., 1929	O 479
Lotz, George Sr.	Feb., 1933	Q 155
Lindner, George	Feb., 1933	Q 160
Litzenburg, Georcia A.	March, 1933	Q 167
Lancaster, George W.	Oct., 1937	R 588
Lewis, George	Aug., 1939	S 369
Long, George L.	Dec., 1940	T 54
Lucas, George	Sept., 1941	T 234
Light, George W.	April, 1943	U 61
Lippold, George E.	Sept., 1946	V 290
Luteman, Garrett J.	March, 1947	V 415
Lindner, George R.	Feb., 1953	X 581
Lambert, Gertrude Mae A.	Sept., 1953	Y 125
Leyh, George Joseph	Jan., 1956	Z 150
Lanam, Gracie Anna	Aug., 1958	1 364

Ladew, Harvey S.		F 5
Little, Hiram H.	April, 1896	G 172

Lee, Harrison G.	Nov., 1903	H 379
Laney, Hervey	Aug., 1904	I 39
Lear, Henrietta	Sept., 1908	I 455
Lowery, Harrison D.	March, 1910	J 140
Livingstone, Hugh F.	May, 1912	J 426
Lloyd, Henry	Feb., 1915	K 286
Lovkus, Helen	Sept., 1928	O 400
Landis, H. Raleigh	June, 1930	P 172
Lippel, Henry	Aug., 1930	P 200
Lashley, Henry W.	March, 1931	P 320
Lancaster, Henry E.	Sept., 1931	P 448
Love, Hugh	Sept., 1933	Q 277
Litzenburg, Hiram L.	Oct., 1936	R 328
Livengood, Henry J.	June, 1938	S 107
Laing, Henry	Oct., 1941	T 247
Lippel, Hattie	March, 1942	T 350
Lapp, Henry A.	April, 1943	U 66
Laughlin, Hice R.	Sept., 1943	U 160
Lepley, Howard Phillip	Oct., 1945	V 60
Little, Harry	Feb., 1955	Y 457
Langham, Herbert W.	May, 1956	Z 255
Lemon, Hazel A.	April, 1959	1 585
Lowery, Hazel	April, 1959	2 10
Laffey, Harry Martin	Aug., 1960	2 525
Liller, Hattie B.	Nov., 1960	3 41
Limbert, Harold	Dec., 1960	3 56

Long, Isaac	Oct., 1905	I 142
Lichtenstein, Isaac R.	Oct., 1920	M 220
Leasure, Isaac	July, 1921	M 343
Love, Isaac	April, 1925	N 400
Little, Ira K.	Nov., 1940	T 39

Logsdon, John		A 164
Loar, Jacob		A 264
Lancaster, John		A 421
Lancaster, Johanna	April, 1938	A 423
Layman, John		A 572
Little, Joseph		C 48
Loar, John	Oct., 1873	D 222

Loar, John E.	March, 1942	T 347
Little, Janet M.	Jan., 1943	T 581
Lydinger, John N.	Aug., 1943	U 142
Loar, John H.	Feb., 1944	U 242
Loar, James B.	June, 1944	U 325
Langan, John A.	April, 1945	U 526
Leasure, John Frederick	May, 1946	V 207
Linaburg, Julius A.	Aug., 1946	V 270
Lester, John George	Sept., 1947	V 547
Lewis, John G.	Oct., 1947	V 567
Lewis, John C.	May, 1948	W 98
Long, Jacob	July, 1949	W 352
Luman, Jessie G.	Sept., 1954	Y 363
Logsdon, James S.	March, 1955	Y 472
LaRue, Joseph Warren	June, 1955	Z 7
Lilly, James	Aug., 1955	Z 39
Llewellyn, Jennie E.	July, 1957	Z 595
Lewis, Jacob M.	Sept., 1957	1 67
Luteman, James H.	June, 1959	2 77
Laffey, James P.	Nov., 1959	2 196
Leader, James A.	June, 1960	2 148

Laing, Kate	Jan., 1919	L 450
Leo, Katie G.	Feb., 1937	R 414
Lark, Kate E.	Dec., 1942	T 556

Lippold, Lewis	Feb., 1873	D 92
Leeds, Louisa C.	June, 1874	D 159
same	June, 1874	D 159
same	June, 1874	D 159
same	June, 1874	D 159
Lowe, Lloyd	July, 1875	D 234
Logsdon, Leonidas	Aug., 1889	E 340
Lowndes, Lloyd	June, 1905	I 72
Leiberman, Lavinia E.	Oct., 1908	I 465
Laney, Laura	Jan., 1909	I 491
Laing, Lydia	March, 1916	K 497
Lee, Lucinda	Aug., 1922	M 503
Levick, Laura V.	Feb., 1923	M 599

Laffey, Michael Francis	Jan., 1928	O 304
Love, Margaret	Nov., 1928	O 424
Logsdon, Meshack B.	Dec., 1928	O 436
Lavin, Mary	Dec., 1930	P 267
Leo, Mary Elizabeth	March, 1931	P 332
Landis, Margaret L.	Feb., 1932	P 530
Laney, Marietta	Feb., 1934	Q 365
Longo, Mike	April, 1934	Q 408
Lancaster, Margaret	March, 1935	R 7
Loar, Mandana L.	Jan., 1936	R 167
Lynn, Margaret Ann	May, 1936	R 247
Loy, Mollie E.	Jan., 1937	R 378
Livingood, Mima E.	April, 1938	S 85
Lippold, Mathilde	May, 1938	S 99
Leasure, Margaret	Jan., 1940	S 459
Long, Missouri	July, 1940	S 599
Lapp, Margaret C.	April, 1944	U 290
Loar, Mary Elizabeth	April, 1945	U 527
Layman, Mary M.	March, 1946	V 158
Lange, Mary Bertha Butler	April, 1946	V 167
Lookenott, Margaret M.S.	July, 1947	V 510
Love, Mary	Sept., 1947	V 550
Long, Myrtle A.	May, 1949	W 316
Lowery, Maggie	May, 1949	W 330
Lashbaugh, Marion Brown	Sept., 1949	W 392
Lewis, Matilda May	Oct., 1950	X 34
Leo, Mary Elizabeth	Sept., 1951	X 237
Laird, Mary B.	April, 1952	X 360
Logsdon, Margaret E.	May, 1953	Y 33
Laughlin, Mary E.	Feb., 1954	Y 221
Lucas, Margaret Walker	April, 1955	Y 522
Lippold, Mary T.	Nov., 1955	Z 104
Lyden, Margaret	March, 1957	Z 464
Lipson, Morris J.	Nov., 1957	1 109
Luteman, Mary D.	June, 1958	1 309
Long, Mollie C.	Sept., 1958	1 390
Lamb, Maria	Sept., 1958	1 403
Lindell, Mary E.	Nov., 1959	2 205
Lambert, Matilda C.	July, 1960	2 479

Leidinger, Nicholas	Dec., 1870	C 184
Lynn, Nannie M.		D 44
Loar, Nathan	Oct., 1873	D 222
Lorisch, Nicholas	June, 1901	H 195
Lawrence, Noah F.	June, 1913	K 35
Lark, Nancy M.	Aug., 1921	M 354
Leidinger, Nicholas	Feb., 1934	Q 372
Lichliter, Norah L.	Dec., 1939	S 441
Leddy, Owen	March, 1879	D 399
Lewis, Owen	June, 1932	Q 25
Leydig, Oscar C.	April, 1960	2 364
Lillis, Patrick	June, 1877	D 329
Logsdon, Peter	March, 1918	L 326
Loughney, Patrick	June, 1922	M 475
Lippold, Peter L.	Aug., 1931	P 415
Lorshbaugh, Philip B.	May, 1941	T 140
Lear, Paul D.	Sept., 1942	T 462
Lacey, Patrick T.	April, 1946	V 199
Lowery, Perry	Jan., 1952	X 304
Loncarevich, Peter	April, 1959	1 596
Logsdon, Raphael		A 166
Lamar, Richard		A 490
Lowndes, Richard T., Jr.	March, 1910	J 130
Leighty, Rebecca J.	March, 1914	K 148
Lancaster, Robert A.	June, 1915	K 354
Lang, Rachel	Oct., 1918	L 417
Lee, Richard	Jan., 1922	M 392
Ladew, Rebecca	Aug., 1928	O 377
Little, Robert W.	April, 1933	Q 200
Levick, Richard C.	May, 1933	Q 222
Little, Rose	March, 1936	R 214
Light, Rebecca Catherine	Feb., 1940	S 496
Lippold, Regina C.	Aug., 1941	T 213
Lewis, Richard Franklin	Jan., 1942	T 317
Loy, Rhoda Luella	Aug., 1943	U 136

Lancaster, R.Hilary	June, 1944	U 317
Lynn, Ruth Gibbons	April, 1945	U 519
Logsdon, Richard P.	Jan., 1946	V 121
Lippold, Ralph P.	Feb., 1952	X 339
Lace, Robert J.	Jan., 1959	1 527
Layman, Richard Olin	June, 1959	2 38
Livengood, Ruth	Nov., 1960	3 19

Lamar, Sarah		A 448
Little, Samuel T.	June, 1882	D 543
Lear, Sophia H.	May, 1893	F 365
Llwellyn, Stephen	April, 1917	L 160
Logsdon, Sarah	Feb., 1919	M 2
Lee, Stephen S.	Aug., 1922	M 513
Little, Sarah D.	Oct., 1922	M 541
Lichtenstein, Sarah	Nov., 1925	N 486
Langham, Susanna	March, 1931	P 339
Lepley, Simon A.	April, 1937	R 455
Lindsay, Sarah	Oct., 1942	T 518
Logsdon, Stanley	Aug., 1945	V 21
Leasure, Sarah	June, 1947	V 493
Lacey, Susan J.	Aug., 1955	X 49
Lewis, Sarah M.	Jan., 1948	W 22
Lammbert, Sophia M.	May, 1957	Z 534

Lavin, Thomas	June, 1877	D 327
Lewis, Theophilus	April, 1908	I 383
Longford, Thomas C.	June, 1918	L 390
Llewellyn, Thomas P.	April, 1924	N 252
Leonard, Thomas A.	Dec., 1928	O 437
Lashley, Thomas B.	Sept., 1933	Q 281
Long, T.Walter	Sept., 1937	R 566
Lewis, Theophilus	Oct., 1938	S 160
LeClear, Thomas	Aug., 1939	S 364
Lowndes, Tasker G.	July, 1952	X 440
Lloyd, Thomas W.	May, 1949	W 306
Logsdon, Thomas	Oct., 1950	X 37
Lee, Thomas F.	Jan., 1956	Z 135
Lewis, Thomas	July, 1950	W 594
Logsdon, Thomas I.	Sept., 1959	2 160
Lloyd, Thomas William	July, 1960	2 475

Long, Upton D.	March, 1869	C 156
same	Nov., 1871	C 209
same	March, 1883	D 588

Lynn, Virginia	Sept., 1872	D 45
Largent, Virginia	May, 1939	S 322
Loar, Violet Courbrough	July, 1956	Z 275
La Velle, Verna	June, 1959	2 52

Lamar, William	Dec., 1802	A 143
Lannen, William		B 135
Lippold, William	May, 1888	E 325
Logsdon, William, Sr.	Feb., 1892	F 269
Lange, William	Dec., 1892	F 334
Leasure, William	March, 1913	K 7
Lashley, William P.	Nov., 1916	L 75
Love, Wilmer W.	Jan., 1918	L 295
Love, William	May, 1918	L 370
Logsdon, William R.	Nov., 1918	L 425
Lewis, William	May, 1919	M 41
Lashley, William	April, 1920	M 156
Leasure, William H.	July, 1921	M 347
Lowery, William	May, 1923	N 57
Ledbetter, William P.	April, 1928	O 326
Lynn, Wilbert H.	April, 1928	O 337
Lambie, William	April, 1929	O 510
Lowery, William	May, 1930	P 157
Layman, William Sheridan	June, 1932	Q 18
Long, William M.	Feb., 1933	Q 174
Lakin, William T.	July, 1934	Q 462
Leasure, William Proctor	Dec., 1939	S 446
Lemmert, William H.	Jan., 1940	S 451
Lowndes, W. Bladen	Oct., 1949	W 410
Lindner, William Louis	Feb., 1955	Y 459
Lange, William Francis	Jan., 1958	1 169

M

McCleary, Andrew		A 205
Majors, Ambrose		A 424
MacDonald, Arch. & Helen	Nov., 1873	D 131
Miller, Albert L.	Jan., 1883	D 584
McFerran, Alexander	June, 1884	E 68
McFarland, Agnes	Oct., 1887	E 268
McKaig, Ada Norman	Jan., 1890	F 60
McGann, Ann	Sept., 1890	F 118
McFerran, Ann	Jan., 1891	F 157
McKee, Ada B.		F 262
McDonald, Archibald	March, 1892	F 284
Morris, Ann R.	Oct., 1892	F 324
Messersmith, Alex	June, 1893	F 382
McVa, Ann	Jan., 1905	G 91
McFerran, Alex	Oct., 1895	G 139
Main, Andrew	June, 1898	G 297
McGill, Agnes	Oct., 1903	H 375
Miller, Anna	Oct., 1905	I 141
McElfish, Amos	June, 1908	I 417
Michael, Andrew S.	Jan., 1916	K 449
McKnight, Annie V.	Dec., 1916	L 97
McFerran, Alexander	Sept., 1919	M 82
Morris, Anna M.	Sept., 1921	M 368
Martin, Alvy H.	June, 1922	M 485
McFarland, Alexander T.	June, 1924	N 270
McFarlane, Annie	April, 1926	N 598
Minke, Anthony A.	Nov., 1927	O 272
Martin, Addison	Nov., 1927	O 283
McDonald, Allan	Sept., 1928	O 397
Mackert, August	Oct., 1928	O 405
McCutcheon, Annie	May, 1929	O 547
Mills, Annie E.	March, 1930	P 116
McIntyre, Annie	Dec., 1930	P 265
Moran, Amanda A.	Jan., 1931	P 286
Miller, Annie E.	Nov., 1931	P 483
McLuckie, A. T.	Nov., 1932	Q 109
Milkowski, Andrew	Jan., 1933	Q 143
McMannis, Andrew	Dec., 1933	Q 321
McMichael, Alice	Nov., 1938	S 199

Murray, Bridget P.	July, 1921	M 344
Middleton, Benjamin F.	June, 1924	N 273
Mooney, Bridget	Nov., 1930	P 250
Martz, Bernard J.	July, 1941	T 181
McCuaig, Barbara Ellen	Aug., 1942	T 441
Matthews, Barbara Anna	April, 1943	U 68
Mattingly, Bernard A.	Jan., 1945	U 436
Mason, Bert A., Sr.	Aug., 1945	V 30
Murphy, Bertha Matilda	Aug., 1952	X 472
McElfish, Bertha M.	July, 1953	Y 66
Miller, Boyd H.	Feb., 1957	Z 452
Mullan, Bernard V.	April, 1958	1 236
McKinley, Bella Marie	Nov., 1958	1 459
Mudd, Barbara H.	Dec., 1959	2 235

Miller, Christopher		A 589
Miller, Charles		C 76
Miller, Catherine	June, 1870	C 173
Miller, Christopher	Feb., 1871	C 187
Mattingly, Cecilia	Sept., 1874	D 187
Manning, Charles P.		D 509
Miller, Conrad, Sr.	June, 1885	E 122
Mullen, Catherine T.	Sept., 1906	I 226
Meister, Catharine	July, 1907	I 303
Miller, Charles C.	April, 1908	I 390
McVeigh, Catharine	May, 1908	I 408
Martin, Catherine	June, 1916	L 24
Matt, Caroline	April, 1917	L 163
McEvoy, Catherine	Dec., 1917	L 280
Myers, Charles H.	Feb., 1918	L 308
Moody, Charles C.	Sept., 1918	L 405
Murphy, Cornelius S.	Nov., 1918	L 430
Meisenzohl, Charles	Aug., 1919	M 67
McEvoy, Charles H.	July, 1920	M 186
Michael, Charles O.	May, 1925	N 427
McDermitt, Catherine	June, 1928	O 355
McCulloch, Champe Carter	May, 1929	O 545
Martin, Conrad	Feb., 1930	P 92
Mactavish, Charles Carroll	Aug., 1931	P 417
Miller, Conrad A.L.	Jan., 1933	Q 152
Miller, Charles	May, 1935	R 32
Metz, Clara J.	March, 1938	S 60

Mulledy, Dennis	Sept., 1897	G 250
Mann, David	Nov., 1909	J 90
Murrie, David	Feb., 1910	J 120
McMullen, Daniel F. et al	April, 1914	K 159
Miller, Donald	June, 1914	K 189
McMullen, Daniel F.	Jan., 1918	L 288
Maloney, Daniel	Jan., 1926	N 527
Murphy, Dennis Ambrose	Aug., 1934	Q 475
McCarty, David S.	July, 1935	R 58
Martin, Daniel	March, 1936	R 202
Mock, Daniel	July, 1936	R 272
Miller, D. Ella	July, 1936	R 274
Miller, David P.	April, 1937	R 472
Martin, Dixon	June, 1944	U 314
McGraw, Donald Thomas	Aug., 1945	V 15
Moore, D.C. (Mrs.)	Aug., 1955	Z 51
McAlpine, David	Jan. 1956	Z 145
Miller, David	April, 1956	Z 215
Mankamyer, Dennis	Aug., 1957	1 25

Musselman, Elizabeth	Feb., 1843	A 520
McCarty, Edward		B 9
Miller, Elizabeth N.		B 156
Mattingly, Ellen		B 122
Mullen, Edward	Sept., 1854	B 84
Mullen, Edward	Jan., 1866	C 89
McMillan, Elizabeth	Oct., 1870	C 182
Mullen, Edward	Aug., 1874	D 168
McKinzie, Elizabeth (Will)	Sept., 1877	D 341
same	March, 1878	D 357
McKinzie, Enoch	Jan., 1884	G 14
McIntire, Elias	Sept., 1895	G 132
Mulvaney, Edward	June, 1899	G 362
Mansfield, Eliza J.	March, 1902	H 260
Miller, Elizabeth	Aug., 1904	I 41
McKenna, Edward	Feb., 1905	I 82
Main, Elizabeth	Oct., 1905	I 151
McKenna, Ellen	Feb., 1908	I 367
McMillan, Elizabeth R.	March, 1909	J 19
McFerran, Emily H.	Nov., 1910	J 206
Mulvany, Elizabeth	May, 1913	K 23

Moore, Ezekiel T.	July, 1913	K 41
McDonald, Ellen	July, 1913	K 48
Macbeth, Estella R.	May, 1915	K 343
Murphy, Ellen	June, 1915	K 359
McAllister, Elizabeth B.	Aug., 1916	L 35
Miller, Ellen	April, 1920	M 157
McCutcheon, Emma James	March, 1926	N 551
Mudge, Elizabeth Mintdrop	Nov., 1929	P 47
McBride, Elizabeth	Nov., 1931	P 479
Mullin, Elizabeth	May, 1933	Q 217
Martin, Elizabeth A.	Oct., 1933	Q 287
Mason, Emily B.	Oct., 1933	Q 292
Magolis, Emma S.	Nov., 1936	R 351
Mahaney, Emily J.	Feb., 1937	R 391
Mauk, Espy J.	Nov., 1938	S 183
MacDonald, Eleanor Humbird	Nov., 1938	S 189
Michael, Eliza E.	Oct., 1939	S 415
McAdams, Elmira F.	Dec., 1939	S 442
Mayer, Elizabeth	July, 1940	S 595
Marsh, Elizabeth M.	Aug., 1940	T 2
Muir, Elizabeth	Nov., 1940	T 42
Murphy, Elizabeth	Feb., 1941	T 82
Morton, Elizabeth	Nov., 1941	T 264
McKenzie, Elizabeth R.	Jan., 1942	T 314
Metger, Earl G.	Oct., 1942	T 515
Murphy, Edward J.	Nov., 1942	T 521
Martin, Ella C.	Nov., 1943	U 196
Menefee, Elizabeth R.	June, 1945	U 569
McDonald, Emma A.	June, 1946	V 248
Meders, Eva B.	April, 1947	V 433
McKenzie, Edward J.	Aug., 1948	W 185
McElfish, Elza	Jan., 1949	W 257
Mangold, Edna Pearl	April, 1949	W 295
Mongold, Elsie	June, 1950	W 572
Moffatt, Ethelwyn F.	Nov., 1951	X 261
Mortzfeldt, Elizabeth	Aug., 1954	Y 323
Minke, Elizabeth	March, 1955	Y 488
Moore, Estella May	Aug., 1955	Z 51
Metz, Elizabeth Preston	Aug., 1956	Z 304
Morris, Earl H.	Aug., 1956	Z 320
Mattingly, Ellen C.	Sept., 1956	Z 343
McGowan, Ella C.	Nov., 1956	Z 389
Mathews, Eda C.	Aug., 1957	1 34
Mullan, Eugene	Feb., 1958	1 174

Mattingly, Francis	Nov., 1859	B 172
McAnally, Felix		B 185
Montgomery, Francis R.		D 516
Mertens, Frederick	Feb., 1886	E 164
Messman, Francis H.	Nov., 1895	G 151
Morris, Frank	Dec., 1912	J 472
Mitchell, Frederick C.	Dec., 1914	K 264
McKaig, Florence	May, 1915	K 340
McMahon, Frank J.	Dec., 1916	L 95
McDermitt, Francis B.	April, 1919	M 32
Moore, Francis	March, 1920	M 135
Maurey, Frank W.	Nov., 1925	N 478
Maurey, Frank W.	Dec., 1925	N 496
McNamee, Francis	Jan., 1926	N 519
McCreary, Francis M.	Sept., 1928	O 390
Molinari, Francesca Barbiera	March, 1930	P 114
Marks, Frances D.	Dec., 1931	P 501
Molinari, Frank	March, 1936	R 207
Maybury, Frances	Aug., 1937	R 544
Michael, Fernando C.	Dec., 1937	S 20
Miller, Frank L.	Aug., 1939	S 360
Mullan, Frank A.	Nov., 1941	T 276
McGettigan, Francis V.	Oct., 1946	V 296
Maffley, Frederick C.	Nov., 1952	X 515
Miller, Freddie A.	Feb., 1956	Z 163
Moore, Francis H.	April, 1957	Z 504
McMillen, Francis Burke	July, 1958	1 343
Martin, Frank A.	July, 1959	2 104
Molinari, Frank, Jr.	Oct., 1959	2 177
Moreland, Ferman Herman	Nov., 1959	2 208

McKenzie, George	Aug., 1872	D 38
McKinzie, Geo. H. et al	Aug., 1872	D 38
Myers, George	March, 1883	D 591
Martin, Gearhart	April, 1886	E 185
Magruder, G. P.	July, 1886	E 198
Miller, George M.	Nov., 1890	F 145
Miller, Geo. Herman L.	Sept., 1896	G 187
McFarland, George W.	Nov., 1917	L 262
Mudge, Gotlieben M.	March, 1925	N 396
Miers, George W.	April, 1925	N 410
Mitchell, George Hamilton	March, 1927	O 156

May, Henry	May, 1933	Q 215
McElfish, Henry C.	Nov., 1933	Q 307
McMullen, Hugh A.	Feb., 1938	S 50
McKee, Henry, Sr.	Dec., 1938	S 217
Miller, Herman	Jan., 1939	S 240
Martin, Harry C.	Aug., 1939	S 362
Matheney, Harry W.	Jan., 1940	S 455
Manley, Harry A.	April, 1943	U 56
Merkel, Hermine	Jan., 1946	V 114
McCulloh, Harry	May, 1947	V 466
Matthews, Henry Washington	Aug., 1947	V 528
Mattingly, Henry T.	Sept., 1949	W 390
McKenzie, Hannah Elizabeth	Jan., 1950	W 473
McLarkie, Henry	May, 1950	W 553
Michael, Henrietta	May, 1953	Y 31
Maravelis, Harry M.	Dec., 1956	Z 397
Murphy, Howard L.	Dec., 1958	1 469
McKee, Henry, Jr.	March, 1959	1 568
McAteer, Henry E.	Aug., 1959	2 138
Mantheiy, Helen Mary	Dec., 1959	2 241
McLuckie, Harry A.	July, 1960	2 470
Miller, Horace G.	Aug., 1960	2 511

Miller, Isaac		A 533
Martin, Ida B.	Aug., 1904	I 38
Moore, Isabella J.	May, 1905	I 110
Martin, Isaac	Feb., 1920	M 119
Miller, Isabella H.	July, 1920	M 184
Miller, Isaac H.	June, 1923	N 72
Myers, Isabella E.	Jan., 1931	P 280
Matlick, Ira L.	Oct., 1932	Q 80
McKee, Ida B.	Dec., 1941	T 299
McCauley, Ida V.	May, 1945	U 540
McElfish, Irvin G.	Sept., 1945	V 49
McKenzie, Ira V.	Oct., 1946	V 295
Michael, Isaac G.	Aug., 1955	Z 51
McDonald, Isaac W.	May, 1958	1 296
Moses, Isabella W.	April, 1959	2 14

Magruder, Jacob N.	Aug., 1862	C 10
Magill, James T.		C 23
Magill, John B.	May, 1857	C 23
McHenry, James J.	June, 1864	C 37
Magruder, Jonathan W.		C 38
Morrison, John J.		C 62
Monroe, Jesse		C 70
Matthews, John		C 103
Miller, Jacob		A 617
Maguire, J. Mason	Oct., 1847	A 652
Meniken, Joseph		B 681
Miller, Joseph	July, 1868	C 145
McCulloh, John L. & Maria	June, 1871	C 206
McElfish, John W.	Aug., 1871	C 205
Myers, Jacob	Dec., 1872	D 69
McKimmy, James	Dec., 1872	D 72
Matthews, James M.	Nov. 1873	D 123
McMahon, John V.L.	July, 1875	D 222
McHugh, James	Aug., 1875	D 238
Miller, John	Aug., 1876	D 290
Magruder, Jonathan W.	March, 1878	D 352
McNamee, John	July, 1878	D 365
McKone, John	July, 1879	D 410
Manning, Jeanette & C.P.		D 517
McCusker, John, Sr.	Oct., 1882	D 562
Maddux, J.B.	Jan., 1883	D 576
McDonald, James	June, 1883	D 616
Mattingly, James	Feb., 1884	E 25
McKenzie, Joseph	April, 1887	E 228
Meyer, John B.	July, 1887	E 246
Mayer, John	May, 1888	E 313
McGonigle, John	Jan., 1889	E 363
McIntire, Jane	June, 1890	F 108
McCaughan, John	Aug., 1890	F 116
Millesson, J.M.		F 284
Matthews, John	May, 1892	F 288
Morrisson, James	Oct., 1892	F 319
McFarland, John A.	April, 1895	G 110
Myers, John of Jacob	July, 1895	G 124
Matthews, John	Nov., 1895	G 143
Mellott, Jeremiah H.	Dec., 1895	G 153
Miller, James B.	Feb., 1899	G 334
McElfish, Joseph	April, 1899	G 348
McCormick, Joseph	Aug., 1901	H 208

Morton, John	Feb., 1902	H 255
Mellinger, John G.	Sept., 1903	H 373
McAleer, James	April, 1906	I 195
Mattingly, John M.	Nov., 1906	I 238
McKenzie, Jeremiah)		I 286
McKenzie, Jeremiah J.)	June, 1907	I 286
Mahaney, J.H.B.	July, 1908	I 430
Malone, John	Feb., 1909	J 2
Madaskie, Joseph	June, 1909	J 55
Meek, John	Oct., 1909	J 78
Myers, Jane M.	Dec., 1909	J 103
Miller, John H.	Feb., 1910	J 123
Markwood, J. Henry	July, 1910	J 172
Morgan, Jonah	Nov., 1910	J 202
Miller, James	Jan., 1911	J 230
Miller, Joseph	July, 1911	J 310
McDonald, John A.	Nov., 1911	J 345
Madore, Jane	Dec., 1911	J 351
Millholland, James A.	Dec., 1911	J 352
McEvoy, Joseph A.	Dec., 1911	J 357
Monaghan, John	June, 1912	J 432
McFarland, John	July, 1912	J 438
Marshall, John H.	Dec., 1912	J 477
McMullen, John P.	March, 1914	K 153
McMullen, John P. et al	April, 1914	K 159
McAlpine, John, Sr.	April, 1914	K 169
McGreevy, John J., Sr.	Dec., 1914	K 256
Merkel, John C.	Dec., 1914	K 259
McFarland, John, Sr.	April, 1915	K 331
Mair, James M.	June, 1915	K 362
Miller, Jacob	Jan., 1916	K 460
Morton, John	Feb., 1916	K 482
McKenzie, John F.	Oct., 1916	L 70
Moser, James	April, 1917	L 166
Mullaney, John P.	Jan., 1918	L 297
Matthews, James H.	July, 1920	M 190
Mackie, John	July, 1920	M 192
Mantheiy, John L.	Feb., 1921	M 263
McCleave, Johns	April, 1921	M 312
Murphy, John J.	March, 1922	M 435
McGeady, John P.	March, 1922	M 439
Morris, Jennie	April, 1922	M 450
Miltenberger, John M.	May, 1922	M 456
Maxwell, Joseph S.	May, 1922	M 458

McDade, James	July, 1922	M 497
Messick, James A.	July, 1922	M 498
Myers, Jacob H.	May, 1923	N 51
Matthews, James L.	Sept., 1923	N 133
McDonald, John James	Aug., 1924	N 304
McCormick, Jane Mary	Sept., 1924	N 318
Metzner, John	April, 1925	N 415
Miller, John Harvey	June, 1925	N 434
MacDonald, James T.	Oct., 1925	N 474
Martens, John E.	March, 1926	N 558
Myers, Jacob L.	March, 1926	N 560
Malloy, Joseph T.	March, 1926	N 577
Morris, John	July, 1927	O 204
Mowbray, Jane Ann	Jan., 1928	O 303
Meyers, John C.	Sept., 1928	O 392
Murray, John F.	March, 1929	O 486
McHenry, James A.	April, 1930	P 139
Moffatt, James E.	Nov., 1930	P 260
Myers, Joseph Nimrod	Jan., 1931	P 284
Michaels, Jacob W.	April, 1931	P 351
Mayers, Joseph Alexander	May, 1931	P 357
Miller, James H.	July, 1931	P 407
Miller, John	Nov., 1931	P 480
Mealing, Jabez J.	Nov., 1932	Q 97
McGowan, John A., Sr.	Feb., 1933	Q 175
Miller, James Wilson	Dec., 1933	Q 328
McGuigan, John	March, 1934	Q 387
Morehead, John E.	Aug., 1934	Q 479
McMurdo, Janet	Dec., 1934	Q 554
McGinis, John	Feb., 1935	Q 586
McCauley, John S.	April, 1935	R 18
Malcolm, Jacob H.	Aug., 1935	R 82
Minnick, Janet	Nov., 1935	R 127
Miller, John Thomas	Feb., 1937	R 406
Morgart, John C.	Sept., 1937	R 548
Martin, John H.	Oct., 1937	R 575
Mahaney, John T.	Dec., 1937	S 24
McCabe, James P.	March, 1938	S 62
McGowan, Joseph	Aug., 1938	S 137
Minnicks, John P.	Sept., 1939	S 380
Metz, Josephine	Nov., 1939	S 428
McBeth, John E.	May, 1940	S 565
Murray, James William	July, 1940	S 592
Mowbray, John, Sr.	Nov., 1940	T 38

Morgan, J. Kenneth	Jan., 1960	2 258
Miller, John Edgar	Jan., 1960	2 264
McKalvey, James	April, 1960	2 357
McKnight, Joseph R.	Aug., 1960	2 510
McAteer, James P.	Aug., 1960	2 520

Miller, Kelita	Sept., 1907	I 321
McCabe, Kate Alice	June, 1947	V 495
Muller, Karl Friedrich	July, 1954	Y 315
McHugh, Katie B.	Sept., 1956	Z 355
MacDonald, Kathryn P.	Sept., 1957	1 70

Mattlingly, Lucy		A 391
Martin, Lenox	Dec., 1812	A 148
same	Jan., 1814	A 148
same	Dec., 1814	A 149
same	Dec., 1814	A 584
McMillan, Lewis	Sept., 1870	C 180
Moffatt, Louisa	April, 1872	D 10
McDearmid, Laura A. & husb.	Nov., 1878	D 375
Meadows, Louis	March, 1881	D 471
Moore, Levi	March, 1883	D 592
Messman, Lorinda A.	Dec., 1883	E 9
McLaughlin, Lydia R.	Jan., 1884	E 13
Miller, Laura Willie	July, 1904	I 31
Mann, Luther A., Sr.	Nov., 1908	I 477
Miller, Lawrence (Lorenz)	April, 1914	K 167
Mayolo, Louis	Feb., 1916	K 477
McDonald, Lida T.	April, 1925	N 416
Morris, Louisa	Feb., 1927	O 128
McAbee, Lillie B.	May, 1930	P 164
Mann, Luther A.	Jan., 1931	P 272
Martin, Leven	Aug., 1931	P 412
Michael, Lawrence	Oct., 1931	P 470
Madore, L.Clark	Feb., 1932	P 528
Miller, Louis J.	June, 1933	Q 242
Morris, Lura	Oct., 1933	Q 299
Madore, Lavina P.	Nov., 1934	Q 525
Middleton, Laura V.	Feb., 1939	S 267
Mendenhall, Laura S.	April, 1940	S 526

McCune, Mary	Oct., 1908	I 456
Morgan, Michael	Dec., 1908	I 486
Major, Mary	Nov., 1909	J 89
Montgomery, Michael M.	Nov., 1909	J 94
McIndoe, Margaret D.	March, 1910	J 132
Mullaney, Mary	April, 1910	J 145
Morgan, Mary L.	Nov., 1910	J 201
Murphy, Mary E.	Feb., 1912	J 489
Matthews, Martha E.	May, 1913	K 29
McCray, Margaret M.	Aug., 1913	K 61
Moffatt, Mary J.	Jan., 1914	K 128
Mann, Mary Willett	Jan., 1916	K 457
McKinnon, Mary	June, 1916	L 15
McCabe, Michael	Dec., 1916	L 99
McCulloh, Maria L.	Feb., 1917	L 134
Malloy, Mary A.	June, 1918	L 387
McCandlish, Margaret L.	March, 1919	M 15
Menahan, Margaret	Aug., 1921	M 350
Mactavish, Maria M.	Dec., 1921	M 387
Miller, Mary E.	March, 1922	M 434
Mair, Mary Ann	Oct., 1922	M 548
McIndoe, Mary	Sept., 1923	N 127
Morehead, Mary	Jan., 1924	N 184
Monahan, Margaret	July, 1924	N 290
Miltenberger, Mary A.	March, 1925	N 390
Mueller, Mary E.	Sept., 1925	N 467
McHugh, Mary	March, 1926	N 549
McDade, Michael	March, 1926	N 562
Marks, Maggie	Aug., 1926	O 43
Meyers, Mary E.	Dec., 1926	O 105
Maxwell, Mary E.	March, 1927	O 153
McKaig, Merwin	Dec., 1927	O 278
McFarland, Mary C.	Jan., 1928	O 292
McAllister, Mary L.	Jan., 1928	O 295
McGowan, Mary B.	Aug., 1928	O 373
McCulloh, Mary E.	Dec., 1928	O 432
Martin, Marcellus	April, 1929	O 504
Miller, Mary Martha	April, 1929	O 521
Mansfield, Mary M.	May, 1930	P 161
McCabe, Margaret Henry	June, 1930	P 171
McCulloch, Mary G.	Oct., 1930	P 216
Miller, Matilda	Oct., 1930	P 224
Malloy, Mary Jane	Oct., 1931	P 469
Miller, Michael	April, 1932	P 555

Moxley, Margaret E.	April, 1932	P 562
Morgan, Mary E.	March, 1933	Q 177
Murray, Mary A.	Feb., 1934	Q 380
Manley, Michael	April, 1934	Q 406
Malamphy, Michael J.	May, 1934	Q 431
McKone, Margaret W.	Nov., 1934	Q 537
Martz, Mary B.	Dec., 1934	Q 549
Martz, Mary F.	March, 1935	Q 595
Mattingly, Mary Ann	March, 1935	R 4
MacKenzie, Margaret	March, 1935	R 5
McLuckie, Margaret	May, 1936	R 240
Miller, Mary	May, 1937	R 495
Michael, Mary	June, 1937	R 516
Miller, Mary Sampson	July, 1937	R 523
McLuckie, Mary	Dec., 1937	S 19
Murphy, Mary K.	Jan., 1938	S 31
Martin, Matthew	Oct., 1938	S 168
Messman, Mary Sell	Oct., 1939	S 392
McEvoy, Mary Shearer	Jan., 1940	S 471
Mattingly, Margaret	Oct., 1940	T 23
McGann, Mary Ann	July, 1941	T 183
Meek, Mary	Aug., 1941	T 210
MacNallin, Mary Amanda C.	Aug., 1941	T 211
Michael, Mary Annie	Dec., 1942	T 562
McMurry, Mary Alberta	Jan., 1943	T 582
Mayer, Margaret	Jan., 1943	T 579
Metz, Minnie	Feb., 1943	T 613
Mullan, Mary E.	March, 1943	U 8
Martin, Mary C.	May, 1944	U 306
Martin, Mary Catherine	May, 1945	U 543
Minke, Margaret Theresa	March, 1945	U 465
Myers, Mary C.	Jan., 1946	V 101
Muncaster, Mary I.	July, 1946	V 260
Michaels, Margaret M.	Oct., 1946	V 320
McDonald, Mary Jane	Aug., 1947	V 527
McGuigan, Mary	Sept., 1947	V 549
Muir, Mary Louise	Aug., 1948	W 182
McElfish, Mary S.	Dec., 1948	W 234
McGuire, Mary E.	May, 1949	W 308
McKenzie, Mary M.	May, 1949	W 317
Mayer, Mary	June, 1949	W 334
Mullan, Mary A.	Aug., 1949	W 359
Murray, Mabel N.	March, 1950	W 503
McMahon, Marshall T.	July, 1950	W 602

Murray, Missouri A.	Jan., 1951	X 90
Mackin, Mary Ann	June, 1951	X 196
Morris, Mattie Viola	June, 1952	X 411
Myers, Mont Zoma	June, 1952	X 452
Morehouse, Mary J.D.	Sept., 1952	X 482
Miller, Mary Anne	Oct., 1952	X 501
Murphy, Mary I.	Nov., 1954	Y 391
McFarland, Maude Viola	Oct., 1955	Z 92
Miller, Michael H.	Nov., 1955	Z 109
Munsie, Mary C.	Dec., 1955	Z 120
Michael, Mary M.)	May, 1956	Z 230
Michael, Margaret A.)	May, 1956	Z 230
Metz, Morris	May, 1956	Z 250
Murphy, Margaret	June, 1956	Z 258
Mullan, Margaret C.	Feb., 1957	Z 462
McGeady, Michael A.	April, 1957	Z 519
Moore, Margaret A.	Aug., 1957	I 30
Miller, Maggie Estella	May, 1958	1 263
Miller, Mary E.	June, 1958	1 311
Meyers, Mary	Sept., 1958	1 402
McGee, Michael F.	June, 1959	2 56
Mullen, Michael E.	June, 1959	2 64
Maybury, Mary	Sept., 1959	2 165
Mattingly, Mary Gertrude	Nov., 1959	2 204
McIntyre, Margaret P.	March, 1960	2 316
Malloy, Margaret	June, 1960	2 465
Monsen, Martha V.	July, 1960	2 478

Magers, Nathan		A 238
Middleton, Nelson		C 47
Miller, Nancy		C 112
Meese, Nelson H.	July, 1908	I 423
Miller, Nancy J.	Dec., 1917	L 283
McGeady, Nora	March, 1922	M 438
Martin, Nathan	Nov., 1931	P 491
Mullan, Norah Ann	Aug., 1933	Q 265
Mansor, Nasib	March, 1942	T 346
Miller, Nellie Elizabeth	Aug., 1949	W 356
Makris, Nicholas	June, 1957	Z 573

McCracken, Ovid		A 130
McElfish, Owen	April, 1897	G 225
McCrea, Oley E.	April, 1956	Z 212
Maxwell, Orin Paine	Nov., 1954	Y 403
McElfish, Ora Marie	March, 1955	Y 460
McArdle, Ola Elmira	Sept., 1958	1 408

Myer, Peter		A 60
Murdock, Patrick		A 122
McMahon, Peter		A 579
Miller, Peter P.	April, 1869	C 136
McDonough, Peter	March, 1886	E 174
Manley, Patrick	May, 1896	G 176
Mooney, Patrick	Feb., 1899	G 337
Martz, Peter	Nov., 1909	J 93
Miller, Pearre C.	Nov., 1910	J 210
Malloy, Patrick	July, 1915	K 388
Martin, Phillis	July, 1916	L 33
McMahon, Philip A.	May, 1918	L 373
Miller, Phillip	March, 1920	M 132
Martin, Patrick H.	March, 1924	N 223
Murphy, Perry R.	Dec., 1925	N 507
Miller, Peter S.	May, 1931	P 375
Miller, Philip	Nov., 1932	Q 108
McCartney, Patrick S.	Dec., 1933	Q 331
Michaels, Peter P.	Feb., 1936	R 191
McGuire, Peter S.	Dec., 1946	V 371
Miller, Philip	Oct., 1947	V 566
Mantheiy, Paul L.	Nov., 1956	Z 393
McCoy, Paul	April, 1957	Z 505

McMinn, Robert		A 20
McKinnie, Richard		B 114
Martin, Rose Ann	Nov., 1874	D 184
McDonald, Robert	Jan., 1877	D 314
Moalin, Rebecca		D 502
McCulloh, Robert C. Heirs	Dec., 1883	D 637
Myers, Rachel,	Jan., 1884	E 11
Maxwell, Robert	Feb., 1886	E 166
McCleave, Robert H.	May, 1886	E 190

McCleave, R.H. Heirs	July, 1886	E 197
McKaig, Reginald H.		E 396
Morris, Robert I.		F 38
Morgan, Richard	April, 1915	K 329
Martin, Ruth Ellen	Nov., 1919	M 96
MacDonald, Robert	Jan., 1925	N 373
McMillen, Robert M.	July, 1925	N 449
McCulloch, Robert C.	May, 1928	O 349
Meager, Richard	May, 1928	O 350
Mattingly, Roselia	Jan., 1931	P 274
McMurdo, Robert	March, 1933	Q 169
McAdams, Robert C.	March, 1935	R 1
Miller, Robert Cookerly	March, 1936	R 206
McMullen, Richard F.	July, 1938	S 120
Marshall, Robert, Sr.	May, 1939	S 331
McCleave, R. Hugh	May, 1946	V 217
Marriott, Rachel Miller	Sept., 1948	W 196
McCardell, Richard P.	Feb., 1949	W 275
Miller, Richard H.	Aug., 1950	W 628
Millholland, Randolph	Nov., 1951	X 262
McFarlane, Robert	Feb., 1953	X 582
Molinari, Ruth Lena	June, 1954	Y 287
Marshall, Robert	Sept., 1954	Y 345
Mitchell, Robert	Feb., 1955	Y 469
McCormick, Robert	May, 1958	1 277
McEvoy, Robert F.	Sept., 1958	1 407
Marshall, Rachel S.	Feb., 1959	1 559
McCulley, Regina M.	April, 1959	2 13
Morgan, Robert A.	June, 1960	2 450

Magruder, Sarah		A 73
McKinzie, Savannah et al	Aug., 1872	D 38
McKaig, Sarah A. Heirs	Sept., 1872	D 301
Miller, Samuel, Sr.	June, 1880	D 450
Monaghan, Sarah	Nov., 1888	E 348
Morris, Susan J.		F 38
Mattingly, Sylvester	April, 1881	F 187
same	April, 1881	F 187
Maryland, State of		G 1
KcKenzie, Samuel	Jan., 1897	G 213
Miller, Samuel J.	May, 1901	H 182
Mansell, Samuel	May, 1907	I 271

Morgan, Samuel C.	July, 1907	I 301
Morris, Susan J.	Oct., 1909	J 79
McFarland, Susannah	May, 1914	K 177
Myers, Samuel C.	March, 1915	K 313
Moore, Sol	Dec., 1924	N 351
McKenna, Susan A.	Oct., 1925	N 471
Malloy, Susan	Oct., 1928	O 414
Matlick, Samantha H.	May, 1936	R 250
Millison, Sallie F.	Aug., 1937	R 530
Morgan, Sarah	Jan., 1939	S 245
Martin, Susan	Aug., 1939	S 365
McKenzie, Samuel B.	Aug., 1939	S 366
Myers, Sarah E.	Feb., 1941	T 79
Myers, Samuel Gilbert	Feb., 1948	W 42
Mills, Savilla W.	April, 1948	W 82
Mickey, Susan E.	May, 1951	X 167
Messersmith, Sherman	April, 1954	Y 248
McKinley, Somers W.	May, 1958	1 275
Mullan, Sadie	Aug., 1958	1 362
Marston, Sarah Ann	Dec., 1958	1 496
Mastrino, Samuel	March, 1960	2 319
Marshall, Sarah E.	March, 1960	2 339

McElfish, Thomas		A 79
McGirr, Thomas	July, 1870	C 175
Malone, Terrence	July, 1872	D 32
McCray, Theodore	Oct., 1875	D 242
McCulloch, Thomas G.	Jan., 1883	D 583
McKaig, Thomas J. Jr.	March, 1886	E 172
McNeill, Thomas	July, 1887	E 248
McCulloh, Thomas G.	Nov., 1890	F 139
McKaig, Thomas J.	May, 1902	F 292
Moran, Thomas	Dec., 1896	G 195
Mullaney, Thomas	Sept., 1901	H 214
Morgan, Thomas	Aug., 1905	I 132
Maguire, Thomas	June, 1908	I 411
McBride, Thomas, Sr.	April, 1909	J 27
Moran, Thomas	March, 1913	K 8
Myers, Thomas F.	March, 1914	K 151
Mills, Thompson	Dec., 1921	M 389
Middleton, Thomas	Nov., 1923	N 155
McDonald, Thomas B.	April, 1924	N 249

McFarlane, Thomas	Oct., 1925	N 477
Merrbach, Theodore	March, 1926	N 567
McAbee, Thomas Edward	Nov., 1927	O 273
Mitchell, Thomas H.	Dec., 1933	Q 323
McKinnon, Thomas	Jan., 1937	R 371
McDonough, Thomas	Oct., 1938	S 176
Morrison, Taylor	Nov., 1939	S 425
Mihailovich, Thomas	Nov., 1939	S 439
Marshall, Thomas C.	Feb., 1940	S 501
Marsh, Theckla O.F.	April, 1940	S 536
Maxwell, Thomas	Sept., 1940	T 16
Morgan, Thomas H.	Aug., 1945	V 34
Myers, Thomas L.	Sept., 1950	W 635
McElfish, Thoms Ernest	March, 1955	Y 475
Mowbray, Thomas, Sr.	April, 1955	Y 525
Miller, Thomas	Oct., 1957	1 86
Mullan, Thomas M.	Oct., 1958	1 421
Moore, Thomas F.)	Feb., 1959	1 534
Moore, Thomas F.)	July, 1959	2 91
Mullaney, Thomas H.	Sept., 1959	2 167
Myers, Thomas L.	May, 1960	2 400

McElfish, Upton B.	Aug., 1871	D 205
McElfish, Upton	Feb., 1911	J 254
Miller, Urban	Feb., 1915	K 281
McCandlish Upton Beall	June, 1915	K 371
Miller, Urban J.	Aug., 1952	X 456

McCulloh, Virginia		E 344
Mayers, Violet Regina	Nov., 1926	O 87
MacTavish, Virginia Scott	Aug., 1931	P 425
Miller, Virginia S.	May, 1933	Q 208
McElfish, Violet L.	Feb., 1957	Z 458
McKay, Virginia Opie	July, 1959	2 89
Miller, Viola S.	June, 1960	2 438

Muncaster, Walter J.	Oct., 1934	Q 519
Menefee, William B.	Nov., 1936	R 348
McIndoe, William A.	April, 1937	R 461
Messman, Wyant C.	May, 1938	S 105
Martens, Walter E.	June, 1940	S 580
Martz, William B.	March, 1941	T 108
Morley, William J.	April, 1941	T 126
Martin, William Addison	Aug., 1942	T 446
Mathews, W.T.	Sept., 1942	T 455
McCullough, William Alexr.	March, 1944	U 269
Miller, William G.S.	Sept., 1944	U 364
McCormick, William Malcolm	Feb., 1945	U 452
Miller, William	Nov., 1945	V 68
Mendenhall, William R.	July, 1946	V 266
McFarland, William Lawrence	March, 1949	W 282
Miller, William M.	March, 1949	W 292
McIndoe, William Haddow	July, 1951	X 198
Morehouse, Wilmot L.	Sept., 1952	X 484
Marvin, Walter Scott	June, 1954	Y 294
Miller, Walter V.	Oct., 1956	Z 376
Malamphy, Wilhelmina	Jan., 1958	1 163
Maddocks, William Leslie	Nov., 1958	1 445
Marshall, William, Sr.	Nov., 1958	1 454
Mulvey, William	Sept., 1959	2 168

Magruder, Zachariah		A 21
McKenzie, Zella	Oct., 1962	4 170

N

Nee, Delia	Nov., 1925	N 488
Newman, Dolia	March, 1930	P 121

Niland, Ellen	Dec., 1891	F 245
same	July, 1895	G 127
Neff, Elizabeth N.	Jan., 1899	G 333
Nash, Elizabeth	June, 1904	I 26
Naismith, Ellen	Dec., 1907	I 340
Norwood, Edward S.	Jan., 1910	J 112
Naughton, Edward J.	April, 1926	O 2
Norris, Esther M.	Nov., 1930	P 258
Northcraft, Elizabeth	Feb., 1932	P 531
Nash, Eva G.	June, 1933	Q 238
Neff, Edward R.	June, 1937	R 508
Noland, Etta V.	Jan., 1939	S 233
Nelson, Elmer E.	Oct., 1939	S 393
Nichols, Ellen N.	Sept., 1941	T 235
Nolan, Elizabeth K.	May, 1943	U 81
Nixon, Eliza E.	April, 1953	Y 18
North, Esther W.	June, 1960	2 452

Naughton, Francis P.	April, 1908	I 384
Naughton, Frances M.	Jan., 1946	V 103
Newcomer, Frank	Sept., 1949	W 395
North, Florence Bergman	April, 1958	1 259

Neill, Grace A.	July, 1884	E 70
Nichols, Grace L.	Jan., 1931	P 290
Neff, Guy R.	Jan., 1936	R 171
Nield, George H.	March, 1942	T 344
North, George Athey	March, 1944	U 256
Nine, Gilbert C.	Jan., 1946	V 108
Nield, George W.	May, 1948	W 103

Naylor, Jesse S.	Sept., 1954	Y 342
Nealis, Joseph Melton	April, 1959	1 592
Nickel, Kate et al	March, 1869	C 133
Nied, Lewis C.	April, 1924	N 255
Noble, Laurie A.	Jan., 1943	T 593
Niner, Louis	Dec., 1943	U 205
Neff, Lillian U.	April, 1957	Z 497
Nasser, Lee	June, 1960	2 453
Nevy, Louis	July, 1960	2 499
Neff, Margaret		A 268
Newens, Mary		A 477
Neff, Michael		C 59
Niland, Matthias	Feb., 1900	H 49
Navin, Mary	June, 1903	H 363
Naughton, Michael	Aug., 1903	H 370
Naughton, Mary	Feb., 1910	J 124
Neilson, Margaret	March, 1918	L 334
Nehring, Mary T.	Oct., 1918	L 411
Norton, Mary E.	Jan., 1918	L 453
Niedballa, Mary	Aug., 1929	O 587
Naughton, Mary	Dec., 1929	P 72
Niland, Mary E.	Dec., 1937	S 16
Nolan, Michael P.	Sept., 1939	S 382
Nolte, Mary J.	Sept., 1939	S 390
Neff, Margaret Jane	April, 1940	S 528
Naumann, Minnie	Dec., 1942	T 576
Norris, Mary Elizabeth	Dec., 1943	U 203
Neal, Mary A.	Feb., 1952	X 336
Neumann, Margaret	April, 1955	Y 509
Nolan, Mary A.	Sept., 1956	Z 347
Noel, Mary S.	Dec., 1956	Z 413
Noonan, Marie R.	July, 1957	Z 583
Nolan, Maud T.	June, 1960	2 457

Neat, Oscar T.	Nov., 1941	T 268
Neff, Peter		A 298
Nolan, Peter	Jan., 1912	J 384
Niland, Patrick F.	June, 1924	N 275
Noland, Pierce M.	Dec., 1926	O 100
Nicklin, Perry A.	May, 1945	U 536
Newman, Robert	Jan.,1816	A 149
same	Jan., 1817	A 157
Nelson, Rose B.	Dec., 1942	T 559
Norris, Robert F.	May, 1955	Y 586
Nickel, Rudolph	June, 1955	Z 3
Nazelrod, Robert G.	Feb., 1960	2 294
Norman, Samuel	Oct., 1888	E 342
Nightengale, Samuel	Nov., 1888	E 346
Naughton, Sarah	April, 1890	F 114
Nichols, Samuel	Aug., 1909	J 74
Nave, Samuel S.	Nov., 1922	M 557
Nicol, Susan	Nov., 1938	S 197
Newman, S.C. (Mrs.)	May, 1943	U 84
Neff, Sallie	June, 1945	U 597
Nichols, Susan	Jan., 1952	X 298
Nicholson, Somerville, Sr.	Nov., 1960	3 25
Neff, Thos. W. & Heirs of John	Nov., 1879	D 414
Neff, Thos. W.	Aug., 1882	D 556
Nash, Thomas	March, 1906	I 190
Norris, Tolbert	Nov., 1933	Q 314
Noland, Virginia C.	Oct., 1947	V 570

Nerring, William	Oct., 1868	C 126
Neff, William	July, 1883	D 617
Norman, William L.	April, 1913	K 14
Nickel, William	March, 1918	L 328
Nehring, William L.	July, 1921	M 338
Niceley, William A.	Jan., 1930	P 84
Naughton, William J.	Nov., 1936	R 344
Nacke, Willie H. F.	June, 1937	R 514
Nicewarner, Walter S.	May, 1956	Z 251
Newberry, William D.	Oct., 1956	Z 363

O

O'Neill, Edward	Sept., 1887	E 262
Oglebay, Ellen J.A.	April, 1904	I 13
O'Donnell, Elizabeth	May, 1916	L 6
Owen, Edwin V.	Feb., 1925	N 375
O'Donnell, Elizabeth	Dec., 1949	W 446
O'Brien, Edward P.	May, 1954	Y 278

Offutt, Frank M.	Dec., 1869	C 158
Offutt, Francis M.	March, 1905	I 87
O'Connor, Francis P.	Nov., 1906	I 247

Oliver, George		C 34

Offman, Henry	Dec., 1903	H 381
Odgers, Harry	Feb., 1904	H 399
Olewine, Harry L.	June, 1911	J 303
Orrick, Helen Marr	Feb., 1919	L 476
Oglebay, Harry C., Sr.	Oct., 1928	O 412

Offutt, James W.		B 81
Otto, Jacob	April, 1870	C 171
Orrick, James C.	Nov., 1891	F 236
Owens, John	April, 1902	H 265
same	Jan., 1903	H 308
Ort, John	Dec., 1908	I 481
O'Toole, John	April, 1909	J 35
Oliver, John	Aug., 1911	J 314
O'Neill, John	Aug., 1921	M 352
Oliver, James M.	Aug., 1924	N 303
O'Connor, John J.	Sept., 1932	Q 77
Oliver, John Arlington	May, 1941	T 139
Ort, John Lewis	Jan., 1960	2 267

Ollrick, Karl (Charles)	Feb., 1917	L 124

Osman, Samuel		A 201
Offutt, Sarah J.		B 82
Ott, Sophia	Jan., 1890	F 49
O'Laughlin, Susan	Oct., 1916	L 57
O'Neal, Samuel A.	Dec., 1923	N 172
Odgers, Stella M.Z.	Oct., 1960	2 591

Ocker, Teresa	Sept., 1873	D 117
O'Brien, Thomas	April, 1927	O 169

Oscius, William		A 523
O'Brien, Winefred	Feb., 1907	I 262
Offman, William	Nov., 1909	J 88
Orrick, William P.	June, 1910	J 167
Oglebay, William H.	Sept., 1912	J 455
O'Connell, William J.	Aug., 1917	L 225
Orendorf, William Walter	April, 1935	R 16

P

Potts, Aaron		B 30
Parker, Amos F.	July, 1900	H 111
Porter, Alexenia E.	Sept., 1912	J 448
Piquett, Alfred C.	Feb., 1933	Q 158
Proctor, Adelaide E.	Feb., 1937	R 390
Prichard, Annie P.	Nov., 1939	S 426
Park, Abraham M.	Dec., 1942	T 575
Pape, Annie	Oct., 1946	V 308
Powell, Anna	June, 1948	W 144
Pendleton, Ambrose	Oct., 1950	X 40
Powers, Anna Elizabeth	March, 1951	X 142
Perry, Albert James, Sr.	Dec., 1954	Y 428
Park, Abraham	Jan., 1955	Y 435
Porter, Anna L.	Feb., 1956	Z 170
Parker, Alice R.	Jan., 1960	2 260
Powers, Anna Catherine	Sept., 1960	2 557
Preston, Amy Metz	Nov., 1960	3 21
Poland, Annie Dorcas	Nov., 1960	3 22

Pegman, Bene S.		A 561
Peters, B.L.	April, 1887	E 228
Porter, Bennett	Nov., 1897	G 264
Poole, Benjamin C.	July, 1925	N 444
Pennington, Betsey	Nov., 1928	O 419

Perry, Charles	May, 1860	B 177
Pagenhart, Charles	Nov., 1870	C 183
Perry, Charles	April, 1872	D 17
Perry, Charles	Sept., 1876	D 294
Priel, Catherine	Sept., 1883	D 625
Parker, Charles H.	Sept., 1895	G 135
Price, Charles	Sept., 1901	H 218
Pagenhart, Charles A.	April, 1905	I 100
Paulus, Catharine	Feb., 1908	I 369
Preston, Catherine	July, 1911	J 312

Porter, Caroline	Feb., 1922	M 412
Porter, Catherine A.	Aug., 1924	N 297
Pferdeort, Charles M.	Nov., 1929	P 39
Pittman, Charles Elmore	Jan., 1931	P 288
Pfaff, Conrad	Jan., 1931	P 292
Purnell, Clayton	April, 1933	Q 194
Porter, Charles W.	Feb., 1943	U 6
Porter, Charles G.	July, 1943	U 122
Porter, Charles Constantine	April, 1944	U 287
Parrish, Charles H.	Aug., 1944	U 345
Perrin, Charles H.	Sept., 1946	V 289
Piper, Charles A.	May, 1960	2 432

Percy, David		B 135
Percy, Douglas	Dec., 1863	C 34
Percy, David T.	Nov., 1873	D 130
Percy, Douglas	Jan., 1886	E 158
Porter, Dena	Nov., 1921	M 378
Pitsnogle, D.E.	Feb., 1937	R 397
Price, David D.	June, 1939	S 353
Powell, David H.	Nov., 1940	T 31
Packi, Domenico Maria	July, 1952	X 450

Peter, Elizabeth		A 34
Percy, Eleanora	July, 1871	C 201
Painter, Elizabeth	May, 1885	E 118
Price, Edward	July, 1897	G 243
Paisley, Eliza J.	Jan., 1902	H 247
Parlaman, Edward G.	May, 1903	H 333
Poole, Elizabeth	April, 1904	I 12
Picken, Elizabeth	April, 1908	I 389
Porter, Eleanor	Feb., 1917	L 133
Peterson, Ellen M.	Dec., 1919	M 104
Prichard, Enoch H.B.	July, 1924	N 280
Pfahler, Elmira	Jan., 1930	P 77
Phillips, Elizabeth A.	Jan., 1931	P 297
Porter, Ella E.	April, 1933	Q 198
Price, Edward M.	Sept., 1933	Q 280
Phillips, Elizabeth B.	Feb., 1932	P 522
Porter, Elizabeth Race	Nov., 1938	S 181

Price, Elizabeth E.	Sept., 1943	U 159
Pierce, Emma V.	March, 1947	V 412
Pratt, Edgar Vanmeter	Oct., 1948	W 199
Porter, Elizabeth Laura Viola	Aug., 1949	W 361
Ponger, Elsie Mae	Aug., 1952	X 458
Pugh, Elizabeth	Sept., 1957	1 76
Price, Enoch Prichard	Sept., 1959	2 147
Piper, Frederick I.	Nov., 1874	D 188
Paulus, Frank	March, 1875	D 203
Petrie, Floyd F.	Feb., 1917	L 122
Pugh, Ferman Gilbert	Dec., 1938	S 204
Porter, Florence	July, 1950	W 592
Perdew, Frank Archibald	Dec., 1954	Y 434
Phillips, Frank T.	June, 1960	2 445
Payne, George		A 15
Preston, George		A 236
Percy, George	April, 1873	D 128
same	Dec., 1873	D 154
Pearre, George A.	June, 1883	D 610
Perry, George C.	Nov., 1886	E 210
Priskorn, Gustave	July, 1891	F 211
Percy, George	Feb., 1878	F 220
Phillips, Griffith	Jan., 1905	I 70
Porter, George W.	Dec., 1916	L 88
Pearre, George A.	Sept., 1923	N 131
Pierce, George B.	May, 1929	O 543
Pearce, George E.	May, 1937	R 502
Pfister, George	Nov., 1940	T 43
Parsons, George W.	April, 1946	V 183
Paulman, George P.	Oct., 1946	V 331
Parsenios, George	Oct., 1959	2 189
Pitzer, Gladys Margaret	March, 1960	2 351
Peters, Henry		A 173
Pigman, Harriet	Aug., 1845	A 566
Pigman, Hanson B.		A 629

Pritchard, Hannah		D 295
same	May, 1884	E 58
Porter, Hiram M.	March, 1905	I 86
Price, Hannah	June, 1914	K 196
Petenbrink, Henry	June, 1936	R 258
Preston, Hannah	Feb., 1938	S 55
Perdew, Harry O.	Dec., 1942	T 561
Pfeiffer, Henry C.	May, 1943	U 82
Poss, Harry G.	June, 1944	U 311
Plunkett, Helen	Oct., 1944	U 375
Porter, Harry Oswald	Feb., 1945	U 447
Pitzer, Harry A.	Oct., 1950	X 29
Paul, Harry F.	Sept., 1953	Y 120
Pennington, Harley D.	Jan., 1956	Z 136
Payne, Henry (James H.)	June, 1958	1 314
Price, Harry Homer, Sr.	July, 1960	2 481
Painter, Ignatius	April, 1890	F 90
Purgit, I.C.	Feb., 1937	R 400
Pheobus, Ida Lee	Feb., 1951	X 109
Powell, Ithan	Oct., 1951	X 258
Pinsley, John	Oct., 1790	A 5
Plummer, Jerome		A 24
Parkison, John		A 28
Prather, James	Jan., 1791	A 140
same	Dec., 1792	A 140
same	Dec., 1794	A 141
same		A 175
Porter, John		A 647
Porter, John B.		B 56
Porter, John		C 24
Percy, James		C 49
Pool, John A. & wife	June, 1865	C 72
Piper, John, Jr.	May, 1881	C 194
Percy, James K.	Nov., 1873	D 126
same	Dec., 1873	D 154
same	March, 1881	D 446
Purcer, Joseph	Sept., 1884	E 78
Porter, John M.	Dec., 1884	E 92

Paulus, John	May, 1887	E 233
Pollock, Jos. W.H.	June, 1888	E 327
Porter, James M.	Dec., 1890	F 151
Pfab, John	Oct., 1892	F 318
Pengelly, John	June, 1895	G 118
Porter, Julia	July, 1895	G 123
Porter, Joseph	Aug., 1895	G 127
Porter, Josiah J.	Feb., 1900	H 47
Pelton, John	April, 1901	H 169
Pascoe, Jane	Jan., 1902	H 239
Porter, Joseph C.	Aug., 1903	H 369
Patterson, John H.	Jan., 1905	I 68
Perry, John H.	May, 1906	I 201
Parsche, John Wm.	July, 1907	I 291
Pratt, James	March, 1911	J 272
Perrie, John	Feb., 1914	K 140
Pfeiffer, John	April, 1915	K 322
Percy, John D.	April, 1916	K 501
Prout, James	Oct., 1916	L 72
Patterson, John W.	May, 1918	L 356
Pressman, John, Sr.	March, 1920	M 142
Phillips, Jeanette	Oct., 1920	M 217
Peel, John	Oct., 1920	M 219
Pitzer, John B., Sr.	Dec., 1925	N 506
Pearce, John F.	April, 1927	O 166
Price, J.E.	Jan., 1928	O 300
Price, John	June, 1930	P 167
Piper, James W.	May, 1931	P 373
Price, James Marshall	June, 1931	P 382
Pierce, John L.	Oct., 1933	Q 288
Poole, John	Feb., 1936	R 186
Price, John J.	Feb., 1937	R 410
Porter, James M.	April, 1937	R 468
Porter, James C.	Oct., 1937	R 578
Porter, J. Frank	May, 1938	S 101
Pierce, James T.	Sept., 1938	S 147
Peebles, John	Feb., 1940	S 486
Pfeiffer, John Casper	March, 1940	S 510
Powell, James C.	Nov., 1941	T 270
Porter, Jessie Jones	March, 1944	U 262
Porter, J. Bradley	Feb., 1946	V 135
Peters, John M.	Sept., 1946	V 279
Porter, John Wesley	March, 1948	W 58
Parise, Joseph	March, 1950	W 515

Perdew, John M.	Dec., 1953	Y 175
Pugh, James L.	Feb., 1954	Y 206
Phillips, John S.	March, 1954	Y 236
Perrin, James Emory	July, 1951	X 203
Peer, Joseph C.	Feb., 1957	Z 443
Pennington, Joseph Parsons	March, 1957	Z 463
Payne, James H. (Henry)	June, 1958	1 314
Parch, John	Aug., 1958	1 370
Patterson, James Edward	Jan., 1959	1 531
Phillips, John F.	June, 1959	2 60
Patchett, Joseph E.	Feb., 1960	2 277

Pfister, Katherine	Oct., 1944	U 378
Pfab, Kennis R.	March, 1955	Y 470

Perry, Lucy		A 523
Pritchard, Lewis	May, 1876	D 283
Pritchard, Louisa	Nov., 1894	G 79
Perrin, Lennox	April, 1896	G 170
Patterson, Louisa A.	Nov., 1899	H 13
Payne, Lydia	Dec., 1900	H 137
Parker, Laura	April, 1904	I 11
Pressmann, Lena C.	Aug., 1911	J 316
Pennell, Lillian	April, 1928	O 335
Popp, Lewis	July, 1928	O 365
Pfeiffer, Louisa	March, 1931	P 321
Passarelli, Lavern	June, 1937	R 507
Patterson, Lloyd W.	June, 1937	R 520
Patrick, Lola Josephine	Dec., 1953	Y 174
Pfeiffer, Laura Belle	Dec., 1954	Y 418
Parker, Laura V.	Feb., 1956	Z 158

Porter, Moses		A 13
Pigman, Mary	May, 1848	A 650
Paugh, Michael	Aug., 1864	C 41
Perdue, Maria	Jan., 1877	D 320
Phillips, Methuselah	March, 1879	D 398
Perry, Marcus	Aug., 1883	D 621

Park, Mary	Oct., 1894	G 68
Poland, Matilda	April, 1900	H 94
Peacemaker, Melvina	July, 1901	H 204
Phillips, Martha	Aug., 1910	J 188
Perry, Marion C.	May, 1914	K 180
Paul, Margaret	June, 1917	L 207
Pearre, Mary W.	Feb., 1918	L 310
Porter, Mary R.	March, 1921	M 286
Pendergast, Margaret A.	March, 1922	M 432
Powers, Michael J.	Jan., 1924	N 199
Porter, Moses	June, 1925	N 431
Powell, Mary F.	April, 1926	N 580
Perrin, Marie	Aug., 1927	O 221
Porter, Michael R.	Nov., 1928	O 420
Pferdeort, Maggie A.	Oct., 1930	P 225
Pudelko, Mary	Oct., 1932	Q 91
Price, Mary M.	Aug., 1934	Q 484
Phillips, Mary H.	Jan., 1938	S 32
Piper, Margaret	Oct., 1938	S 180
Price, Mary A.	Jan., 1942	T 318
Pantuso, Michelena (Michelia)	April, 1943	U 37
Phillips, Martin T.	Dec., 1944	U 422
Pearce, Matilda Agnes	Dec., 1945	V 87
Porter, Mary A.	Dec., 1945	V 94
Pugh, Mary A.	Feb., 1947	V 407
Parker, Margaret	June, 1948	W 140
Peebles, Mary A.	May, 1950	W 545
Patterson, Mary Florence	Dec., 1951	X 273
Peel, Mary	Aug., 1953	Y 102
Peskin, Morton W.	Jan., 1957	Z 431
Phillips, Milton J.	May, 1957	Z 541
Phillips, Mary C.	Feb., 1959	1 538

Pigman, Nathaniel	Aug., 1845	A 566
Phillips, Nannie G.	Jan., 1908	I 361
Phillips, Nannie	Oct., 1909	J 82
Porter, Norman	Aug., 1917	L 227
Piper, Nellie G.	Nov., 1929	P 35
Poland, Nancy Catherine	Jan., 1937	R 373
Pigman, Nora C.	Jan., 1937	R 380

Price, Owen, Sr.	May, 1915	K 341
Porter, Oscar	Sept., 1944	U 373
Phillips, Peter	Jan., 1894	G 15
Pryle, Patrick	March, 1909	J 21
Pressman, Peter	March, 1934	Q 400
Parker, Robert		A 158
Puder, Robert H.	May, 1885	E 116
Parker, Rebecca	April, 1901	H 177
Paul, Robert C.	June, 1903	H 357
Perry, Roger	Dec., 1914	K 254
Powers, Rachel P.	Nov., 1919	M 98
Perrin, Rebecca S.	April, 1924	N 256
Porter, Rose A.	Sept., 1932	Q 62
Porter, Rachel	Oct., 1935	R 115
Pierce, Robert E.	Aug., 1944	U 343
Perrin, Rosie H.	Aug., 1956	Z 307
Phenix, Rebecca S.	Feb., 1960	2 282
Pariser, Rae	May, 1960	2 403
Pomeroy, Raymond S.	Dec., 1960	3 67
Prather, Sarah		A 229
Powell, Stephen	Jan., 1888	E 289
Perry, Sarah	April, 1895	G 113
Porter, Samuel	June, 1900	H 104
Porter, Sally	Feb., 1907	I 260
Petrie, Samuel M.	July, 1916	L 30
Porter, Sarah B.	Feb., 1917	L 126
Poland, Sallie E.	Nov., 1927	O 265
Poling, Sallie J.	July, 1931	P 409
Praeger, Saul	Aug., 1932	Q 52
Peters, Samuel	April, 1936	R 220
Pearce, Susan F.	Dec., 1945	V 88
Pierce, Sarah Letitia	Feb., 1952	X 322
Plosz, Steve	April, 1957	Z 506

Q

Quantz, Catherine	March, 1887	E 227
Quantz, Charles H.	Aug., 1919	M 64
Quinn, Benjamin	March, 1952	X 350
Quinn, James	Dec., 1948	W 237
Quinn, James F.	Feb., 1959	1 535
Quigley, Mary	Aug., 1908	I 442
Quigley, Mary J.	Jan., 1914	K 122
Quarles, Mollie D.	April, 1936	R 227
Quinn, Sarah	July, 1919	M 58

R

Rompf, Anna M.	March, 1954	Y 229
Robertson, Amelia	Nov., 1954	Y 388
Rafferty, Anastasia	May, 1955	Y 571
Roberts, Annie Cornwall	Oct., 1958	1 412
Rice, Ammy	Jan., 1959	1 522

Rensky, Benjamin	Nov., 1890	F 148
Ryland, Bridget T.	March, 1920	M 139
Richmond, Benjamin A.	March, 1922	M 423
Rice, Bernadette P.	Dec., 1925	N 514
Ridgely, Banner I.	May, 1942	T 405
Rice, Benjamin W.	Dec., 1952	X 542
Ritchie, Bertha Catherine	May, 1954	Y 276
Rapp, Benno	Sept., 1958	1 379

Reid, Charity		A 207
River, Catherine	Jan., 1843	A 511
Reed, Charles W.	June, 1845	A 552
Ridgely, Catherine	Dec., 1848	A 680
Robinette, Cassandra		B 34
Rice, Catherine		C 44
Russell, Catherine	June, 1883	D 615
same	Jan., 1890	F 50
Rawlings, Charles M.	Sept., 1897	G 256
Roth, Christiana	June, 1899	G 359
Riehl, Christina	April, 1902	H 262
Reichert, Casper	Sept., 1904	I 44
Rodenhauser, Catherine E.	Jan., 1905	I 74
Roberts, Christopher	Feb., 1906	I 167
Reichelt, Charles F. August	Aug., 1907	I 304
Ritter, Catharine	July, 1908	I 432
Robinson, Claude E.	Aug., 1913	K 57
Rogan, Catharine	Oct., 1913	K 70
Rohman, Casper	Nov., 1918	L 428
Rase, Catharine	July, 1919	M 60
Richardson, Charles A.	Feb., 1920	M 131
Reig, Caroline	Jan., 1922	M 395
Ryan, Catherine	June, 1923	N 70
Rose, Catherine E.	Jan., 1924	N 178

Ryan, Charles	Aug., 1930	P 210
Reynolds, Charles Correll	Nov., 1932	Q 96
Repp, Charles Sherman	Jan., 1933	Q 146
Ruppenkamp, Catherine M.	Jan., 1934	Q 342
Roeder, Christian	March, 1934	Q 383
Roby, Clifton V.	Oct., 1936	R 321
Ring, Charles S.	Oct., 1937	R 573
Robinette, Cora L.	Jan., 1938	S 41
Rockey, Charles M.	Feb., 1940	S 490
Rudolph, Conrad	May, 1942	T 390
Raley, Charles Vinant	Nov., 1944	U 399
Rankin, Clarence W.	March, 1946	V 147
Richardson, Clara	Feb., 1947	V 390
Ryland, Coleta M.	July, 1950	W 593
Rephann, Catherine	May, 1950	W 539
Rizer, Clarence Francis	Feb., 1953	X 585
Ricker, Charles Clinton	May, 1953	Y 46
Raygor, Charles William	April, 1955	Y 569
Raupach, Charles F.	Feb., 1956	Z 180
Reith, Clara G.	May, 1956	Z 243
Robinette, Charles E.	July, 1957	Z 525
Roeder, Charles A.	Aug., 1957	1 43
Reuschel, Carl G.	April, 1958	1 245
Rawlings, Caroline Virginia	July, 1960	2 485

Rice, David	Jan., 1888	E 287
Ross, David	Dec., 1896	G 199
Rohrback, Dorothea	Aug., 1900	H 119
Ritchie, David	June, 1908	I 419
Roland, David F.	Jan., 1927	O 121
Rees, Daniel L.	April, 1935	R 23
Robertson, David G.	April, 1948	W 73
Robinette, Delia	May, 1949	W 319
Root, Duncan Walter	Nov., 1950	X 47
Robertson, Dorothy I.	Aug., 1958	1 365

Russell, Elnathan		A 353
Robosson, Elijah	Feb., 1838	A 421
Robosson, Emeline	Feb., 1838	A 421
Richardson, Ellen	April, 1897	G 227

Robertson, Elizabeth	March, 1900	H 54
Reinhard, Emma	June, 1903	H 348
Ring, Elizabeth	July, 1904	I 34
Robinette, Emmaline H.	Aug., 1908	I 439
Reynolds, Ellen	Nov., 1914	K 246
Roeder, Elisabeth	March, 1916	K 491
Rhoden, Elnorah	Nov., 1916	L 77
Roman, Eloise	March, 1919	M 8
Rank, Elizabeth	Feb., 1921	M 266
Rees, Eliza	Aug., 1922	M 509
Reynolds, Ellen	July, 1923	N 101
Roberts, Elizabeth H.	Nov., 1929	P 41
Richardson, Elizabeth	March, 1931	P 333
Reynolds, Emmett	Feb., 1932	P 519
Reed, Elizabeth V.	April, 1932	P 571
Robinson, Eugenia H.	Nov., 1933	Q 315
Rephann, Emelia Catherine	Nov., 1937	R 591
Roberts, Elias J.	Jan., 1941	T 70
Rank, Elizabeth Ann	Feb., 1942	T 333
Rice, Edgar Will	March, 1943	U 26
Radcliffe, Eva B.	June, 1943	U 90
Robb, Emma L.	April, 1948	W 94
Reinhart, Ella May	July, 1948	W 153
Rooney, Ella M.	Feb., 1949	W 269
Roberts, Edwin J.	June, 1949	W 335
Roe, Elizabeth D.	April, 1950	W 524
Riggleman, Elizabeth	Sept., 1951	X 241
Reed, Edward C.	Oct., 1952	X 493
Rogan, Earl R.	Sept., 1953	Y 119
Reid, Ella Regina	Feb., 1954	Y 209
Reynolds, Edgar	Aug., 1954	Y 320
Rooney, Ellen E.	Oct., 1954	Y 384
Rees, Elizabeth	Jan., 1955	Y 442
Rexroad, Emma	May, 1955	Y 573
Roberts, Elizabeth T.	March, 1956	Z 191
Robertson, Elizabeth E.	Nov., 1957	1 101

Reid, Francis		A 398
Rice, Frederick of Andrew		A 494
Rawdon, Freeman		C 115
Robbins, Fannie S.	Dec., 1882	D 570
Rice, Fannie M.	Jan., 1886	E 156

Rossworm, Frances	July, 1889	F 26
Rees, Francis	July, 1901	H 201
Ruppenkamp, Frederick	Nov., 1907	I 331
Ricker, Frank A.	March, 1915	K 311
Rossworm, Fitus	April, 1919	M 17
Richards, Flora A.	May, 1923	N 61
Robison, Frank	Nov., 1933	Q 304
Rice, Fannie	Oct., 1934	Q 512
Rephann, Frank	Sept., 1936	R 318
Renner, Finley Smith	April, 1939	S 302
Raley, Frank C.	Aug., 1942	T 451
Rodda, Francis T.	Feb., 1946	V 134
Rowe, Frank Stuart	Jan., 1948	W 20
Rephann, Frederick	Aug., 1951	X 213
Reed, Frank L.	Aug., 1955	Z 56
Rossi, Frank	March, 1958	1 225
Rephan, Flora Jane	Feb., 1959	1 555
Ruppert, Frank J.	March, 1960	2 312

Robinette, George, Sr.		A 56
Rizer, George	Feb., 1805	A 151
Robinette, George of N.		A 318
Reinhart, George		A 461
Rice, George		B 79
Rizer, George		C 97
Riley, Geo. & Davis K. Duling	July, 1855	C 163
Rabold, George E.	Nov., 1878	D 375
Reuschlein, George	Nov., 1880	D 456
Richardson, George	April, 1890	F 82
Rossworm, George	Feb., 1892	F 260
Robinette, Gilles	Feb., 1896	G 156
Robertson, George H.	June, 1899	G 363
Reid, George M.	Oct., 1901	H 226
Rushton, George R.	March, 1904	I 4
Rainsford, George E.	Nov., 1905	I 150
Robinette, George E. W.	May, 1906	I 204
Reid, George	Oct., 1908	I 460
Reidler, George	April, 1922	M 448
Rice, George F.	Aug., 1923	N 112
Ridenbaugh, George W.	Aug., 1924	N 298
Robinson, George S.	Feb., 1931	P 300
Rice, George Parry Samuel	March, 1931	P 335

Ruppert, George W.	June, 1932	Q 17
Reuschel, George	Nov., 1933	Q 308
Reinhard, George A.	Sept., 1934	Q 492
Reuschlein, George	Jan., 1936	R 165
Rephorn, George	March, 1936	R 217
Rice, George Wesley	Feb., 1937	R 422
Robinette, George B.	Nov., 1939	S 427
Rodenhauser, George	Feb., 1940	S 497
Reese, Grace S.	June, 1942	T 416
Reed, Grover C.	Nov., 1942	T 524
Robinson, George W.	May, 1943	U 80
Reuschline, George L.	Nov., 1945	V 77
Rowley, Gertrude	March, 1946	V 149
Ridgway, George William	Oct., 1951	X 255
Rice, Goldie L.	Nov., 1953	Y 164
Robison, George M.	May, 1954	Y 265
Ruhl, George	Dec., 1956	Z 402

Ross, Henry		B 143
Rohrback, Harmon		B 194
Ruekle, Henry		C 67
Rembold, Henry	Feb., 1879	D 391
Rephann, Henry	March, 1894	G 28
Rompf, Herman	Aug., 1899	G 366
Rehs, Henry	Aug., 1899	G 368
Rank, Henry	March, 1904	I 7
Ryan, Hannah	Sept., 1906	I 224
Robinson, Harriet	June, 1907	I 289
Roberts, Hilleary F.	Oct., 1919	M 85
Reuschlein, Henry	March, 1928	O 317
Randall, Honorah H.	May, 1931	P 374
Roberts, Hannah	Aug., 1934	Q 478
Roman, Henry A.	May, 1935	R 28
Ruehl, Henry	Feb., 1936	R 188
Rice, Harriet A.	March, 1937	R 450
Rizer, Hervey Lee	Jan., 1939	S 253
Radcliffe, Harry Richard	April, 1940	S 541
Robinson, Howard T.	Dec., 1942	T 553
Ruppenthal, H.M.	July, 1945	V 11
Rector, Harry A.	Nov., 1945	V 81
Rice, Hannah C.	March, 1946	V 144
Richmond, Hannah	March, 1947	V 427

Ruppert, Henry A.	Nov., 1949	W 437
Robinson, Hazel M.	May, 1950	W 546
Rephan, Howard	April, 1951	X 155
Ricker, Henry Ludwig	Jan., 1953	X 567
Roemmelmeyer, H.D.	Feb., 1955	Y 462
Rainalter, Herman C.	Oct., 1955	Z 81
Rowe, Harry R.	May, 1957	Z 546
Richard, Herbert N.	June, 1957	Z 559
Rannells, Hettie V.	Dec., 1958	1 473

Richards, Isaac	Sept., 1887	E 256
Roby, Isabella	April, 1922	M 447
Rockkind, Isaac	March, 1928	O 313
Rosenbaum, Ira	Jan., 1932	P 505
Ravenscroft, Ida B.	June, 1944	U 319
Richards, Ida Bell	March, 1945	U 479
Ryan, Ira Talmage	Aug., 1951	X 223
Rosenberg, Isidor	Jan., 1956	Z 153
Rhoads, Ida M.	Feb., 1960	2 298

Reid, John M.		A 203
Rice, John		A 217
Robinette Joseph		A 356
Robinette, Jasper	Aug., 1836	A 396
Rutan, John		A 434
Rush, John		A 500
Rhind, John	June, 1864	C 38
Ritter, Jacob	May, 1866	C 76
Robertson, James		C 78
Ramsey, Jane C.		C 83
Rizer, Jacob	Jan., 1866	C 89
Ross, James	Jan., 1869	C 130
Roman, J. Philip	March, 1871	C 191
Russell, John E.	Jan., 1872	C 213
Ries, John	Sept., 1872	D 48
Rhind, John	Nov., 1875	D 252
Rice, Joshua	April, 1876	D 267
Rabold, John C.	Nov., 1878	D 374
Reynolds, John	July, 1880	D 452
Ross, Julia A.	Nov., 1887	E 274

Robinette, Jasper	Oct., 1892	F 326
Ryland, Jacob	May, 1894	G 43
Robinette, Jeremy	Dec., 1895	G 149
Ravenscroft, John F.	March, 1900	H 56
Rodda, Justus A.	March, 1900	H 75
Reese, John David	May, 1901	H 190
Rephann, John	July, 1904	I 35
Rogan, John	Nov., 1907	I 332
Riehl, John	May, 1908	I 395
Rizer, Jacob	May, 1909	J 46
Ricker, John	April, 1910	J 152
Robinette, Jesse	March, 1915	K 309
Rankin, Jane	April, 1915	K 323
Resley, John Mac L.	Jan., 1916	K 463
Rees, John B.	March, 1916	K 495
Reed, James	Dec., 1916	L 90
Rankin, James A.	Jan., 1919	L 452
Rowley, Jane	May, 1919	M 42
Ruppenkamp, Joseph H.	Nov., 1919	M 91
Robinette, John C.	Aug., 1920	M 193
Roth, John M.	Feb., 1924	N 213
Ruppert, Jacob W.	July, 1924	N 292
Robb, Josephine M.	July, 1924	N 294
Reuschlein, John W.	Oct., 1924	N 333
Ruppert, Joseph H.	Feb., 1926	N 548
Roberts, Jane H.	June, 1926	O 20
Rephan, Justus	July, 1927	O 194
Robinette, Jeremiah	Sept., 1927	O 246
Rupp, John	June, 1928	O 352
Ruppenkamp, John Frederick	June, 1928	O 353
Roberts, J.B.G.	Aug., 1929	O 584
Root, James E.	Aug., 1929	O 585
Robertson, J.F.	Jan., 1930	P 87
Regel, Johanna	July, 1930	P 184
Rees, James B.	Oct., 1930	P 241
Raflo, Jennie	Feb., 1931	P 304
Retzer, Joseph	March, 1931	P 336
Ravenscroft, John F.	April, 1932	P 569
Reid, James Alfred	June, 1932	Q 29
Rankin, James, Sr.	Oct., 1932	Q 90
Rank, John	Nov., 1932	Q 100
Rohman, John J.N.	May, 1933	Q 211
Rowan, James J.	July, 1933	Q 252
Reed, Johanna	Jan., 1934	Q 345

Race, Lewis	Jan., 1879	D 378
Rank, Lewis	March, 1889	E 376
Rosenmerkel, Luther	March, 1910	J 129
Rice, Laura	June, 1914	K 199
Rice, Lydia M.G.	Jan., 1917	L 119
Rank, Louis	April, 1922	M 442
Riley, Laban	Jan., 1924	N 187
Raupach, Lydia V.	June, 1926	O 24
Rush, Luverna	March, 1928	O 323
Rice, Lee Andy Jackson	March, 1929	O 489
Robertson, Lillie May	May, 1932	P 580
Rice, Lizzie J.	March, 1937	R 440
Rowell, Louis Osgood	June, 1943	U 101
Rosenbaum, Lewis	Feb., 1948	W 43
Richards, Lydia	April, 1948	W 77
Ruby, Leona Nora	Dec., 1951	X 271
Rawlings, Lloyd	June, 1954	Y 282
Riley, Louis	April, 1956	Z 217
Read, Louisa A.	June, 1957	Z 552
Rusmisel, Levi Clyde	Feb., 1960	2 300

Robinette, Moses		A 106
Rizer, Mary Magdalena		A 293
Rawlings, Moses	Feb., 1839	A 433
same	Feb., 1840	A 457
same	Feb., 1841	A 479
same	Feb., 1842	A 499
same	Jan., 1843	A 507
same	Feb., 1844	A 535
Rizer, Martin, Jr.	Feb., 1845	A 545
same	Feb., 1846	A 591
same	Feb., 1847	A 616
Rawlings, Moses	Nov., 1855	B 98
same	Nov., 1859	B 172
Ransom, Mary E.	June, 1862	C 48
same	Dec., 1864	C 44
Rizer, Mary	Jan., 1866	C 89
Riley, Margaret	Oct., 1869	C 153
Ross, Moses A.	Sept., 1870	C 177
Resh, Matthias	Sept., 1870	C 178
Rabold, Matthias Y.	May, 1884	E 61
Russell, Martha	Nov., 1884	E 84

Rausch, Mattie	Aug., 1951	X 220
Rees, Mary C.	Oct., 1953	Y 133
Rosenmerkel, Mollie J.	Nov., 1954	Y 416
Ryland, Mary E.	March, 1955	Y 473
Retallick, Mary Ann	May, 1955	Y 591
Rank, Mary J.	Sept., 1955	Z 63
Rose, Mary C.	Nov., 1955	Z 112
Rice, Millard M.	Sept., 1957	1 58
Race, Milton W.	Feb., 1958	1 198
Reed, Mary E.	Sept., 1958	1 385
Rusmisel, Margaret L.	June, 1959	2 34

Robinette, Nathan		A 377
Ridgely, Nancy		B 122
Read, Nelson C., Sr.	Aug., 1886	E 204
Read, Nelson C.	June, 1907	I 278
Robinson, Nannie F.	Jan., 1951	K 268
Rawlings, Newton T.	June, 1916	L 11
Ryland, Norman F.	April, 1921	M 296
Reider, Nicholas	June, 1925	N 441
Randall, Norman L.	March, 1953	Y 11
Russler, Nelson W.	Aug., 1957	1 52

Rice, Olin R.	Jan., 1928	O 298
Robison, Olin D.	July, 1932	Q 46
Rice, O.E.	Sept., 1935	R 96
Rodenhauser, Oscar W.	Dec., 1944	U 417
Ruehl, Otto Henry	March, 1958	1 214
Ryan, Okey C.	Oct., 1960	2 589

Rahrig, Peter	Aug., 1885	E 132
Rafferty, Patrick	April, 1908	I 380
Raybould, Phoebe	Jan., 1914	K 120
Rogers, Patrick	Dec., 1916	L 93
This will revoked and set aside, Court Proceedings Liber 22, Folios 316 to 340		
Rogers, Patrick	Jan., 1917	L 105
Rooney, Patrick	April, 1922	M 445

Renner, Sarah P.	May, 1939	S 318
Rephann, Sarah Alice	May, 1942	T 401
Rice, Sarah E.	Jan., 1943	T 596
Roland, Sarah	June, 1946	V 242
Richards, Sarah Ella	Feb., 1948	W 36
Robson, Sol	Sept., 1950	X 11
Reid, S. Margaret	Jan., 1952	X 286
Ruehl, Sophia C.	Nov., 1952	X 526
Ritchie, Sarah	Dec., 1958	1 499

Reid, Thomas		A 177
Robosson, Thomas		A 419
Riley, Tobias		A 515
Ryland, Thomas		B 19
Reichert, Therese	Nov., 1904	I 60
Rice, Thomas B.	Aug., 1907	I 306
Rowe, Thomas	Nov., 1910	J 203
Richards, Thomas Milton	May, 1912	J 427
Ross, Truman F.	Dec., 1920	M 240
Ruppert, Teresa	July, 1922	M 496
Richards, Thomas Davis	Nov., 1938	S 196
Rosenbaum, Toni	Feb., 1947	V 402
Reinhart, Thomas D.	March, 1948	W 64
Richardson, Thomas	Aug., 1949	W 382
Reichert, Theresa M.	Dec., 1949	W 448
Ryan, Tobitha	Aug., 1951	X 221
Rider, Theresa Elizabeth	Nov., 1953	Y 168
Richardson, Thomas W.	Jan., 1959	1 518
Rahrig, Thomas O.	March, 1960	2 340

Raley, Vincent	Oct., 1895	G 138
Rahrig, Valentine	Jan., 1908	I 354
Robertson, Viola P.	Nov., 1938	S 188
Roberts, Vincent E.	Feb., 1940	S 482
Rossnova, Vincenza	Feb., 1946	V 130
Rieg, Vincent I.	Feb., 1959	1 561
Rice, Verdie May	Dec., 1960	3 52

S

Scott, Ann	Nov., 1832	A 333
Smith, Alexander		A 436
Scott, Ann		A 529
Sides, Aaron		A 655
Selby, Arthur		B 150
Stark, Adam	Nov., 1870	C 183
Steinlein, Adam	July, 1871	C 201
Sloan, Alex and Sarah	Nov., 1873	D 129
Sloan, Alexander	Oct., 1874	D 173
Shepherd, Amos P.	May, 1875	D 209
Spier, Andrew	Jan., 1887	E 219
Scott, Archer	May, 1891	F 191
Shuck, Albert G.	Sept., 1892	F 316
Saylor, Anna	Oct., 1892	F 325
Shuck, Albert G., estate of.	Feb., 1894	G 22
Schriver, Anthony	Oct., 1902	H 293
Shaw, Alexander	July, 1905	I 121
Siebert, Adam	Dec., 1907	I 344
Somerville, Agnes	Jan., 1908	I 349
Schyler, Andrew	June, 1909	J 44
Sloan, Ann	Aug., 1910	J 186
Seifarth, Andrew, Sr.	Oct., 1913	K 88
Seifert, Albert	Feb., 1915	K 293
Smith, Albert F.	June, 1918	L 385
Snyder, Andrew H.	Aug., 1923	N 116
Somerville, Archibald A.	April, 1924	N 240
Stromberg, Annie J.	Feb., 1925	N 381
Shupe, Annie E.	July, 1925	N 447
Spier, Andrew	July, 1925	N 454
Shahan, Albert	Feb., 1926	N 529
Shaw, Andrew B.	Aug., 1927	O 224
Shinholtz, Asa H.	Jan., 1928	O 291
Shuck, Anna M.	March, 1928	O 321
Smyth, Andrew A.	Feb., 1929	O 477
Schleuss, Albert V.	April, 1929	O 514
Spitznas, Anna Martha	April, 1929	O 523
Stubblefield, Anna Fox	Oct., 1929	P 18
Swimley, Asbury C.	Jan., 1930	P 80
Smith, Albert	Feb., 1930	P 100

Shellhori, Balsor		A 29
Skimmings, Barbara		B 168
Seve, Bernard	1866	C 71
Spriggs, Burgess	Feb., 1873	D 90
Simpkins, B.B.	April, 1873	D 108
Stern, Bernard	Dec., 1895	G 145
same	Dec., 1895	G 147
Shipley, Bernard D.	Sept., 1902	H 290
Shuck, Benjamin W.	Dec., 1911	J 359
Slater, Beuna V.	May, 1914	K 174
Sturtz, Bessie G.	Jan., 1923	M 579
Shearer, Bessie	Oct., 1930	P 236
Slezak, Berta	June, 1939	S 333
Stahl, Bettie W.	April, 1942	T 384
Stickley, Bertha E.	April, 1943	U 34
Smith, Bessie	Jan., 1947	V 379
Stark, Bessie M.	March, 1951	X 137

Squire, Catherine		A 151
Smith, Christian		A 610
Smith, Catherine	Jan., 1855	B 89
Smouse, Catherine		B 133
Stotler, Christian		B 154
Somercamp, Charles F.	Jan., 1870	C 160
Shriver, C.C.	Nov., 1873	D 132
Slack, Cornelius	July, 1874	D 173
same	Nov., 1875	D 251
Staup, Catherine	Feb., 1874	D 221
Slack, Cornelius	June, 1877	D 331
Steele, Claude	Dec., 1883	E 2
Schiller, Conrad	Nov., 1887	E 276
Shober, Casper C.		F 151
Saturday, Charles	Feb., 1892	F 264
Seifker, Conrad E.	Jan., 1893	F 336
Schulz, Catherine	Aug., 1894	G 60
Smith, Conrad	Oct., 1896	G 190
Schaidt, Catherine	Aug., 1899	G 370
Sonnenberg, Charles	June, 1901	H 192
Shuck, Charles H.	Jan., 1902	H 245
Schmidt, Christian Frederick	May, 1903	H 335
Schramm, Christina	Oct., 1903	H 376
Schneider, Conrad	Oct., 1910	J 198

Sluss, Charles	Oct., 1914	K 232
Shaw, Caroline E.	Nov., 1914	K 243
Shaffer, Caroline	Sept., 1915	K 398
Stickley, Charles	July, 1916	L 28
Shea, Catharine	June, 1917	L 203
Shannon, Charles T.	Feb., 1918	L 315
Schadt, Conrad	June, 1918	L 376
Spitznas, Charles A.	June, 1918	L 382
Smith, Charles C.	Aug., 1918	L 398
Speelman, Charles H.	Oct., 1918	L 421
Stewart, Charles	March, 1920	M 138
Shafer, Charlottie	Jan., 1921	M 247
Sommerlott, Charles, Sr.	May, 1922	M 461
Showacre, Charles F.	Sept., 1923	N 134
Stotlemyer, Christina	Feb., 1924	N 208
Starner, Charles H.	April, 1924	N 254
Schwankhaus, Catherine	Dec., 1924	N 356
Stowers, Charles G.	May, 1927	O 179
Schlundt, Catherine	June, 1927	O 180
Sonnerberg, Catherine	Jan., 1929	O 452
Smith, Caroline McLain	April, 1929	O 516
Scudder, Chauncey T.	Oct., 1929	P 17
Spriggs, Charles T.Z.	June, 1930	P 173
Stark, Charles W.	March, 1932	P 551
Schoenadel, Charles Wm.	Aug., 1932	Q 47
Spoerl, Clara B.	April, 1933	Q 191
Straub, Catherine Magdalene	May, 1936	R 253
Small, Charles Franklin	Aug., 1936	R 285
Schuh, Charles	April, 1937	R 465
Strohmenger, Clara C.	April, 1938	S 73
Smith, Conrad G.	Oct., 1938	S 163
Snyder, Catherine C.	March, 1939	S 276
Sively, Charles P.	Feb., 1941	T 86
Smith, Charles Edward	June, 1941	T 156
Shaffer, Clara V.	May, 1943	U 79
Schoenadel, Charles	May, 1945	U 550
Sturtz, Cora Jane	July, 1945	V 6
Schultz, Clara	Nov., 1945	V 86
Stewart, Clay Wilson	April, 1946	V 197
Shroyer, Cora M.	June, 1947	V 492
Shanholtz, Charles W.	Oct., 1947	V 562
Schutz, Charles A.	May, 1948	W 109
Shaffer, Caroline K.	Feb., 1949	W 265
Smouse, Charles Arthur	March, 1951	X 135

Sampsell, Cora M.	April, 1951	X 160
Springer, Carrie	Sept., 1951	X 238
Simpson, Charles J.	Feb., 1952	X 313
Strong, Carrie Messman	May, 1952	X 387
Smith, Charles G.	Dec., 1953	Y 182
Sander, Carl A.	Dec., 1954	Y 421
Shaffer, Charles Wesley	Jan., 1955	Y 446
Steiner, Carrie W.	March, 1956	Z 187
Stevenson, Catherine	March, 1956	Z 201
Seaver, Clara T. Walsh	April, 1956	Z 224
Smith, Charles	April, 1957	Z 514
Schmutz, Carl F.	May, 1957	Z 527
Stein, Clarence H.	June, 1957	Z 554
Smith, Charles H.	Jan., 1958	1 147
Schlund, Charles Edward	May, 1958	1 276
Stegmaier, Clara Catherine	Aug., 1958	1 368
Smith, Charles L.	April, 1959	2 11
Shumaker, Clara Barbara	June, 1959	2 54
Shriver, Clifton V.	Aug., 1959	2 132
Stickley, Charity M.	March, 1960	2 323
Schafer, Clarence F.	April, 1960	2 375
Sisk, Carl M.	Dec., 1960	3 48

Simpkins, Dickerson		A 296
Shriver, David		B 53
Smouse, Daniel		B 125
Sullivan, Daniel		E 284
Steyer, Daniel R.		F 189
Street, Enos A.	May, 1892	F 298
Seckman, David F.	May, 1893	F 364
Schneider, Dorothea	Sept., 1894	G 63
Stewart, D. Shriver	Oct., 1897	G 259
Sparks, D.F.	Feb., 1902	H 254
Sloan, David	June, 1908	I 416
Smyth, David K.	May, 1915	K 298
Smith, Denton	April, 1923	N 35
Schleigh, Daniel H.	July, 1924	N 283
Smouse, Daniel	July, 1929	O 580
Sloan, Duncan R.	June, 1934	Q 458
Sloan, Dixon Connolly	June, 1947	V 502
Scott, Delia Hollingsworth	Oct., 1949	W 421
Smith, Daisy	Nov., 1955	Z 114

Smith, Della Estella	Feb., 1957	Z 446
Stakem, Daniel	Aug., 1957	1 45
Steele, David M.	Nov., 1959	2 206

Shipley, Eliza		A 505
Swearengen, Eli		A 558
Scott, Eliza	March, 1834	A 347
Spellman, Edmond		C 13
Stone, Earl S.	Nov., 1864	C 42
Sigler, Elizabeth		C 96
Spangler, Elizabeth	June, 1865	C 72
Stark, Elizabeth	Nov., 1870	C 184
Steinlein, Eleanora	Jan., 1872	C 212
Sultzer, Emma		D 8
Semmes, Eleanora	Jan., 1875	D 196
Street, Enos A.	May, 1892	F 298
Shuck, Eliza L.	Sept., 1893	F 393
Shuck, Edward E.	Feb., 1894	G 22
Shuck, Elizabeth C.	Feb., 1894	G 22
Stewart, Elizabeth	April, 1895	G 107
Shriver, Edwin T.	Feb., 1896	G 158
Sharp, Ellen	Jan., 1901	H 145
Smith, Eliza	Dec., 1902	H 299
Stubblefield, Ellen S.	March, 1906	I 178
Sullivan, Ellen	June, 1908	I 414
Stephens, Eliza	Oct., 1910	J 197
Strube, Elizabeth	Sept., 1912	J 458
Sloan, Elizabeth A.	Dec., 1915	K 403
Sullivan, Ellis L.	Feb., 1919	L 488
Shields, Edward H.	April, 1919	M 34
Sturtz, Ellen	June, 1919	M 51
Snyder, Ella F.	Feb., 1921	M 274
Skidmore, Elsie T.	Oct., 1921	M 375
Smith, Ernest	July, 1922	M 493
Steiding, Elizabeth J.	June, 1923	N 84
Schilling, Edward	Feb., 1925	N 387
Stakem, Ellen	Sept., 1929	O 592
Shiffler, Ellen G.	Dec., 1929	P 64
Seifarth, Elizabeth	Feb., 1930	P 108
Stitcher, Ellen L.	Oct., 1930	P 238
Shaw, E. Lee	Dec., 1930	P 262
Stottler, Emma C.	Feb., 1931	P 310

Spaight, Edward J.	Dec., 1932	Q 119
Stakem, Esther M.	Feb., 1933	Q 162
Spicer, Edward B.	Nov., 1933	Q 310
Sampsell, Edward H.	March, 1935	R 2
Sprigg, Ellen B.	Feb., 1936	R 195
Swart, Edgar	Aug., 1939	S 377
Sellers, Ella C.	Sept., 1939	S 387
Schramm, Ernest	Feb., 1940	S 498
Sanner, Elizabeth M.	May, 1940	S 546
Strieby, E. Grace	Jan., 1941	T 68
Showacre, Edward A.	April, 1941	T 117
Shaffer, Effie A.	Nov., 1941	T 267
Sanner, Emma K.	Dec., 1942	T 570
Shearer, Elizabeth G.	Aug., 1944	U 341
Skidmore, Elijah E.	May, 1945	U 565
See, Elizabeth Wachter	Feb., 1946	V 124
Smith, Edward L.	May, 1946	V 228
Sell, Emma M.	Dec., 1948	W 251
Stone, Emma C.	Aug., 1949	W 357
Smith, Esther J.	April, 1950	W 520
Schramm, Elizabeth	Jan., 1951	X 99
Steele, Elizabeth	Sept., 1951	X 243
Schaidt, Ernest F.	June, 1952	X 408
Seem, Emma R.	Aug., 1954	Y 332
Smallwood, Edith M.	Jan., 1955	Y 444
Stegmaier, Elizabeth Mary	June, 1955	Z 24
Stowell, Edward A.	Jan., 1956	Z 142
Sloan, Ella Frederick	Sept., 1956	Z 341
Shoupe, Elizabeth B.	June, 1957	Z 548
Stafford, Eleanor Osborne	July, 1957	1 6
Schmutz, Esther C.	March, 1958	1 215
Scott, Elva Claire	Sept., 1958	1 383
Sollars, Ellwood	Nov., 1958	1 460
Spence, Ella M.	May, 1959	2 31
Shuck, Edgar W.	July, 1959	2 87

Sapp, Frederick		A 163
Shriver, Fred. Wm.		B 97
Schilling, Frederick	July, 1871	C 199
Seuff, Fred. Chas. Theodore	April, 1885	E 106
Seiss, Francis	Dec., 1885	E 148
Screen, Francis	Dec., 1901	H 232

Schlund, George	July, 1907	I 297
Small, George	July, 1914	K 214
Sills, George W.	Nov., 1916	L 74
Schafer, George F.	May, 1917	L 179
Shaffer, G. Henry	June, 1917	L 210
Stark, George H.	Oct., 1917	L 258
Stucklauser, Gustav	April, 1918	L 350
Stephenson, Gavin R.	Aug., 1918	L 400
Smith, George C.	Feb., 1921	M 261
Stark, George	Feb., 1922	M 420
Sanders, George C.	July, 1922	M 492
Staup, George W.	Sept., 1924	N 321
Sell, G. Albert	June, 1925	N 437
Schwarzenbach, George	March, 1926	N 574
Smith, George	Jan., 1928	O 305
Sell, George J.	Feb., 1928	O 309
Seifarth, George	April, 1929	O 532
Sturtz, George	Oct., 1929	P 32
Stafford, George W.	April, 1930	P 137
Schriver, George	April, 1931	P 346
Schmutz, George J.	Sept., 1932	Q 69
Snyder, George A.	Jan., 1933	Q 136
Shoemaker, Grace C.	July, 1934	Q 464
Savage, George M.	April, 1935	R 14
Schafer, George J.	May, 1936	R 254
Shaffer, George Washington	Aug., 1936	R 304
Sharrett, George O.	Sept., 1936	R 309
Shuck, George C.	Dec., 1936	R 353
Steckman, George C.	May, 1937	R 501
Schwarzenbach, George	June, 1939	S 349
Swach, George J.	July, 1941	T 180
Stitcher, George J.	Aug., 1941	T 214
Stern, George	March, 1942	T 341
Schaidt, Gustave	May, 1942	T 388
Shoemaker, George Guy	May, 1944	U 302
Stotlemyer, George W.	Feb., 1946	V 123
Schultz, George H.	Nov., 1946	V 354
Shipper, George	Nov., 1946	V 356
Sliger, George T.	April, 1947	V 450
Sowers, Geneva	Aug., 1947	V 541
Stump, Genevieve Anna	Nov., 1947	V 581
Schade, George	June, 1948	W 139
Shaffer, George L.	May, 1950	W 547
Smith, George Albert	Sept., 1952	X 477

Schad, Henrya	Nov., 1939	S 430
Schmidt, Helen V.	Nov., 1939	S 437
Sanner, Harry D.	May, 1940	S 547
Sauser, Harry S.	April, 1941	T 125
Smith, Henry Clay	June, 1941	T 160
Spiker, Harry G.	March, 1942	T 349
Smith, Harry L.	Oct., 1942	T 492
Schaidt, Henry W.	Dec., 1946	V 364
Sweene, Henry J.	March, 1948	W 67
Seem, Harrison E.	Feb., 1949	W 272
Shaw, Henry C.	June, 1949	W 341
Sheffler, Hannah	March, 1951	X 120
Sharp, H. Hall	Nov., 1954	Y 402
Sturtz, Henry	Aug., 1955	Z 60
Strieby, Harry E.	May, 1956	Z 227
Smith, Harry L.	Dec., 1956	Z 409
Seaber, Harry W.	July, 1958	1 358
Smith, Harold Watson	Feb., 1960	2 296
Schwarzenbach, Henrietta	Oct., 1960	2 599

Smenner, Isabella M.	March, 1863	C 20
Schupfer, Ignatius	Aug., 1892	F 309
Swain, Isaac O.	April, 1894	G 30
Smith, Isaac	Oct., 1900	H 124
Sinclair, Isabella	Feb., 1901	H 153
Somerville, Isabella C.	May, 1915	K 347
Smith, Isaac H.	Feb., 1929	O 483
Stegmaier, Ignatius B.	Feb., 1934	Q 373
Shuey, Ida Virginia	Dec., 1934	Q 551
Shearer, Isaac	Dec., 1936	R 360
Stakem, Isaac A.	May, 1948	W 114
Sparks, Isabella	July, 1948	W 157
Steinla, Irene G.	May, 1949	W 313
Schafter, Ilda Turner	July, 1949	W 344
Spiker, Isabel E.	Nov., 1952	X 505
Stafford, Ira Hayes	July, 1957	1 1

Schellhaus, John P.	Aug., 1873	D 116
Stewart, Janet	April, 1875	D 205
Sloan, John	March, 1877	D 322
Schilling, John Conrad	Jan., 1879	D 384
Stephens, James	May, 1880	D 448
Spiker, John & wife	July, 1880	D 460
Scherzer, John B.	April, 1881	D 480
Somerville, John	Jan., 1883	D 586
Smith, John	Nov., 1884	E 87
Searight, Joseph D.	Feb., 1885	E 99
Smith, John	July, 1885	E 130
Smouse, John J.	April, 1886	E 183
Shriver, Joseph	Aug., 1887	E 254
Shuck, Jacob	Feb., 1888	E 300
Schilling, John	June, 1889	E 394
Schaidt, John C.		F 47
Swift, John	April, 1890	F 81
Smith, James M.	Sept., 1890	F 120
Steyer, John B.		F 189
Steyer, Jacob		F 189
Schachte, Joseph		F 255
Stover, James, Sr.	Nov., 1891	F 247
Stover, John F.	Sept., 1892	F 314
Sander, John W.	Sept., 1896	G 188
Smith, Joseph	Oct., 1899	G 388
Shannon, John B.	Dec., 1899	H 1
Stewart, James	Feb., 1901	H 146
Schilling, John Conrad	March, 1901	H 154
Sloan, Jennette	April, 1901	H 174
Sheridan, John	Feb., 1902	H 252
Schaidt, John	Oct., 1904	I 51
Seiss, J. Frank	Dec., 1904	I 63
Shaw, John	April, 1905	I 95
Saul, John	Feb., 1907	I 261
Steckman, Johnson	April, 1907	I 270
Shupe, Jacob B.	June, 1907	I 279
Smith, John	July, 1910	J 176
Stewart, John	Sept., 1910	J 180
Stevens, James	Aug., 1911	J 309
Stevens, John	Nov., 1913	K 102
Sturts, John	Nov., 1913	K 104
Skilling, John D.	Feb., 1915	K 289
Snyder, John H.	July, 1915	K 380
Sloan, John	Oct., 1915	K 409

Sigler, John	Feb., 1940	S 488
Sell, John F.	April, 1940	S 545
Stegmaier, Joseph V.	May, 1940	S 570
Stitcher, Joseph F.	May, 1940	S 571
Scott, Jean	Sept., 1940	T 15
Squires, John E.	Oct., 1940	T 22
Schaefer, John	June, 1941	T 163
Sloan, James M.	Sept., 1941	T 243
Schauwecker, John F.	Oct., 1941	T 249
Spear, J. Hall	Oct., 1941	T 258
Scheller, John A.	March, 1942	T 355
Smith, J. George	March, 1943	U 17
Somerville, John F.	Sept., 1943	U 169
Shaffer, John R.	Aug., 1944	U 358
Shaw, John K.	June, 1945	U 566
Schmidt, John	June, 1945	U 593
Shaffer, John L.	Oct., 1945	V 61
Stewart, Joseph C.	April, 1946	V 185
Spoerl, John P.	April, 1947	V 435
Steen, Joseph W.	Nov., 1947	V 578
Shriver, James C.	Feb., 1948	W 35
Shaw, James P.	April, 1948	W 70
Shaw, John K.	June, 1948	W 125
Stewart, John Marshall	May, 1949	W 311
Summers, James O.	Aug., 1949	W 367
Stump, John J.	Dec., 1949	W 455
Snyder, John W.	Feb., 1950	W 475
Seggie, James Lenard	Aug., 1950	W 618
Smith, Joseph J.	Jan., 1951	X 87
Seaders, John F.	Oct., 1951	X 249
Sweene, John A., Sr.	June, 1952	X 399
Smith, John Henry	Feb., 1952	X 333
Sigler, John William	Sept., 1954	Y 348
Stark, Joseph R.	March, 1955	Y 493
Scott, James H., Sr.	May, 1955	Y 579
Schwarzenbach, John	June, 1955	Z 9
Spiker, Jacob M.	June, 1955	Z 18
Singer, John A.	Sept., 1955	Z 69
Stickley, James W.	June, 1956	Z 266
Stewart, James A.	July, 1956	Z 294
Stafford, John Miller	Jan., 1957	Z 428
Sutherland, James H.A.	Jan., 1957	Z 434
Shiflett, John J.	March, 1957	Z 477
Sturtz, Jonathan Walter	Sept., 1957	1 73

Shepherd, Lucius P.	Aug., 1920	M 196
Spier, Louis	Oct., 1920	M 227
Shaffer, Lucy K.	June, 1922	M 480
Stratton, Lula Louise	March, 1924	N 235
Stein, Louis	March, 1926	N 553
Schadt, Louisa	July, 1926	O 29
Shuckhart, Linnie	March, 1927	O 149
Swankhaus, Lena M.	July, 1927	O 198
Smith, L. McClellan	June, 1929	O 566
Stewart, Lucy Cleveland	Sept., 1929	P 9
Stott, Laura Davis	July, 1933	Q 246
Stevens, Lloydburton	Feb., 1935	Q 587
Smith, Laura V.	Aug., 1935	R 92
Shaffer, Lloyd L.	Aug., 1937	R 537
Smith, Lydia	Sept., 1941	T 229
Schaidt, Leander, Sr.	June, 1943	U 93
Stump, Lawson (Mrs.)	June, 1943	U 100
Shryock, Lucy Willson	March, 1945	U 485
Sindy, Leroy Wallace	Nov., 1946	V 344
Shaffer, Louisa K.	Aug., 1952	X 646
Struckman, Lena Barley	Nov., 1956	Z 391
Shafer, Lottie May	March, 1957	Z 466
Smith, Lillian Wright	Feb., 1958	1 189
Seaman, Lee Herbert	Nov., 1958	1 444
Soterakos, Louis P.)		2 574
Soterakos, Leonidas)	Sept., 1960	

Snook, Matthias	Dec., 1790	A 1
Slicer, Mary		A 223
Soyster, Michael		A 473
Scott, Martha	March, 1834	A 347
Stotler, Maria	Feb., 1852	B 50
Shryer, Mary Cathe		B 177
Startzman, Mary	April, 1867	C 139
Stewart, Miller & Patsy E.	Nov., 1869	C 155
Strominger, Michael	March, 1871	C 193
Semler, Martin	Jan., 1872	C 215
Snyder, Mary	Oct., 1872	D 54
Schindler, Mary	Feb., 1881	D 469
Shugh, Mary J.	Dec., 1883	E 5
Steyer, Margaret	Dec., 1889	
Shober, Margaret		F 151

Schutz, Mary Jane	Feb., 1939	S 284
Shryock, Mabel	April, 1939	S 315
Stevens, Minnie	May, 1939	S 330
Schulz, Minnie M.	Dec., 1939	S 444
Swauger, Mary E.	Jan., 1940	S 467
Stafford, Martha	Oct., 1940	T 25
Skilling, Margaret E.	Nov., 1941	T 289
Strohmenger, Mary S.	Jan., 1943	T 586
Straub, Mary M.	Jan., 1943	T 600
Shaffer, Margaret B.	April, 1943	U 38
Shaffer, Mary K.	June, 1943	U 106
Smith, Mary Amanda	Aug., 1943	U 133
Shepherd, Mary L.	Oct., 1943	U 177
Sigler, Maria (Mrs. W.T.)	Dec., 1943	U 211
Scott, Marion D.	June, 1944	U 322
Sell, Michael	April, 1945	U 515
Scott, Mollie L.	July, 1945	V 3
Stitcher, Mary E.	Aug., 1945	V 17
Stallings, Mary Elizabeth	Oct., 1945	V 53
Sibley, Minnie Ida	Nov., 1945	V 82
Smith, Mary B.	April, 1946	V 164
Stern, Martha W.	Oct., 1946	V 322
Shuck, Minerva Elizabeth	Feb., 1949	W 279
Shaw, Mary E.	June, 1949	W 337
Seibert, Mary M.	July, 1950	W 604
Schulte, Myrtle D.	Nov., 1952	X 509
Shroyer, Minnie	May, 1953	Y 34
Shupe, Minnie	Nov., 1954	Y 395
Shaffer, Mary Agnes	Feb., 1955	Y 455
Sloan, Mary Elizabeth	June, 1955	Z 16
Stuby, Melissa C.	Nov., 1955	Z 110
Sloan, Mary Virginia	Jan., 1956	Z 151
Stegmaier, Michael L.	March, 1956	Z 182
Stafford, Mary	March, 1957	Z 493
Smith, Matilda	Dec., 1957	1 130
Skelley, Michael W.	March, 1958	1 223
Sharp, Matilda M.	March, 1959	1 570
Snyder, Mary Ellen	July, 1959	2 103
Shultice, Mary E.	May, 1960	2 417
Seifert, M. Edna	Nov., 1960	3 33

Smouse, Peter Bender	Dec., 1953	Y 178
Schultz, Paul J.	Feb., 1956	Z 172
Stakem, Patrick J.	Aug., 1959	2 143
Staup, Peter	Dec., 1960	3 54

Swan, Robert	Nov., 1824	A 229
same	Feb., 1825	A 237
same	March, 1826	A 250
same	Oct., 1830	A 305
same		A 378
Spangler, Rebecca		B 153
Saylor, Rachel	April, 1867	C 95
Smalley, Rose	May, 1873	D 110
Semmes, R.T.& A.H.B.	Feb., 1875	D 281
Schaidt, Rosena		F 47
Starrett, Rebecca	April, 1893	F 352
Somerville, Robert A.	Jan., 1904	H 390
Snively, Robert	Feb., 1909	J 14
Sipes, Rosilla	July, 1909	J 64
Somerville, Robert L.	March, 1911	J 284
Shriver, Robert	March, 1912	J 403
Snyder, Ross K.	Dec., 1914	K 262
Siegmund, Rosella	April, 1921	M 308
Smith, Robert	April, 1923	N 46
Semmes, Richard T.	Aug., 1924	N 309
Staup, Rebecca S.	Sept., 1924	N 320
Schell, Rebecca J.	May, 1927	O 171
Simpson, Robert & Jane	April, 1929	O 519
Scarpelli, Rose	July, 1932	Q 42
Smith, Rosalia B.	Oct., 1932	Q 88
Spangler, Robert P.	March, 1937	R 438
Smith, Robert	Sept., 1939	S 385
Stakem, Richard.F.	Aug., 1941	T 201
Strachan, Robert L.	Sept., 1941	T 237
Swayne, Rawley K.	July, 1942	T 429
Sizer, Robert J.	May, 1943	U 86
Stewart, Russell E.	Jan., 1947	V 376
Spicer, Richard J.	Jan., 1949	W 254
Stallings, Robert L.	July, 1952	X 434
Shepherd, Rowland, Jr.	Oct., 1957	1 85
Schultz, Rachel E.	April, 1958	1 242
Skidmore, Royal C.	Feb., 1959	1 536

Screen, Sarah Elizabeth	May, 1958	1 262
Snowden, Simon H.	Aug., 1958	1 377
Sweitzer, Sarah A.	Dec., 1959	2 237

Stanton, Thomas		A 55
Stephens, Thomas		B 103
Street, Thomas	Jan., 1875	D 192
Sullivan, Timothy J.	Jan., 1917	L 111
Smouse, Thomas F.	Sept., 1928	O 402
Schwarzer, Teresa	Dec., 1931	P 497
Stakem, Thomas C.	Dec., 1940	T 45
Sperry, Theophilus	Feb., 1941	T 92
Snelson, Thomas	June, 1959	2 42

Sinclair, Vally V.	Oct., 1931	P 473
Shaffer, Virginia (Jennie E.)	Feb., 1938	S 54
Schramm, Viola K.	July, 1938	S 119
Sides, Valentine	July, 1952	X 419

Shaw, William		A 133
Sanford, William		A 246
Selby, Walter		A 710
Startzman, William		B 27
Sprigg, William O.	May, 1862	C 8
same	July, 1863	C 27
same	Feb., 1868	C 123
Shircliff, William	June, 1871	C 195
Syers, William Thomas	Feb., 1874	D 145
Shuck, Walter L.	Feb., 1894	G 22
Staples, William	March, 1899	G 338
Small, William Henry	Nov., 1911	J 346
Smith, Wilhelmina	Nov., 1913	K 105
Schell, William	June, 1917	L 193
Stevenson, William J.	June, 1918	L 383
Shober, William F.	Feb., 1919	L 474
Straub, Wendel	June, 1920	M 170
Smith, Wolfgang	Nov., 1920	M 230
Sinclair, William F.	Oct., 1922	M 484

Siebert, William	Oct., 1922	M 551
Strickler, William M.	Oct., 1923	N 139
Shryer, Walter	Sept., 1924	N 312
Smith, William Walter	Dec., 1926	O 101
Shepherd, Will H.	Feb., 1927	O 134
Stratton, Wilfred J.	March, 1928	O 312
Sleeman, William, Sr.	Nov., 1929	P 44
Schimp, William E.	May, 1930	P 150
Swauger, William F.	March, 1931	P 317
Skilling, William Quail	Feb., 1932	P 523
Schafer, William	June, 1932	Q 30
Shaffer, William A.	March, 1933	Q 168
Slider, William	Oct., 1933	Q 294
Sigler, William T.	Dec., 1933	Q 319
Smith, William L.	June, 1934	Q 456
Seifers, William F.	Oct., 1934	Q 517
Slingloff, William	May, 1936	R 241
Shultice, William Waverly	July, 1937	R 528
Sperry, William Lincoln	June, 1938	S 106
Smith, Wilhelmina F.	Dec., 1938	S 216
Seaber, William H.	Jan., 1940	S 450
Stonestreet, Wilmer S.	Sept., 1940	T 13
Soethe, William L.	July, 1944	U 333
Sitt, William Theodore	Oct., 1946	V 325
Stoll, William F.	Oct., 1947	V 553
Smith, William Black	Oct., 1948	W 212
Stewart, William	Dec., 1948	W 243
Schell, Willie G.	April, 1949	W 303
Schafer, William H.	June, 1950	W 563
Spates, William James	June, 1950	W 574
Shryock, W.A.	June, 1951	X 187
Sonner, W.B.	Sept., 1951	X 233
Shaffer, Warren E.	Feb., 1952	X 332
Skidmore, William H.	Jan., 1953	X 569
Simpson, William Harmon	Dec., 1953	Y 177
Sherman, William L.	Dec., 1953	Y 189
Shertzer, Wilhelmina	June, 1954	Y 292
Stakem, Winifred Ann	May, 1955	Y 583
Sanner, Walter Ross	Sept., 1956	Z 329
Seel, Walter W.	Oct., 1956	Z 374
Shumaker, Wilson W.	Jan., 1957	Z 415
Suder, William E.	Aug., 1959	2 141
Schlund, Walter P.	Sept., 1959	2 145
Schell, William G.	Dec., 1960	3 75

Smith, Yost	May, 1858	B 136
Shryer, Zachariah	Dec., 1864	C 45
Smith, Zella Agnes	Feb., 1945	U 454

T

Trost, Adam	Feb., 1876	D 258
Thomson, Alexander		D 511
Tilghman, Anna B.	June, 1882	D 547
Tomlinson, Amanda	Aug., 1887	E 251
Twigg, Argyle	Oct., 1887	E 272
Twigg, Alley	July, 1893	F 381
Trail, Amanda	April, 1894	G 30
Turner, Alonzo B.	June, 1903	H 361
Taylor, Annie F.	Jan., 1912	J 367
Twigg, Argyle	Oct., 1913	K 83
Tasker, Alice V.	April, 1917	L 165
Tabler, Augustus M.	Oct., 1917	L 261
Turner, Annie J.	Feb., 1919	L 486
Twigg, Annie M.	Feb., 1924	N 207
Tiley, Amelia Jane	July 1926	O 31
Thuss, August	Sept., 1926	O 59
Thomas, Alice	July, 1929	O 573
Tharp, Annie M.	Nov., 1931	P 489
Twigg, Ashby	Sept., 1935	R 97
Turner, Ada V.	Sept., 1936	R 315
Thomas, Albert E.	Oct., 1936	R 339
Trescher, Anna Viola	May, 1938	S 96
Thompson, Agnes	Dec., 1942	T 547
Twigg, Alvin Walter	May, 1945	U 533
Tennant, Agnes	Oct., 1947	V 573
Taylor, Andrew J.	Jan., 1952	X 309
Turner, Arnold	Aug., 1953	X 97
Thumel, A. Bernard	April, 1955	Y 503
Teufel, Alvina	Dec., 1957	1 136
Thorpe, Annie G.	Feb., 1958	1 197
Torkington, Alice	April, 1958	1 235
Tosh, Alice K.	May 1958	1 281
Twigg, Anna Mary	Nov., 1958	1 466
Taccino, Angelina	May, 1960	2 413
Thompson, Ada M.	July, 1960	2 473

Tomlinson Benjamin		A 425
Twigg, Benjamin L.		F 203
Twigg, Barbara E.	Nov., 1929	P 33
Totten, Bessie May	April, 1937	R 458
Tennant, Bessie	Aug., 1941	T 200
Thomas, Bruce Waugh (Mrs.)	April, 1947	V 461
Twigg, Blanche Ray	Nov., 1949	W 429
Taylor, Bertie Ring	March, 1950	W 492
Troxell, Bertha Elizabeth	Aug., 1950	W 624
Thomas, Bertie May	Jan., 1960	2 254

Twigg, Catherine	Oct., 1854	B 87
Thruston, Charles M.	Feb., 1873	D 94
Thomas, Charles	May, 1897	G 228
Twigg, Catherine	Oct., 1904	I 57
Twigg, Charles H.	Oct., 1907	I 324
Tribut, Christina	Oct., 1909	J 76
Thomasen, Charles N.	April, 1916	K 499
Tagen, Catherine	Oct., 1917	L 257
Thomas, Clara B.	June, 1921	M 331
Tully, Catherine R.	Aug., 1922	M 506
Trescher, Charles F.	Jan., 1924	N 190
Turner, Charles J.	Jan., 1926	N 526
Thayer, C. W.	April, 1932	P 554
Taylor, Charles H.	Nov., 1936	R 349
Twigg, Charles J.	June, 1945	U 582
Thomspon, Charles E.	April, 1946	V 161
Tice, Carlista	Sept., 1949	W 385
Tharp, Charles E.	Feb., 1956	Z 173
Tomlinson, Cecil	Feb., 1957	Z 447

Trail, David		B 68
Timney, Daniel	Feb., 1939	S 261
Tennant, David	May, 1942	T 412

Twigg, Eli		B 86
Toban, Elizabeth	1861	B 185
Trimble, Enoch	Nov., 1882	D 564
Thrasher, Elizabeth A.	May, 1883	D 605

Ternant, George J.	Jan., 1952	X 294
Taschenberger, Gertrude M.	March, 1954	Y 232
Trieber, Grace E.	Dec., 1958	1 502
Taylor, George	Dec., 1959	2 242
Tomlinson, Hannah		A 440
Trimble, Henry		D 523
Toy, Henry & wife	Feb., 1883	D 588
Thoma, Henry	May, 1906	I 206
Thomas, Henry	Sept., 1911	J 324
Taylor, Henry	Sept., 1916	L 52
Thomas, Henry J.	Dec., 1923	N 171
Templeton, Isabel D.	June, 1913	K 32
Turvey, John		A 16
Twigg, John		A 198
Trimble, John		A 220
Twigg, James		B 85
Taylor, James		B 156
Tibbs, James	Sept., 1870	C 179
Tauber, John A.	Oct., 1876	D 299
Thruston, Juliana		D 504
same		D 507
same		D 510
same, Heirs of		D 525
Thomas, James B.	Jan., 1885	E 98
Thomas, John	Dec., 1888	E 350
Tennant, Janet	Jan., 1889	G 326
Trenton, Joseph S.	Dec., 1902	H 306
Trigg, Jennie Wagner	June, 1906	I 212
Trescher, John	April, 1908	I 386
Thompson, James	Aug., 1909	J 69
Taylor, Jeremiah	April, 1913	K 11
Timmons, Joseph	Jan., 1916	K 453
Thompson, Joseph F.	Aug., 1917	L 230
Tuvin, Jacob	Sept., 1919	M 78
Twigg, John D.	Nov., 1920	M 234
Thomas, Jane	June, 1923	N 67
Trost, John J.	May, 1925	N 422

Tomlinson, Mary		C 36
Twigg, Mary C.		F 203
Tangye, Mary	Jan., 1893	F 339
Tearney, Michael	Aug., 1898	G 305
Thomas, Mary Ann	Sept., 1899	G 374
Twigg, Michael C.S.	March, 1918	L 339
Taylor, Mary R.	March, 1919	M 6
Townsend, Mary E.	Sept., 1919	M 73
Taylor, Mary	April, 1923	N 38
Turner, Mary L.	Oct., 1924	N 329
Trieber, Mary E.	July, 1926	O 27
Taylor, Mary L.	Oct., 1926	O 75
Tracy, Michael	Nov., 1929	P 48
Trent, Martha	March, 1930	P 118
Tibbitts, Mamie	Sept., 1931	P 455
Trieber, Margaret D.	Jan., 1935	Q 568
Taylor, Mary A.	Oct., 1935	R 123
Trezise, Martha J.	March, 1936	R 212
Trieber, Mary J.	Sept., 1937	R 561
Tipka, Mary A.	March, 1939	S 281
Toomey, Margaret J.	March, 1940	S 519
Tole, Mary E.	March, 1952	X 343
Thomas, Martha J.	Dec., 1952	X 538
Trainer, Mary C.	March, 1955	Y 478
Turner, Mary Alice	April, 1957	Z 502
Turner, Martha Landonian	May, 1957	Z 546
Taylor, Mary C.	Nov., 1957	1 108
Taylor, Maude E.	July, 1959	2 93

Trail, Nathan	Dec., 1893	G 2
same	April, 1894	G 30
Townsend, Neenah D.	May, 1949	W 323
Tansey, Nellie	March, 1956	Z 189

Ternent, Oscar G.	Sept., 1951	X 239
Tabler, Orpha	June, 1960	2 443

Thrasher, Presely J.	May, 1883	D 603
Tansey, Patrick	Aug., 1909	J 70
Timmon, Parmelia M.	Jan., 1924	N 193
Twigg, Robert		A 75
Taylor, Reuben, Sr.		A 211
Twigg, Rebecca		A 249
Twigg, Ruth		A 417
Turner, Rozin	July, 1868	C 121
Thruston, Rosalie B.	June, 1882	D 547
Tully, Redmond	Sept., 1895	G 136
Tennant, Robert	Dec., 1899	H 4
Taylor, Robert E.	Dec., 1904	I 64
Tennant, Robert	Aug., 1905	I 131
Taylor, Reuben	March, 1910	J 137
Tennant, Robert	May, 1926	O 10
Turner, R. Peyton	Jan., 1937	R 364
Tucker, Rachel V.	Sept., 1940	T 6
Totten, Robert, Mellier	Feb., 1942	T 325
Thompson, Robert	Jan., 1944	U 237
Thuss, Rose Caroline	May, 1950	W 550
Taylor, Ruth E.	April, 1959	1 595
Townsend, Singleton		A 401
Twigg, Sarah		B 35
Trent, Samuel		B 72
Tearney, Sarah M.	Jan., 1898	G 277
Taylor, Sarah M.	Jan., 1908	I 355
Tanzer, Sigmund	Jan., 1912	J 360
Thomas, Susan M.	Feb., 1914	K 134
Tacey, Sally E.	Jan., 1919	L 465
Thrasher, Solomon J.	June, 1927	O 189
Tabler, Sevilla (Seville)	Nov., 1928	O 428
Twigg, Sallie M.	Feb., 1935	Q 593
Thrasher, Shobe	July, 1936	R 277
Thomas, Sarah D. Avirett	Oct., 1942	T 493
Treiber, Sarah Ann	April, 1947	V 442
Turner, Sarah W.	Sept., 1949	W 401
Twigg, Sophia	Sept., 1950	X 18
Thompson, Stephen B.	Feb., 1952	X 315
Tribut, Sophia B.	Jan., 1958	1 170

Thistle, Thomas	Oct., 1803	A 144
same	Dec., 1803	A 144
same	Jan., 1805	A 144
same	Jan., 1806	A 145
same	Dec., 1812	A 148
same	Jan., 1814	A 148
same	Dec., 1814	A 149
same	Jan., 1816	A 149
same	Aug., 1817	A 157
same	Jan., 1817	A 159
same	Oct., 1818	A 170
same	Feb., 1819	A 177
Trail, Thomas		A 453
Taylor, T. Buckey	Nov., 1905	I 157
Thumel, Theodore A.	Dec., 1933	Q 326
Thomas, Thomas	March, 1939	S 287
Thoma, Theodora C.	March, 1942	T 334
Twigg, Theresa	Oct., 1953	Y 144

Thompson, William	June, 1842	A 503
Taylor, William I.		D 489
Thrasher, William A.	July, 1882	D 549
Ternent, William	Nov., 1906	I 247
Thomas, William	May, 1909	J 49
Trimble, Winfield S.	April, 1924	N 258
Toner, William	Jan., 1926	N 515
Same. (Rescinded)	(See Court Procs. Liber 30,Folio 497)	
Toner, William	April, 1927	O 161
Twigg, William H.	July, 1931	P 405
Turner, William Edward	Dec., 1932	Q 129
Toomey, Willie S.	Oct., 1933	Q 290
Torrington, William J.	July, 1944	U 339
Twigg, William A.	Sept., 1945	V 41
Twigg, William L.	March, 1955	Y 482
Tansill, William Bailey	Nov., 1955	Z 98
Trail, William H.	March, 1956	Z 199
Theis, Wilbert Reynolds	April, 1956	Z 226

U

Uhl, Anna Barbara	May, 1956	Z 253
Uhl, Charles		A 259
Uhl, Charles W.	Oct., 1918	L 416
Uhl, Cecil R.	April, 1945	U 503
Uhl, Daniel		A 705
Umbel, Daniel	Jan., 1873	D 73
Umphenour, John	April, 1864	C 40
Umphenour, James H.	Sept., 1864	C 42
Uhl, J. W. Edgar	Jan,, 1942	T 319
Umphenour, Mary C.	April, 1864	C 40
Uhl, Nevin	Feb., 1951	X 111
Usinger, Stephen		D 488
Uhlman, Sigfried	July, 1920	M 178
Uhlman, Theresa	July, 1920	M 181
Uhl, William Walter	July, 1943	U 126

V

Vocke, Antoinette	May, 1909	J 50
Vogtmann, Ann C.	Sept., 1918	L 408
Vogel, Annie E.	Oct., 1931	P 460
Valentine, Amanda M.	Sept., 1933	Q 283
Van Meter, Annie M.	July, 1945	V 2
Valentine, Alice M.	March, 1946	V 146
Van Pelt, Amanda Florence	Dec., 1960	3 53
Vaughan, Benjamin G.		A 539
Valentine, Benjamin R.	Sept., 1920	M 207
Vincent, Benjamin M.	July, 1953	Y 82
Valentine, Catherine		A 555
Vogtmann, Conrad	April, 1911	J 289
Vogtmann, Christian	Feb., 1934	Q 360
Valentine, Charles Elmer	Jan., 1946	V 106
Van Pelt, Charles Edward	May, 1948	W 111
Valentine, Clyde A.	May, 1957	Z 528
Vogel, Edward J.	May, 1939	S 332
Van Pelt, Elizabeth	July, 1945	V 10
Van Meter, Edwin V.	Oct., 1952	X 503
Vandegrift, Edgar D.	Dec., 1955	Z 124
Vernall, Emma	Oct., 1957	1 92
Valentine, Frederick		A 241
Vogel, Frederick William	Jan., 1940	S 460
Vann, Frank T.	March, 1950	W 512
Valentine, George W.	March, 1924	N 232
Vogtman, George	Aug., 1930	P 202
Valentine, George P.	Jan., 1941	T 78

Vogtman, Henry	Sept., 1872	D 43
Valentine, Henry	Dec., 1930	P 268
Vogel, Henry	Jan., 1936	R 160
Van Meter, Isaac	Nov., 1911	J 340
Valentine, John		B 175
Velkel, John	June, 1889	E 399
Van Meter, Jacob C.	May, 1896	G 175
Vocke, J. (Mrs.)	May, 1909	J 50
Vogtmann, John	May, 1911	J 291
Valentine, Jacob Albert	Nov., 1915	K 430
Valentine, John F.	April, 1921	M 295
Vogtman, Josephine	Aug., 1938	S 142
Vandegrift, John I	June, 1946	V 237
Vernay, Joseph H.	April, 1952	X 384
Volk, Lloyd D.	Nov., 1939	S 438
Valentine, Lorenzo	Dec., 1951	X 275
Van Meter, Marion Estelle	April, 1930	P 136
Vanorsdale, M.A.	Dec., 1944	U 410
Vocke, Mary C.	May, 1947	V 420
Vogel, Mary Lulu	Nov., 1949	W 433
Van Meter, Milton G.	Sept., 1954	Y 359
Vanorsdale, Nora B.	Aug., 1946	V 275
Virts, Oscar C.	March, 1941	T 109
Valentine, Rebecca	July, 1929	O 583
Van Newkirk, R.G.	Jan., 1936	R 182
Valentine, Rudolph F.	Aug., 1947	V 542
Van Fleet, Roy E.	Dec., 1960	3 74

Valentine, Sarah E.	March, 1917	L 147
Van Ormer, Sarah B.	March, 1952	X 355
Van Pelt, Thomas	May, 1943	U 88
Valentine, Ursula D.	March, 1933	Q 171
Van Buskirk, William	Feb., 1916	K 470
Vogtman, William	June, 1945	U 599

W

White, A. Gertrude	Jan., 1947	V 375
Williamson, Annie L.	July, 1948	W 161
White, Anna E.	Oct., 1948	W 206
Woerner, Annie M.	July, 1949	W 348
Wiseman, Albert R.	Jan., 1951	X 82
Will, Augustine L.	March, 1954	Y 228
Weber, Albert L.	July, 1954	Y 299
White, Adrian C.	Sept., 1954	Y 347
Witt, Anthony Theodore	March, 1955	Y 489
Willison, Annie L.)	Jan., 1957	Z 419
Willison, Anna L.)	same	Z 419
Willison, Archibald	May, 1957	Z 540
Wagner, Anna B.	Oct., 1957	1 96
Willison, Arthur W.	May, 1958	1 268
Weber, Anna Agnes	Oct., 1958	1 427
Waitekunas, Adolph	Dec., 1959	2 221
Willison, Amanda L.	Aug., 1960	2 523
Weber, Arthur J.	Sept., 1960	2 544
Wiley, Benjamin		A 326
Wheinheim, Barbara	May, 1916	L 4
Welsh, Bridget	April, 1920	M 151
Wentling, Bertha May	July, 1935	R 57
Willison, Blue	May, 1942	T 397
Waingold, Benjamin	Jan., 1945	U 428
same - Codicil to will rescinded. See Court Proceedings Liber J-12 Folio 282, 6/8/45		U 428
Wilson, Belle L.	Feb., 1947	V 409
Wilson, Bess	May, 1948	W 100
Wolfe, Betty V.H.	Oct., 1949	W 408
Wolford, Baird A.	Jan., 1950	W 464
Wakeman, Bessie L.	Oct., 1958	1 411
Willison, Cornelius		A 42
Wallace, Charles	Oct., 1876	D 304
Woods, Charles L.	Nov., 1876	D 308
Weber, Christian	May, 1877	D 324
White, Charles	June, 1891	F 203
Willard, Charles D.		F 262
Walker, Catherine C.	June, 1900	H 108
Weyand, Catherine	Sept., 1901	H 221

Wade, Charles H.	Oct., 1904	I 49
Wilson, Catharine	Jan., 1909	J 1
Walker, Charles H.	April, 1912	J 414
Wilson, Conda	Jan., 1913	J 481
Weiskettle, Charles	Oct., 1915	K 421
Williamson, Charles Francis	Nov., 1915	K 416
Williams, Catherine	Feb., 1918	L 312
Weisenborn, Conrad	Nov., 1920	M 235
Workman, Cass B.	May, 1923	N 53
Wilson, Charlotte V.	July, 1924	N 289
Wagner, Catherine	Oct., 1924	N 336
Wolfe, Clara V.	Feb., 1925	N 378
Wildman, Charles H.	May, 1925	N 428
Willison, Carl C.	June, 1925	N 429
Workman, C.I.	Feb., 1930	P 111
Wilhelm, Clara E.	March, 1930	P 126
Wade, Charles L.	Feb., 1931	P 308
Wegman, Charles	March, 1932	P 535
Wagner, Catherine	April, 1932	P 563
Wolford, Charles H.	Dec., 1932	Q 128
Whisner, Charles N.	Sept., 1940	T 9
Welsh, Charles J.	Dec., 1940	T 58
Wallace, Christina W.M.	Nov., 1941	T 279
Willard, Charles D.	Aug., 1944	U 347
White, Charles A.	Oct., 1944	U 397
Wickard, Clara L.	April, 1945	U 498
Watson, Charles G.	Nov., 1945	V 85
Wilson, Clay	Feb., 1946	V 136
Wagus, Clara	July, 1947	V 512
Willison, Charles W.	Aug., 1947	V 537
Wagner, Clersy Ellen	Feb., 1948	W 45
Warnick, Charles A.	Nov., 1948	W 218
Walters, Carrie	Nov., 1948	W 225
Walsh, Caroline W.	May, 1950	W 544
Weires, Christopher	Oct., 1950	X 22
Wiegand, Charlotte	July, 1953	Y 74
Walters, Charles W.	Aug., 1953	Y 92
Ward, Cecelia J.	April, 1954	Y 257
White, Clifton	June, 1954	Y 298
Wright, Clara Belle	Nov., 1955	Z 115
Wilson, Chester H.	March, 1956	Z 194
Wickard, Charles H.	Aug., 1956	Z 312
Wotring, Charles L.	Nov., 1956	Z 387
Wilkinson, Clara R.	Dec., 1957	1 135

Webster, Cornelius H.	Nov., 1958	1 463
Wilson, Charles H.	April, 1959	2 15

Watt, Devecmon		B 70
White, David and wife	Dec., 1862	B 200
Wilt, David	May, 1868	C 119
Williams, David	April, 1905	I 94
Williams, Daniel J.	May, 1911	J 294
Williams, Daniel	Dec., 1919	M 106
Walker, David	April, 1930	P 142
Wilt, Daniel M. L.	May, 1933	Q 219
Wilson, David L.	Nov., 1936	R 343
Wigfield, Dennis	Sept., 1945	V 38
Wilson, Dennis A. (Dick)	April, 1951	X 153
Willison, Dora E.	April, 1951	X 156
Williams, David C.	May, 1952	X 395
Waddell, Douglas	Feb., 1959	I 539

Wilson, Edward		A 85
Wiatt, Edward	June, 1821	A 190
same	Jan., 1821	A 193
Williams, E.H.		A 683
Wilhelm, Elizabeth Ann	March, 1866	C 89
Winter, Eli	Oct., 1873	D 222
Wallace, Esbella	Oct., 1876	D 305
Wolf, Elizabeth	Dec., 1880	D 467
Wright, Elizabeth	Aug., 1882	D 558
Williams, Eli		F 209
Willard, Elizabeth E.		F 262
Wilson, Elizabeth Jane	April, 1905	I 106
Wehner, Elizabeth	Sept., 1905	I 134
Wilson, Eli	Jan., 1909	I 496
Wiebrecht, Elizabeth	March, 1912	J 400
Welsh, Elizabeth	Feb., 1913	J 492
Welsh, Edward H.	Jan., 1914	K 131
Williamson, Eugene L.	Jan., 1916	K 458
Wigfield, Elijah	Nov., 1917	L 268
Welsh, Ellen S.	June, 1923	N 75
Willison, Emily	July, 1923	N 88
Wilhelm, Elizabeth	March, 1926	N 562 A

Wunder, Edward J.	April, 1926	N 589
Webb, Edward F.	Nov., 1928	O 422
Wilhelm, Emma I.	April, 1929	O 505
Wehner, Ella Louise	Nov., 1929	P 54
Winters, Elijah	May, 1934	Q 437
Winter, Elijah S.	July, 1934	Q 460
Wilson, Emma Lee	Sept., 1934	Q 498
Wheeler, Edward L.	July, 1937	R 524
Walker, Eva Carns	Aug., 1937	R 534
Wenrich, Enoch L.	Sept., 1940	T 18
Wilson, Eli Walter	May, 1942	T 404
Willison, Emma	April, 1947	V 444
Willison, Edward C.	April, 1948	W 74
Wilson, Ernest D.	Dec., 1949	W 453
Wolford, Evelyn M.	March, 1951	X 122
Williamson, Elizabeth G.	May, 1951	X 162
Walkenshaw, Elizabeth	Feb., 1954	Y 208
Wilson, Emlie C.	Dec., 1954	Y 424
White, Emory L.	June, 1958	1 325
Wahl, Edgar H.	Oct., 1958	1 430
Windemuth, Elizabeth	July, 1959	2 119
Webster, Edna Esther	Feb., 1960	2 278
Walters, Eva M.	Aug., 1960	2 573
Wigfield, Emory J.	Nov., 1960	3 31

Wunder, Frederick	May, 1889	E 391
Willard, Florence M.		F 262
Wenk, Frederick	Nov., 1912	J 469
Willetts, Francis	Dec., 1915	K 436
Weiland, Frederick	Dec., 1915	K 443
Watson, Frances A.	Feb., 1922	M 406
Willetts, Frances S.	April, 1922	M 449
Weber, Frederick	Dec., 1924	N 354
Williams, Ferdinand	Sept., 1926	O 58
Williams, Flora F.	June, 1927	O 186
Walker, Frank	May, 1931	P 352
Wahl, Frank J.	Dec., 1931	P 496
Willetts, Frank	April, 1938	S 74
Wilson, Francis R.	Jan., 1939	S 247
Wiegand, Frederick W.	May, 1942	T 387
Williams, Frank J.	May, 1947	V 475
Walker, Frank L.	July, 1948	W 167

Williams, Florence Henrietta	Aug., 1949	W 360
Wilson, Frank M.	March, 1950	W 483
Warner, Fred M.	Sept., 1951	X 234
Wolfhope, Francis A.	Sept., 1956	Z 338
Weber, Frederick	Nov., 1956	Z 384
Whiting, F. Brooke	Aug., 1957	1 17
Weires, Florence Wilma	April, 1958	1 249

Whitney, Gilbert		A 18
Walker, Gracy	April, 1848	A 652
Winter, George		C 105
Wagner, George	June, 1893	F 370
Walters, George	Sept., 1902	H 292
Weber, George	July, 1903	H 366
Wadsworth, George A.	March, 1908	I 374
Wehner, George	Feb., 1911	J 242
Willison, George A.	June, 1913	K 38
Wills, George Edward	Nov., 1913	K 97
Webester, George W.	Dec., 1916	L 83
Webster, George W.	same	L 83
Woerner, George W.	Feb., 1922	M 410
Willison, George S.	May, 1924	N 264
Winebrenner, George W.	Feb., 1927	O 129
Wellington, George L.	March, 1927	O 150
Winters, Gertrude	June, 1932	Q 33
Wittig, George J.	July, 1935	R 61
Willison, George	Oct., 1935	R 118
Wineberner, George Washington	Dec., 1935	R 140
Winfield, George	April, 1940	S 537
Windemuth, George	Jan., 1941	T 65
Webster, George W.F.	Sept., 1941	T 225
Weaver, George W.	April, 1944	U 277
Witt, George W.	April, 1944	U 295
Williams, George E.	Nov., 1945	V 74
Winters, George W. Sr.	Nov., 1946	V 347
White, Gertrude A.	Jan., 1947	V 375
Wilson, George O.	Jan., 1951	X 104
Weltman, George Franklin	Feb., 1954	Y 214
Williams, George Oliver	April, 1958	1 247
Wagner, George Albert	Oct., 1960	2 585

Wilson, Isaac		A 86
Ward, Isaac		A 468
Wilson, Isaac C.		C 23
Winebrenner, Isaac	April, 1895	G 109
Warfield, Isabella	Oct., 1904	I 53
Wilson, Isabella	June, 1913	K 33
Weiskettel, Isabella	May, 1928	O 344
White, Irvin Blaine	Aug., 1929	O 590
Worgan, Isabella N.	Jan., 1949	W 261
Whorton, Ida V.	June, 1956	Z 262

Wall, John		A 19
Willison, Jeremiah		A 108
Willison, John		A 202
Warwick, Joseph		A 282
Waugh, Joseph		A 303
Wright, John B.		A 315
Witt, John		A 397
White, James		A 471
Waltz, John		A 542
Welch, Jacob		A 548
Willison, John		A 664
Wright, John		B 47
Wilson, Jonathan		B 99
Widener, John B.	Nov., 1857	B 131
same	Dec., 1863	B 201
White, John W.		C 40
Winter, John	Jan., 1868	C 120
Winter, Joseph N.	Jan., 1868	C 120
Wilson, James	Feb., 1871	C 188
Watkins, Joseph	March, 1872	D 6
Winter, Jacob, Jr.	Oct., 1873	D 222
Wentling, John	June, 1876	D 288
Werkmeister, John A.	Dec., 1877	D 346
Wintermeier, John	April, 1879	D 400
Widener, John B.	July, 1879	D 409
Wilson, Jackson	April, 1880	D 437
Wegman, John D.		D 497
Widener, John B.	Nov., 1883	D 635
Warren, James	Sept., 1884	E 76
Wilson, John	July, 1886	E 200
Wagner, James C.		E 284

White, James H.	Nov., 1928	O 423
Williams, James D.	May, 1929	O 537
Walsh, John W.	Dec., 1929	P 70
Workman, John F.	Oct., 1930	P 229
Wolf, John W.	Aug., 1931	P 432
Wolf, Julia A.	April, 1934	Q 424
Wheeler, James W.	April, 1935	R 17
Weber, John	April, 1935	R 25
Wolford, John Wesley	Nov., 1935	R 133
Wright, John	April, 1936	R 228
Wilkinson, Josephine	May, 1937	R 479
Williams, Josiah	July, 1937	R 521
Williams, Jane	Feb., 1939	S 270
Williams, James B.	Feb., 1940	S 493
Wegman, John J.	Jan., 1941	T 66
Whittaker, John B.	July, 1943	U 125
Weinberg, Joseph	Aug., 1943	U 144
Weaver, Joseph E.	Aug., 1944	U 354
Wilson, J. Homer	March, 1945	U 483
Wagus, James Henry	Aug., 1945	V 24
Wempe, John R.	Sept., 1945	V 50
Whetstone, Joseph	Oct., 1946	V 307
Weimer, Josephine	Aug., 1947	V 533
Wagner, Julius V.	Feb., 1949	W 274
White, James H.	Aug., 1949	W 368
Watkinson, Joseph T., Sr.	Dec., 1949	W 452
Willison, James	Nov., 1950	X 49
Wolford, John C.	April, 1952	X 366
Williams, John	May, 1952	X 396
Ways, John W.	Oct., 1952	X 497
Wise, John A.	Aug., 1954	Y 334
Wolfe, Jennie May	Oct., 1954	Y 372
Walton, J. Frederick	Nov., 1955	Z 103
Weaver, Jennie	July, 1956	Z 291
Wheeler, John D.	July, 1956	Z 303
Workman, John J.	Feb., 1957	Z 449
Weber, Johanna Margaret	Jan., 1958	1 149
Wiebel, John G.	March, 1960	2 344
Warnick, James W.	April, 1960	2 382

Ward, Mary E.	Sept., 1865	C 61
same	March, 1870	C 168
Wilson, Mary	May, 1874	D 149
Wolf, Marguard	Jan., 1880	D 418
Wagner, Millard F.		E 284
Wagner, Mary A.		E 284
Winter, Mary S.		F 91
Watson, Mary	Jan., 1891	F 167
Watkins, Margaret J.	June, 1890	F 280
Weedy, Margaret	Sept., 1892	F 312
Wiesenmiller, Margaretta	Nov., 1894	G 81
Wolz, Mary B.	April, 1900	H 80
Whisner, Mary Ann	July, 1902	H 277
Wright, Mary Elizabeth	Jan., 1903	H 313
Wilson, Moses	Aug., 1902	H 279
Wineland, Marx	Oct., 1906	I 235
Wills, Mary A.	May, 1908	I 393
Walsh, Mary E.	Aug., 1910	J 182
Wilson, Martin L.	Jan., 1911	J 235
Winter, Mary Louisa	Jan., 1915	K 270
Willison, Mary	May, 1915	K 338
Ward, Michael J.	July, 1915	K 372
Wenseck, Margaret G.	Oct., 1916	L 65
Wempe, Mary C.	Aug., 1917	L 231
Wilson, Moses R.	May, 1918	L 358
Weslow, Mary C.	Nov., 1918	L 432
Wehner, Mary	Dec., 1918	L 440
Wempe, Margaret A.	Sept., 1920	M 200
Wempe, Martin	Dec., 1920	M 245
Wempe, Mary A.	June, 1921	M 329
Weiskettel, Minnie	July, 1921	M 334
Williams, Margaret E. B.	Feb., 1922	M 403
Walker, Mary C.	July, 1923	N 89
Walker, Maryland	Jan., 1924	N 182
Wills, Martha E.	Jan., 1925	N 369
Wilson, Martha	April, 1925	N 399
Willison, Missouri E.	July, 1925	N 451
Wilderman, Mary A.	Nov., 1925	N 490
Welsh, Mary P.	Nov., 1926	O 85
Wilson, Mary E.	Jan., 1927	O 124
Walker, Mary Gertrude	July, 1927	O 199
Walbert, Mary A.	Aug., 1927	O 222
Workman, Margaret P.	Sept., 1928	O 399
Wertz, Marquis L.	March, 1931	P 326

Wilson, Nathan	Feb., 1872	D 7
same	Dec., 1880	D 464
Windermuth, Nicholas	Sept., 1883	D 629
Willison, Nancy	March, 1896	G 167
Willison, Nellie M.	April, 1920	M 149
Wharton, Nancy Millholland	Jan., 1933	Q 140
Weaver, Noble P.	April, 1943	U 49
Weber, Nicholas J.	Oct., 1944	U 387
Wentling, Nina May	May, 1956	Z 237
Wolford, Nettie R.	Jan., 1958	1 152
Watkins, Nannie Lee	Nov., 1959	2 195

White, Otho B.	Dec., 1868	C 157
Willard, Oscar A.		F 262
Wilson, Oliver S.	Feb., 1923	N 7
Wilson, Owen	March, 1945	U 480
Ward, Olive D.	Dec., 1953	Y 185
Williams, Oliver D.	Feb., 1954	Y 216
Wenrich, Orville M.	Aug., 1954	Y 325
Wilson, Olive May	May, 1960	2 411

Warnick, Patsy	May, 1869	C 137
Weyand, Peter		D 514
Weyland, Philip	Nov., 1890	F 146
Weis, Peter	April, 1900	H 77
Wright, Peter E.	Jan., 1918	L 284
White, Patrick F.	July, 1922	M 489
Whetstone, Peter	Nov., 1928	N 156
Wagner, Peter H.	Sept., 1927	O 253
Wilson, Peter	Jan., 1929	O 445
Warfield, Peregrine	June, 1932	Q 27
Wiegand, Priscilla	Jan., 1947	V 389
Waldstein, Paula	April, 1948	W 71
Williams, Paul A.	July, 1959	2 101

Wilson, Thomas R.	May, 1856	B 105
Wheatley, Thomas		B 160
Wilson, Thomas R.	Oct., 1859	B 174
White, Thomas F.	May, 1860	B 176
same	May, 1861	B 189
Wilson, Thomas		C 43
Wright, Thomas		C 91
Ward, Thomas	Oct., 1870	C 181
Whelan, Thomas	Dec., 1875	D 248
Wright, Thomas E.	Dec., 1883	E 5
Wagner, Thomas		E 284
Woods, Terrence	Oct., 1901	H 222
Walker, Tabitha	Feb., 1910	J 118
Walker, Teresa	Sept., 1911	J 320
Wilson, Thornton	Feb., 1923	N 1
Wilson, Thomas J.	Aug., 1930	P 203
Whitman, Temperance	April, 1931	P 344
Welsh, Theodore	Jan., 1938	S 42
Whelan, Thomas Joseph	Aug., 1944	U 349
Wallace, Theodore A.	April, 1950	W 517
Woolard, Thomas E.	Nov., 1952	X 527
Winters, Thomas F.	Dec., 1952	X 535
Winn, Thomas P.	Jan., 1953	X 570
Willison, Thomas	Sept., 1953	Y 111

Whytock, Virginia T.	June, 1916	L 12
Wilson, Virgie M.	Jan., 1930	P 89
Whitfield, Virginia	May, 1930	P 160
Wilson, Verdeen B.	Sept., 1935	R 103
Wolford, Virgil T.	Dec., 1952	X 539

Wooden, William		A 364
Ward, William		A 438
Walker, William		A 647
Weber, William	Feb., 1850	B 17
Wiland, William		B 76
Wright, William		B 123
Wickard, William	Feb., 1868	C 114
Ward, William	Aug., 1869	C 155
same	March, 1877	D 308

Y

Yeager, Annie	Oct., 1902	H 295
Young, Annie E.	Sept., 1920	M 204
Young, Arch A.	May, 1929	O 535
Yinger, Caspar		B 18
Young, Charles	Oct., 1875	D 244
Young, Carrie M.	Jan., 1931	P 293
Yeager, Catherine	Nov., 1939	S 422
Yost, Daniel & Sarah	Feb., 1872	D 7
Yoder, Elizabeth		B 93
Young, Eliza Alice	Oct., 1939	S 406
Yarnall, Elizabeth T.	July, 1950	W 579
Yost, Eliza	Aug., 1956	Z 322
Yost, Ella E.	July, 1959	2 126
Yager, Frederick	Nov., 1887	E 278
Young, George		A 469
Young, George G.	Feb., 1948	W 32
Yeager, George	July, 1953	Y 73
Yaldwin, John		A 570
Young, John	July, 1869	C 144
Young, James	April, 1880	D 438
Yates, Joseph	Sept., 1898	G 309
Young, John H.	Feb., 1906	I 169
Yates, John W.	Oct., 1912	J 461
Young, John W.	July, 1916	L 25
Yantz, James	March, 1917	L 153
Youngerman, John C.	Dec., 1932	Q 123

Yates, Jennie	Sept., 1934	Q 497
Young, James R.	Feb., 1939	S 263
Yates, James Ellis	March, 1939	S 296
Yantz, Jessie W.	April, 1939	S 313
Youngerman, Justus	Oct., 1941	T 259
Young, James A.	July, 1943	U 117
Yates, Jane	April, 1945	U 528
Young, Joseph W., Sr.	March, 1957	Z 492
Yergan, Martha A	Aug., 1885	E 135
Young, Martin Luther	Dec., 1904	I 66
Yungerman, Melchior	Sept., 1912	J 452
Yenshaw, Michael	Oct., 1913	K 89
Yeargen, Maria	Oct., 1914	K 236
Young, Maude E.	Nov., 1952	X 520
Yingling, Mary Lula	Sept., 1956	Z 353
Young, Nancy		A 514
Yoder, Norman S.	Feb., 1946	V 132
Yates, Owen Reginald	Aug., 1941	T 189
Yeart, Peter	July, 1851	B 37
Yarnall, Peter	July, 1866	C 77
same	Jan. 1903	H 315
Yanezich, Peter	Oct., 1955	Z 96
Yoder, Rachael	Dec., 1883	E 5
Yungerman, Rose M.	May, 1951	X 178
Yokum, Riley Hess	Aug., 1957	1 55
Young, Robert W.	June, 1958	1 313
Yantz, Rebecca	March, 1960	2 322
Yost, Sarah M.	Nov., 1925	N 492
Young, Samuel D.	June, 1926	O 18
Yeager, Susan Lambie	Oct., 1955	Z 79

Yurgen, William	June, 1908	I 413
Young, William D.	Sept., 1917	L 246
Yingling, Walter A.	Dec., 1939	S 448
Yonker, Wade Hampton	Dec., 1950	X 65

Z

Zihlman, Julia	Aug., 1925	N 463
Zink, John J.	June, 1926	O 14
Zimmerly, John M.	Aug., 1933	Q 275
Zink, John	June, 1936	R 259
Zitzman, John	April, 1944	U 292
Zapp, Maggie	Sept., 1886	E 209
Zapp, Maria	Feb., 1904	H 393
Zimmerla, Marshelene	Sept., 1919	M 75
Zink, Mary C.	Aug., 1931	P 435
Zais, Mary Louise	Dec., 1932	Q 122
Zais, Morris Edward	Dec., 1935	R 142
Zimmerla, Nathan Thomas	April, 1911	J 285
Zimmerman, Philip M.	Dec., 1946	V 368
Zimerla, Raymond Lenwood	Jan., 1959	1 513
Zimmerman, Wilhelmina	Dec., 1887	E 295
Zimmer, Wilhelmina	Sept., 1898	G 312
Zilch, William C.	Jan., 1947	V 383
Zais, Walter L.	Feb., 1957	Z 439

ADDENDA

Anderson, Polly Jane	Nov., 1960		3 29
Alderton, Rebecca Grace	July, 1954		Y 302
Albright, Samuel R.	April, 1936		R 231
Buchanan, Howard	Aug., 1936		R 308
Bancord, John	Aug., 1877		D 336
Bancord, John, Jr.	May, 1877		D 338
Brandler, J.N.M.	Dec., 1895	Orph. Ct.	CP 4 368
Biddinger, Sampson & Henry	Jan., 1872		C 213
Bell, William	Nov., 1874		D 176
Cain, Patrick	Dec., 1951		X 284
Cross, Uriah	Jan., 1875		D 203
Doerner, Anna L.	Nov., 1957		1 100
Dawson, Harry	Oct., 1957		1 87
Darr, Nial Vincent	Oct., 1960		3 2
Groening, Caroline	March, 1900		H 69
Griffith, Hampton P.	Nov., 1947		V 588
Gnau, Kunigunda C.	Jan., 1911		J 237
Grimes, Kathrine Heller	Aug., 1958		1 360
Holsinger, David	Nov., 1897		G 266
Hendrickson, Perry	March, 1906		I 181
Lee, James F.	Aug., 1922		M 517
McCullough, Christopher R.	March, 1956		Z 195
Moore, George			A 227
Michael, George			B 180
McCulloh, George			B 89
Miller, Joseph M.	March, 1960		2 332
Pugh, Thomas W.	Nov., 1849		W 434
Powell, Thelma L.	Aug., 1953		Y 100
Preston, Thomas	Jan., 1954		Y 191
Pitzer, Theodosia	Dec., 1956		Z 411

ADDENDA

Rice, Martin V.	Dec., 1899	H 3
Shriver, Henry	Feb., 1947	V 398
Street, John M.	Sept., 1920	M 213
Trail, Amanda	May, 1896	G 174
Wagner, Adam	Oct., 1924	N 334
Zembower, Alice Pearl	Jan., 1957	Z 426